W9-BSP-014

# A Year Full of Recipes

365 RECIPES, ONE FOR EVERY DAY OF THE YEAR
PLUS 1 FOR A LEAP YEAR

First published in 2012

LOVE FOOD is an imprint of Parragon Books Ltd

Parragon
Queen Street House
4 Queen Street
Bath BA1 1HE, UK

Copyright © Parragon Books Ltd 2012

LOVE FOOD and the accompanying heart device is a registered trademark of Parragon Books Ltd in Australia, the UK, USA, India, and the EU.

www.parragon.com/lovefood

All rights reserved. No part of this publication may be reproduced, stored in a retrieval system, or transmitted, in any form or by any means, electronic, mechanical, photocopying, recording, or otherwise, without the prior permission of the copyright holder.

ISBN: 978-1-4454-8969-8

Printed in China

Cover and internal design by Lexi L'Esteve
Project managed by Natalie Coates
New photography by Mike Cooper
New home economy by Lincoln Jefferson
Additional design by Siân Williams
Introduction and additional recipes by Christine France

**Notes for the Reader**

This book uses standard kitchen measuring spoons and cups. All spoon and cup measurements are level unless otherwise indicated. Unless otherwise stated, milk is assumed to be whole, butter is assumed to be salted, eggs are large, individual vegetables are medium, and pepper is freshly ground black pepper. Unless otherwise stated, all root vegetables should be washed and peeled before using.

For the best results, use a meat thermometer when cooking meat and poultry—check the latest USDA government guidelines for current advice.

Garnishes and serving suggestions are all optional and not necessarily included in the recipe ingredients or method. The times given are only an approximate guide. Preparation times differ according to the techniques used by different people and the cooking times may also vary from those given. Optional ingredients, variations, or serving suggestions have not been included in the calculations.

Recipes using raw or very lightly cooked eggs should be avoided by infants, the elderly, pregnant women, and people with weakened immune systems. Pregnant and breast-feeding women are advised to avoid eating peanuts and peanut products. People with nut allergies should be aware that some of the prepared ingredients used in the recipes in this book may contain nuts. Always check the packaging before use.

# CONTENTS

# INTRODUCTION

For those of us who regularly cook meals for family and friends, the one thing that can turn this everyday activity into a chore is its repetitive nature. However good a cook you are, providing meals for a family all year round can soon drain your bank of ideas. Special occasions often provide an extra challenge, especially if you're not used to cooking more demanding, skillful recipes.

So if, like most of us, you have developed a lack of culinary inspiration, this is the book for you. Every page is packed full of creative recipe ideas for every single day of the year, whether it's for those quick weekday meals or for dinner party dishes. There are tempting cakes and desserts, plus some classics for special occasions and festive celebrations.

Chilly fall and winter days call for warming, hearty dishes that are slow-cooked and economical, too, making the best of comforting, seasonal ingredients. In the spring and summer months, we tend to focus on lighter, refreshing dishes that use the best fresh, young produce, either to cook outdoors or to take outdoors to eat when the weather permits. It's always plenty of fun to have a barbecue or an impromptu picnic, so inside you will find loads of easy dishes for alfresco eating of all kinds, including healthy, colorful salads, flavorful grills, and even campfire treats.

## EVERYDAY INSPIRATION

Feeding a family every day can be demanding, especially if you're catering for different ages and tastes while trying to make sure everyone maintains a healthy balanced diet. This book will prove to be an invaluable store of recipes to fall back on, any day of the week.

Whether you are looking for ideas for healthy lunch box snacks when the children go back to school, or you are in need of nutritious, sustaining food to help you through the working day, there are plenty of ideas to choose from to keep your diet varied and interesting.

Cakes and other baked items have their place in everyday cooking, too, as well as on special celebrations. You'll find some irresistible sweet treats to cover every season, including special occasions, when you need a sophisticated, indulgent sweet dish to impress your guests.

## THE STAPLES

A well-stocked pantry or cupboard is invaluable at any time of year. Then, all you should need to buy are the fresh foods in season to complete the dish. Start with this list of basic standbys, then add your own useful favorites:

Canned foods:
- Italian tomatoes
- corn kernels
- beans, such as red kidney, navy beans, chickpeas, lentils

Jars:
- honey, corn syrup, maple syrup
- olive oil
- extra virgin olive oil
- cooking oil, such as sunflower oil or peanut oil
- Worcestershire sauce
- wine vinegar
- soy sauce

Dry goods:
- flour, such as all-purpose flour, as well as cornstarch
- sugar: granulated sugar, brown sugar, and confectioners' sugar
- dried pasta and noodles
- rice and grains, such as bulgur wheat and rolled oats
- dried beans
- dried fruits, such as apricots, raisins, and golden raisins

Frozen:
- vegetables: peas, broccoli
- pastry: phyllo, piecrust, puff

Herbs and spices:
- sweet spices, such as vanilla beans, allspice, cinnamon, nutmeg, ginger
- dried herbs, such as bay leaves, thyme, parsley, oregano, sage, rosemary

## HOW TO USE THIS BOOK

Whether you're cooking everyday family meals or cooking to impress your friends for special dinner parties, this book will be an invaluable resource, guaranteeing that you always have a suitable choice of dishes on hand. It's designed so that you can easily dip in and out of the pages for ideas and inspiration.

You'll find this book is simple to use because there are two useful separate indexes. The first index lists all the recipes alphabetically by name in the usual way for easy reference. A second index lists by the main ingredient or food type, so you can quickly check all the recipes that use your main ingredient; for example, all the beef recipes are listed together, all the chicken ones, and so on. So, if you're trying to decide how to cook some chicken for dinner, it's easy to see at a glance what's in the book and find not just one, but several ideas for chicken dishes. All that's left to do is to start cooking and enjoy eating your way through the whole year!

# JANUARY

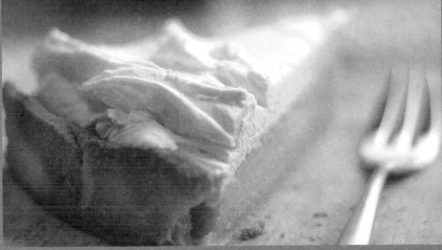

# BAKED HAM WITH HOISIN & HONEY GLAZE

SERVES: 6–8 ⋮ PREP TIME: 20 MIN. PLUS 20 MIN. STANDING TIME ⋮ COOK TIME: 1 HR. 45 MIN.

## INGREDIENTS

4¼-pound city ham

2 bay leaves

2 garlic cloves, crushed

1 tablespoon Dijon mustard

2 tablespoons hoisin sauce

2 tablespoons honey

1. Preheat the oven to 350°F. Put the ham into a large saucepan with the bay leaves and cover with cold water. Bring to a boil, cover, reduce the heat, and simmer gently for 10 minutes. Drain well.

2. Put the ham into a roasting pan and cover loosely with aluminum foil. Bake in the preheated oven for 1 hour.

3. Remove the ham from the oven (do not turn off the oven). Remove the foil and place the ham on a board. Carefully remove the skin with a sharp knife, leaving an even layer of fat on the meat. Score lines through the fat layer, crisscrossing to make a diamond pattern. Return the meat to the roasting pan.

4. Put the garlic, mustard, hoisin sauce, and honey into a bowl and stir to combine. Spread half the mixture over the fat layer of the meat, pressing it into the cuts.

5. Return the ham to the oven and bake for 15 minutes. Remove from the oven, spread with the remaining glaze, then bake for an additional 15 minutes, until golden brown.

6. Cover loosely with foil and let stand for 20 minutes before carving into slices. Skim the fat from the juices and serve them with the meat, as a sauce.

# HEARTY BEEF STEW

SERVES: 4    PREP TIME: 30 MIN. PLUS 15 MIN. STANDING TIME    COOK TIME: 2 HR. 15 MIN.

## INGREDIENTS

3-pound boneless chuck steak, cut into 2-inch pieces

2 tablespoons vegetable oil

2 onions, cut into 1-inch pieces

3 tablespoons all-purpose flour

3 garlic cloves, finely chopped

4 cups beef stock

3 carrots, cut into 1-inch lengths

2 celery stalks, cut into 1-inch lengths

1 tablespoon ketchup

1 bay leaf

¼ teaspoon dried thyme

¼ teaspoon dried rosemary

8 white round or Yukon gold potatoes (about 2 pounds), cut into large chunks

salt and pepper

1. Season the steak generously with salt and pepper. Heat the oil in a large flameproof casserole dish over high heat. When the oil begins to smoke slightly, add the steak, in batches, if necessary, and cook, stirring frequently, for 5–8 minutes, until well browned. Using a slotted spoon, transfer to a bowl.

2. Reduce the heat to medium, add the onions to the casserole dish, and cook, stirring occasionally, for 5 minutes, until translucent. Stir in the flour and cook, stirring continuously, for 2 minutes. Add the garlic and cook for 1 minute. Beat in 1 cup of the stock and cook, scraping up all the sediment from the bottom of the casserole dish, then stir in the remaining stock and add the carrots, celery, ketchup, bay leaf, thyme, rosemary, and 1 teaspoon of salt. Return the steak to the casserole dish.

3. Bring back to a gentle simmer, cover, and cook over low heat for 1 hour. Add the potatoes, replace the lid, and simmer for an additional 30 minutes. Remove the lid, increase the heat to medium, and cook, stirring occasionally, for an additional 30 minutes, or until the meat and vegetables are tender. Remove the bay leaf.

4. If the stew becomes too thick, add a little more stock or water and adjust the seasoning, if necessary. Let stand for 15 minutes before serving.

# TURKEY & LENTIL SOUP

SERVES: 4    PREP TIME: 30 MIN.    COOK TIME: 50 MIN.

## INGREDIENTS

1 tablespoon olive oil

1 garlic clove, chopped

1 large onion, chopped

3 cups sliced white button mushrooms

1 red bell pepper, seeded and chopped

6 tomatoes, peeled, seeded, and chopped

5 cups chicken stock

⅔ cup red wine

½ cup cauliflower florets

1 carrot, chopped

1 cup red lentils

2½ cups chopped cooked turkey

1 zucchini, chopped

1 tablespoon shredded fresh basil

salt and pepper

sprigs of fresh basil, to garnish

1. Heat the oil in a large saucepan. Add the garlic and onion and cook over medium heat, stirring, for 3 minutes, until slightly softened. Add the mushrooms, red bell pepper and tomatoes and cook for an additional 5 minutes, stirring. Pour in the stock and red wine, then add the cauliflower, carrot, and red lentils. Season with salt and pepper. Bring to a boil, then lower the heat and simmer the soup gently for 25 minutes, until the vegetables are tender and cooked through.

2. Add the turkey and zucchini to the pan and cook for 10 minutes. Stir in the shredded basil and cook for an additional 5 minutes, then remove from the heat and ladle into serving bowls. Garnish with basil and serve.

HEARTY
BEEF STEW

# BARLEY, LENTIL & ONION SOUP

**SERVES: 6    PREP TIME: 20 MIN. PLUS 30 MIN. DRYING TIME    COOK TIME: 2 HR. 40 MIN.**

## INGREDIENTS

2 tablespoons pearl barley

⅔ cup water

7 cups vegetable stock

3 onions, thinly sliced into rings

¾ cup dried green lentils

½ teaspoon ground ginger

1 teaspoon ground cumin

3 tablespoons lemon juice

2 tablespoons chopped fresh cilantro

salt and pepper

## TO GARNISH

2 onions, halved and thinly sliced

⅓ cup vegetable oil

2 garlic cloves, finely chopped

**1.** Put the barley into a large saucepan, pour in the water, and bring to a boil. Reduce the heat, cover, and simmer gently, stirring frequently, for about 30 minutes, until all the liquid has been absorbed.

**2.** Add the stock, onions, lentils, ginger, and cumin and bring to a boil over medium heat. Reduce the heat, cover, and simmer, stirring occasionally, for 1½ hours, adding a little more stock, if necessary.

**3.** Meanwhile, make the garnish. Spread out the onions on a thick layer of paper towels and cover with another thick layer. Let dry out for 30 minutes. Heat the oil in a skillet. Add the onions and cook over low heat, stirring continuously, for about 20 minutes, until well browned. Add the garlic and cook, stirring continuously, for an additional 5 minutes. Remove the onions with a slotted spoon and drain well on paper towels.

**4.** Season the soup with salt and pepper, stir in the lemon juice and cilantro, and simmer for an additional 5 minutes. Serve garnished with the browned onions.

# SESAME BEEF

**SERVES: 4–6**    **PREP TIME: 20 MIN.**    **COOK TIME: 10 MIN.**

## INGREDIENTS

1 pound tenderloin steak, cut into thin strips

1½ tablespoons sesame seeds

½ cup beef stock

2 tablespoons soy sauce

2 tablespoons grated fresh ginger

2 garlic cloves, finely chopped

1 teaspoon cornstarch

½ teaspoon crushed red pepper

3 tablespoons sesame oil

1 large head of broccoli, cut into florets

1 yellow bell pepper, seeded and thinly sliced

1 fresh red chile, finely sliced

1 tablespoon chili oil, or to taste

chopped fresh cilantro, to garnish

cooked wild rice, to serve

1. Mix the beef strips with 1 tablespoon of the sesame seeds in a small bowl.

2. In a separate bowl, stir together the stock, soy sauce, ginger, garlic, cornstarch, and crushed red pepper.

3. Heat 1 tablespoon of the sesame oil in a large wok or skillet. Stir-fry the beefstrips for 2–3 minutes. Remove and set aside, then wipe the wok with paper towels.

4. Heat the remaining sesame oil in the wok, add the broccoli, yellow bell pepper, red chile, and chili oil, and stir-fry for 2–3 minutes.

5. Stir in the stock mixture, cover, and simmer for 2 minutes.

6. Return the beef to the wok and simmer until the juices thicken, stirring occasionally. Cook for an additional 1–2 minutes. Sprinkle with the remaining sesame seeds.

7. Garnish with fresh cilantro and serve over wild rice.

## 06 JANUARY

# BAKED TUNA & RICOTTA RIGATONI

| SERVES: 4 | PREP TIME: 5 MIN. | COOK TIME: 30 MIN. |
|---|---|---|

### INGREDIENTS

butter, for greasing

1 pound dried rigatoni

1 (5-ounce) can chunk light tuna, drained and flaked

1 cup ricotta cheese

½ cup heavy cream

2½ cups freshly grated Parmesan cheese

¾ cup drained, sliced sun-dried tomatoes in oil

salt and pepper

1. Preheat the oven to 400°F. Lightly grease a large ovenproof dish with butter. Bring a large, heavy saucepan of lightly salted water to a boil. Add the rigatoni, bring back to a boil, and cook according to the package directions, until just tender but still firm to the bite. Drain the pasta and let stand until cool enough to handle.

2. Meanwhile, mix together the tuna and ricotta cheese in a bowl to form a soft paste. Spoon the mixture into a pastry bag and use to fill the rigatoni. Arrange the filled pasta tubes side by side in the prepared dish.

3. To make the sauce, mix together the cream and Parmesan cheese in a bowl and season with salt and pepper. Spoon the sauce over the rigatoni and top with the sun-dried tomatoes, arranged in a crisscross pattern. Bake in the preheated oven for 20 minutes. Serve hot, straight from the dish.

## 07 JANUARY

# SPAGHETTI CARBONARA

| SERVES: 4 | PREP TIME: 10 MIN. | COOK TIME: 20 MIN. |
|---|---|---|

### INGREDIENTS

1 pound dried spaghetti

1 tablespoon olive oil

8 ounces rindless pancetta or bacon, chopped

4 eggs

½ cup light cream

2 tablespoons freshly grated Parmesan cheese

salt and pepper

1. Bring a large, heavy saucepan of lightly salted water to a boil. Add the spaghetti, bring back to a boil, and cook according to the package directions, until just tender but still firm to the bite.

2. Meanwhile, heat the oil in a heavy skillet. Add the pancetta and cook over medium heat, stirring frequently, for 8–10 minutes.

3. Beat the eggs with the cream in a small bowl and season with salt and pepper. Drain the pasta and return it to the saucepan. Transfer the contents of the skillet to the saucepan, then add the egg mixture and half the cheese. Stir well, then transfer the spaghetti to a serving dish. Serve sprinkled with the remaining cheese.

# PENNE IN TOMATO SAUCE WITH TWO CHEESES

SERVES: 4    PREP TIME: 20 MIN.    COOK TIME: 35 MIN.

## INGREDIENTS

1 pound dried penne

1 cup diced Fontina cheese, Gouda cheese, or Muenster cheese

⅔ cup freshly grated Parmesan cheese

### TOMATO SAUCE

2 tablespoons butter

2 tablespoons olive oil

2 shallots, finely chopped

2 garlic cloves, finely chopped

1 celery stalk, finely chopped

1 (14½-ounce) can diced tomatoes

2 tablespoons tomato paste

brown sugar, to taste

1 teaspoon dried oregano

½ cup water

salt and pepper

1. For the tomato sauce, melt the butter with the oil in a saucepan. Add the shallots, garlic, and celery and cook over low heat, stirring occasionally, for 5 minutes, until softened. Stir in the tomatoes, tomato paste, sugar, oregano, and water and season with salt and pepper. Increase the heat to medium and bring to a boil, then reduce the heat and simmer, stirring occasionally, for 15–20 minutes, until thickened.

2. Meanwhile, bring a large, heavy saucepan of lightly salted water to a boil. Add the penne, bring back to a boil and cook according to the package directions, until just tender but still firm to the bite. Drain and return to the pan.

3. Add the tomato sauce and the cheeses to the pasta and toss well over low heat until the cheeses have melted. Transfer to a serving dish and serve immediately.

## 09 JANUARY

# WINTER SALAD SLAW

SERVES: 4–6    PREP TIME: 15 MIN.    COOK TIME: NO COOKING

### INGREDIENTS

1½ cups finely shredded green cabbage

2 carrots, shredded

1 celery stalk, thinly sliced

3 scallions, thinly sliced

1 Red Delicious or Pink Lady apple

2 tablespoons lime juice

2 tablespoons toasted pumpkin seeds

### DRESSING

½ cup plain yogurt

2 tablespoons mayonnaise

2 tablespoons finely chopped parsley

salt and pepper

1. Put the cabbage, carrots, celery, and scallions into a large bowl and mix together. Coarsely grate the apple and discard the core, then sprinkle with the lime juice and add to the vegetables.

2. To make the dressing, mix together the yogurt, mayonnaise, and parsley, then season with salt and pepper.

3. Pour the dressing over the prepared vegetables and toss well to coat evenly. Sprinkle with the pumpkin seeds and serve cold.

## 10 JANUARY

# HOT BANANA BUTTERSCOTCH

SERVES: 4    PREP TIME: 5 MIN.    COOK TIME: 2–3 MIN.

### INGREDIENTS

4 tablespoons unsalted butter

3 tablespoons raw brown sugar

4 large bananas, thickly sliced

3 tablespoons lemon juice

2 tablespoons light corn syrup

freshly grated nutmeg, for sprinkling

vanilla ice cream, whipped cream, or Greek-style yogurt, to serve

1. Melt the butter in a wide saucepan and stir in the sugar. Heat, stirring, until bubbling, then add the banana chunks. Cook over fairly high heat, stirring continuously, for 1–2 minutes, until bubbling and golden.

2. Stir in the lemon juice and corn syrup, then cook for an additional minute, until bubbling and golden.

3. Sprinkle with nutmeg and serve with ice cream.

# STANDING RIB ROAST

SERVES: 8    PREP TIME: 25 MIN. PLUS 30 MIN. RESTING TIME    COOK TIME: 2½ HR.

## INGREDIENTS

olive oil, for rubbing

6½-pound standing rib roast

½ tablespoon all-purpose flour

1 cup beef stock

1 cup red wine

seasonal vegetables, to serve

### YORKSHIRE PUDDING

2 cups all-purpose flour, sifted

6 eggs

½ teaspoon salt

2½ cups milk

2 tablespoons vegetable oil or lard

### ROASTED POTATOES

4½ pounds russet or new potatoes, peeled

⅓ cup sunflower oil, goose fat, or duck fat

salt and pepper

1. For the Yorkshire pudding, mix together the flour, eggs, and salt in a bowl, then gradually add the milk as you stir with a balloon whisk. When smooth, set aside but do not chill.

2. Preheat the oven to 425°F. For the roasted potatoes, bring a large saucepan of lightly salted water to a boil, add the potatoes, bring back to a boil, and cook for 10 minutes. Drain the potatoes and toss them in oil and salt and pepper. Put them in a roasting pan in a single layer.

3. Rub a generous amount of olive oil and salt and pepper into the beef, then place in a roasting pan. Transfer to the preheated oven and roast for 30 minutes.

4. Reduce the temperature to 325°F. Transfer the potatoes to the oven and roast with the beef for 60 minutes. Remove the beef from the oven—a meat thermometer should read 145°F for medium–rare, 160°F for medium, and 170°F for well done—and increase the oven temperature to 425°F. Cover the beef with aluminum foil and let rest for 30 minutes. Meanwhile, place a roasting pan in the bottom of the oven.

5. Remove the roasting pan from the bottom of the oven and add the vegetable oil. Put it back in the oven for 5 minutes, then remove it and add the Yorkshire pudding batter. Put it back in the hot oven for about 20 minutes.

6. Meanwhile, make the gravy. Remove the beef from the pan and stir the flour into the leftover juices, add the stock and wine, then simmer over medium heat until reduced by about half.

7. Remove the Yorkshire pudding and the potatoes from the oven. Cut the Yorkshire pudding into eight pieces. Cut the rib bones off the meat and carve the beef. Serve with the roasted potatoes, gravy, and seasonal vegetables.

# 12 JANUARY

# CHICKEN SOUP WITH RICE

SERVES: 6    PREP TIME: 15 MIN.    COOK TIME: 40 MIN.

## INGREDIENTS

2 tablespoons olive oil

3 leeks, chopped

6 skinless, boneless chicken thighs, diced

¼ cup long-grain rice

5½ cups vegetable stock

dash of Worcestershire sauce

6 fresh chives, chopped

6 thin bacon strips

2 tablespoons chopped fresh parsley

salt and pepper

1. Heat the oil in a saucepan. Add the leeks and cook over low heat, stirring occasionally, for 5 minutes, until softened. Add the chicken, increase the heat to medium, and cook, stirring frequently, for 2 minutes. Add the rice and cook, stirring continuously, for another 2 minutes.

2. Pour in the stock, add the Worcestershire sauce and chives, and bring to a boil. Reduce the heat, cover, and simmer for 20–25 minutes. Check the chicken is tender and cooked through.

3. Cook the bacon in a nonstick skillet over medium heat, turning occasionally, until crisp. Remove and let cool, then crumble.

4. Season the soup with salt and pepper and stir in the parsley. Ladle into serving bowls, sprinkle with the crumbled bacon, and serve.

# 13 JANUARY

# FRANKFURTER & BEAN CASSEROLE

SERVES: 4    PREP TIME: 15 MIN.    COOK TIME: 35 MIN.

## INGREDIENTS

8 frankfurters

2 tablespoons olive oil

1 large onion, chopped

2 garlic cloves, chopped

1 green bell pepper, seeded and sliced

1 (14½-ounce) can diced tomatoes

2 tablespoons tomato paste

1 (15-ounce) can navy beans

mashed potatoes or rice, to serve

1. Prick the frankfurters all over with a fork. Heat 1 tablespoon of the oil in a large, heavy skillet. Add the frankfurters and cook over low heat, turning frequently, for 5 minutes, until evenly browned and heated through. Remove them from the skillet and keep warm. Drain off the oil and wipe out the skillet with paper towels.

2. Heat the remaining oil in the skillet. Add the onion, garlic, and green bell pepper to the skillet and cook for 5 minutes, stirring occasionally, or until softened.

3. Add the tomatoes to the skillet and let the mixture simmer for about 5 minutes, stirring occasionally, or until slightly reduced and thickened.

4. Stir the tomato paste, navy beans, and frankfurters into the mixture in the skillet. Cook for 4–5 minutes, or until the mixture is piping hot. Add 4–5 tablespoons of water if the mixture becomes too dry during cooking.

5. Transfer to serving plates and serve with mashed potatoes.

CHICKEN SOUP
WITH RICE

# NEW ENGLAND CLAM CHOWDER

**SERVES: 4**  **PREP TIME: 15 MIN.**  **COOK TIME: 25 MIN.**

## INGREDIENTS

2 pounds hardshell clams, such as littlenecks

4 bacon strips, chopped

2 tablespoons butter, plus extra for sautéing

1 onion, chopped

1 tablespoon chopped fresh thyme

1 large potato, diced

1¼ cups milk

1 bay leaf

1½ cups heavy cream

1 tablespoon chopped fresh parsley

salt and pepper

**1.** Scrub the clams. Discard any with broken shells and any that refuse to close when tapped. Put them into a large saucepan with a splash of water. Cook over high heat for 3–4 minutes, until they open. Discard any that remain closed. Strain, reserving the cooking liquid. Let stand until cool enough to handle, reserving eight for the garnish.

**2.** Remove the clams from their shells, chopping them coarsely if large, and reserve.

**3.** In a clean saucepan, sauté the bacon with a little butter until browned and crisp. Drain on paper towels. Add the butter to the same saucepan, and when it has melted, add the onion. Sauté for 4–5 minutes, until soft but not browned. Add the thyme and cook briefly before adding the diced potato, reserved clam cooking liquid, milk, and bay leaf. Bring to a boil, then reduce the heat and let simmer for 10 minutes, or until the potato is just tender.

**4.** Discard the bay leaf, then transfer to a food processor and process until smooth, or push through a strainer into a bowl.

**5.** Add the clams, bacon, and cream. Simmer for 2–3 minutes, until heated through. Season with salt and pepper. Stir in the chopped parsley and serve, garnished with the reserved clams in their shells.

# WINTER BEEF STEW WITH HERB DUMPLINGS

**SERVES: 4**     **PREP TIME: 30 MIN.**     **COOK TIME: 2 HR. 25 MIN.**

## INGREDIENTS

3 tablespoons all-purpose flour

1¾ pounds chuck steak, cubed

3 tablespoons olive oil

12 shallots, peeled and halved

2 carrots, cut into sticks

1 parsnip, sliced

2 bay leaves

1 tablespoon chopped fresh rosemary

2 cups hard cider

2 cups beef stock

1 tablespoon soy sauce

18 canned chestnuts, drained

salt and pepper

## HERB DUMPLINGS

1 cup all-purpose flour, plus extra for flouring

1½ teaspoons baking powder

¼ cup vegetable shortening

2 tablespoons chopped fresh thyme

1. Preheat the oven to 325°F. Put the flour into a clean plastic food bag or on a plate and season generously with salt and pepper. Toss the beef in the seasoned flour until coated.

2. Heat 1 tablespoon of the oil in a large, flameproof casserole dish over medium–high heat. Add one-third of the beef and cook for 5–6 minutes, turning occasionally, until browned all over—the meat may stick to the casserole dish until it is properly sealed. Remove the beef with a slotted spoon. Cook the remaining two batches, adding another tablespoon of oil, as necessary. Set aside when all the beef has been sealed.

3. Add the remaining oil to the casserole dish with the shallots, carrots, parsnip, and herbs and cook for 3 minutes, stirring occasionally. Pour in the cider and beef stock and bring to a boil. Cook over high heat until the alcohol has evaporated and the liquid reduced. Add the soy sauce, then cook for an additional 3 minutes.

4. Stir in the chestnuts and beef, cover, and cook in the preheated oven for 1 hour 35 minutes.

5. Meanwhile, to make the herb dumplings, combine all the ingredients in a bowl and season with salt and pepper. Mix in enough water to make a soft dough. Divide the dough into walnut-size pieces and, using floured hands, roll each piece into a ball.

6. Add to the casserole dish, cover, and cook for an additional 25 minutes, or until the dumplings are cooked, the stock has formed a thick, rich gravy, and the meat is tender. Remove the bay leaves and season with salt and pepper before serving.

## 16 JANUARY

# CHICKEN WITH TOMATO & CINNAMON SAUCE

**SERVES: 4    PREP TIME: 15 MIN.    COOK TIME: 1 HR**

### INGREDIENTS

4 tablespoons butter

2 tablespoons olive oil

4 chicken parts, such as breasts and/or thighs

1 onion, finely chopped

2 garlic cloves, finely chopped

1 celery stalk, finely chopped

1 (14½-ounce) can diced tomatoes

2 tablespoons tomato paste

1 teaspoon Dijon mustard

brown sugar, to taste

2 tablespoons lemon juice

3 tablespoons chicken stock

1 teaspoon dried oregano

¾ teaspoon ground cinnamon

salt and pepper

**1.** Melt the butter with the oil in a flameproof casserole dish. Season the chicken well with salt and pepper, add to the casserole dish, and cook over medium heat, turning frequently, for 8–10 minutes, until evenly browned. Remove from the casserole dish and set aside.

**2.** Add the onion, garlic, and celery to the casserole dish and cook over low heat, stirring occasionally, for 5 minutes, until softened. Stir in the tomatoes, tomato paste, mustard, sugar, lemon juice, stock, oregano, and cinnamon, then season with salt and pepper. Increase the heat to medium and bring to a boil, then reduce the heat and simmer, stirring occasionally, for 15 minutes.

**3.** Return the chicken to the casserole dish and spoon the sauce over it. Cover and simmer, stirring occasionally, for 30 minutes, or until a fork can be easily inserted into the thickest part of the meat with ease and the juices run clear. A meat thermometer should read 170°F when inserted into the thickest part of the meat, without touching the bone. Serve immediately.

## 17 JANUARY

# SHRIMP STIR-FRY

**SERVES: 4    PREP TIME: 10 MIN.    COOK TIME: 5–6 MIN.**

### INGREDIENTS

2 tablespoons sunflower oil

1 garlic clove, thinly sliced

½ teaspoon crushed red pepper

1 large red bell pepper, seeded and thinly sliced

1 large yellow bell pepper, seeded and thinly sliced

1 bunch scallions, sliced diagonally

1 pound large cooked, peeled shrimp

¼ cup oyster sauce

2 tablespoons soy sauce

juice of 1 lime

cooked rice noodles or rice, to serve

**1.** Heat the oil in a wok, add the garlic and crushed red pepper, and stir-fry for 30 seconds.

**2.** Add the red and yellow bell peppers and stir-fry for 2–3 minutes. Add the scallions and shrimp and stir-fry for an additional 2–3 minutes.

**3.** Stir in the oyster sauce, soy sauce, and lime juice and cook until heated through.

**4.** Serve with rice noodles.

# CHICKEN POT PIE

**SERVES: 4–6     PREP TIME: 30 MIN. PLUS 15 MIN. COOLING TIME     COOK TIME: 1 HR. 15 MIN.**

## INGREDIENTS

1 tablespoon olive oil

3 cups sliced white button mushrooms

1 onion, finely chopped

6 carrots, sliced

2 celery stalks, sliced

4 cups chicken stock

6 tablespoons butter

½ cup all-purpose flour, plus extra for dusting

2 pounds skinless, boneless chicken breasts, cut into 1-inch cubes

¾ cup frozen peas

1 teaspoon chopped fresh thyme

3 rolled dough pie crusts, thawed, if frozen

1 egg, lightly beaten

salt and pepper

1. Heat the olive oil in a large saucepan over medium heat. Add the mushrooms and onion and cook, stirring frequently, for about 8 minutes, until golden. Add the carrots, celery, and half the stock and bring to a boil. Reduce the heat to low and simmer for 12–15 minutes, until the vegetables are almost tender.

2. Melt the butter in another large saucepan over medium heat. Whisk in the flour and cook, stirring continuously, for 4 minutes, until the flour is light tan in color. Gradually whisk in the remaining chicken stock. Reduce the heat to medium–low and simmer, stirring, until thickened.

3. Stir in the vegetable mixture, add the chicken, peas, and thyme, and season with salt and pepper. Bring back to a simmer and cook, stirring continuously, for 5 minutes. Taste and adjust the seasoning, if necessary, and remove from the heat.

4. Preheat the oven to 400°F.

5. Divide the filling among six large ramekins (individual ceramic dishes), filling them to within ½ inch of the top. Roll out the dough on a lightly floured work surface and cut out six circles 1 inch larger than the diameter of the ramekins.

6. Put the circles on top of the filling, then fold over ½ inch all the way around to make a rim. If you prefer, pinch with your fingertips to form a crimped edge. Cut a small cross in the center of each dough circle.

7. Put the ramekins on a baking sheet and brush the tops with the beaten egg. Bake in the preheated oven for 35–40 minutes, until the pies are golden brown and bubbling. Remove from the oven and let cool for 15 minutes before serving.

# PEARS WITH CARAMEL

**SERVES: 4**     **PREP TIME: 15 MIN.**     **COOK TIME: 50 MIN.**

## INGREDIENTS

1 tablespoon unsalted butter, plus extra for greasing

4 large pears

ice cream, to serve

### CRUMB TOPPING

1 cup all-purpose flour

1½ teaspoons baking powder

1 stick unsalted butter, diced

⅓ cup raw brown sugar

2 tablespoons chopped hazelnuts

### CARAMEL

3 tablespoons light corn syrup

3 tablespoons raw brown sugar

1 tablespoon unsalted butter

2 tablespoons light cream

½ teaspoon vanilla extract

1. Preheat the oven to 400°F. Grease an ovenproof dish.

2. To make the crumb topping, put the flour and baking powder in a large mixing bowl, then use your fingertips to rub in the unsalted butter until crumbly. Stir in ¼ cup of the sugar and the chopped hazelnuts, place in the prepared dish, and cook in the preheated oven for 5–10 minutes, until heated through.

3. To make the caramel, put the corn syrup into a saucepan over low heat. Add the sugar, unsalted butter, cream, and vanilla extract, and bring gently to a boil. Simmer for 3 minutes, stirring continuously, then remove from the heat and set aside.

4. Put the unsalted butter in a skillet and melt over low heat. Meanwhile, peel and coarsely chop the pears, then add them to the skillet and cook, stirring gently, for 3 minutes. Stir in the caramel and continue to cook, stirring, over low heat for an additional 3 minutes.

5. Transfer the pear-and-caramel mixture to an ovenproof pie plate. Arrange the crumb topping evenly over the top, then sprinkle with the remaining sugar. Bake in the preheated oven for 25–30 minutes, or until the topping is golden brown.

6. Serve hot with ice cream.

# GOLDEN RAISIN & PLUM CRISP

**SERVES: 4**     **PREP TIME: 15 MIN. PLUS 8 HR. SOAKING TIME**     **COOK TIME: 35 MIN.**

## INGREDIENTS

1 cup chopped prunes

1½ cups golden raisins

3¼ cups water

3 tablespoons raw brown sugar

1 teaspoon allspice

1 tablespoon dark rum (optional)

ice cream, to serve

### CRUMB TOPPING

1 cup all-purpose flour

1½ teaspoons baking powder

½ teaspoon allspice

1 stick unsalted butter, diced

⅓ cup raw brown sugar

1. Put the prunes and golden raisins in a large bowl, cover with the water, and let soak overnight or for at least 8 hours.

2. Preheat the oven to 350°F.

3. Drain the fruit, reserving the soaking liquid. Put the fruit in a large saucepan with the sugar and 2½ cups of the soaking liquid. Bring to a boil, then reduce the heat and simmer for about 10 minutes, or until the fruit has softened.

4. Meanwhile, to make the crumb topping, put the flour, baking powder, and allspice in a bowl, then use your fingertips to rub in the butter until crumbly. Stir in ¼ cup of the raw brown sugar.

5. Remove the fruit from the heat, stir in the allspice and the rum, if using, then pour into an ovenproof pie plate. Carefully arrange the crumb over the fruit in an even layer—keep your touch light or the crumb will sink into the filling and turn mushy. Sprinkle the remaining sugar over the topping, then transfer to the preheated oven and bake for 25 minutes, or until the crumb topping is golden brown.

6. Serve hot with ice cream.

PEARS WITH
CARAMEL

## 21 JANUARY

# GROUND BEEF & MASHED POTATOES

SERVES: 6    PREP TIME: 20 MIN.    COOK TIME: 55 MIN.

### INGREDIENTS

2 tablespoons sunflower oil

1 onion, finely chopped

2 carrots, finely chopped

2¼ pounds fresh ground beef

1 tablespoon chopped fresh thyme

2 tablespoons rolled oats

1 cup beef stock

9 parsnips (about 2¼ pounds), finely chopped

9 russet potatoes (about 2¼ pounds), finely chopped

1 stick butter

½ cup heavy cream

salt and pepper

fresh flat-leaf parsley sprigs, to garnish

1. Heat the oil in a skillet. Add the onion and carrots and cook over low heat, stirring occasionally, for 5 minutes, until softened. Add the beef, increase the heat to medium, and cook, stirring frequently and breaking it up with a wooden spoon, for 8–10 minutes, until evenly browned.

2. Stir in the thyme and oats, then pour in the stock. Season with salt and pepper and bring to a boil. Reduce the heat, cover, and simmer, stirring occasionally, for 25–30 minutes, until thickened.

3. Meanwhile, cook the parsnips and potatoes in a large saucepan of lightly salted boiling water for 10–15 minutes, until tender but not falling apart. Remove from the heat and drain. Return the vegetables to the pan and add the butter and cream. Season with salt and pepper, then mash well until smooth.

4. Divide the mashed potatoes and parsnips among serving plates. Top with the beef mixture, garnish with parsley sprigs, and serve.

## 22 JANUARY

# GOLDEN CHICKEN CASSEROLE

SERVES: 4    PREP TIME: 20 MIN.    COOK TIME: 1 HR.

### INGREDIENTS

8 chicken parts, such as thighs and drumsticks

2 tablespoons olive oil

1 large onion, sliced

1-inch piece fresh ginger, finely chopped

3 carrots, sliced

2 yellow bell peppers, seeded and sliced

juice of 1 orange

⅔ cup chicken stock

fresh thyme sprig

salt and pepper

1. Preheat the oven to 350°F. Season the chicken with salt and pepper.

2. Heat the oil in a large saucepan or flameproof casserole dish, add the chicken pieces, and cook, turning occasionally, for 4–5 minutes, until golden brown. Remove from the pan and keep warm.

3. Add the onion to the pan and sauté, stirring, for 2–3 minutes. Stir in the ginger, carrots, and yellow bell peppers.

4. Return the chicken to the pan and add the orange juice, stock, and thyme. Bring to a boil, then cover and cook in the preheated oven for 40–45 minutes, or until a fork can be easily inserted into the thickest part of the meat with ease and the juices run clear. A meat thermometer inserted into the thickest part of the meat, without touching a bone, should read 170°F. Serve.

# SILKY SMOOTH FISH CASSEROLE

SERVES: 6–8      PREP TIME: 20 MIN.      COOK TIME: 1 HR. 10 MIN.

## INGREDIENTS

9 russet potatoes (about 2½ pounds)

1¼ sticks butter, plus extra for greasing

2 cups milk

2 pounds firm white fish fillets, such as halibut, red snapper, or Alaskan pollock

3 bay leaves

½ cup all-purpose flour

handful of fresh parsley, chopped

8 ounces cooked, peeled shrimp

4 hard-boiled eggs, shelled and quartered

4 tablespoons butter, melted

salt and pepper

cooked peas, to serve

1. Peel and quarter the potatoes. Bring a large saucepan of lightly salted water to a boil, add the potatoes, and cook for 15–20 minutes, or until tender. Drain and mash the potatoes thoroughly with half of the butter and 2 tablespoons of the milk. Season with salt and pepper, cover, and keep warm.

2. Preheat the oven to 400°F. Rinse the fish under cold running water and pat dry with paper towels. Place the fish fillets in a shallow saucepan and pour the remaining milk over them. Add the bay leaves and place over low heat. Bring the milk to a gentle simmer and poach the fish for 4 minutes (it shouldn't be completely cooked because it will be baked later). Remove from the saucepan and place on a plate, discard the bay leaves, and reserve the milk. Remove and discard any remaining bones and skin from the fish, then flake the flesh into large chunks. Put the flaked fish in a bowl, cover, and set aside.

3. Melt the remaining butter in a saucepan, then stir in the flour to make a paste and cook, stirring occasionally, for 3 minutes. Gradually add the reserved milk, a ladleful at a time, and mix into the paste. Add the parsley, cooked fish, shrimp, and eggs. Carefully fold together, and season with salt and pepper.

4. Grease a pie plate with butter and fill it with the fish mixture. Spoon the mashed potatoes on top, smoothing the surface level. Drizzle the melted butter over the potatoes, place in the preheated oven, and bake for 30–40 minutes, until the top is golden brown. Serve with peas.

# SLOW-COOKED POTATO STEW

SERVES: 4     PREP TIME: **20 MIN.**     COOK TIME: **1 HR**

## INGREDIENTS

1½ pounds white round or Yukon gold potatoes, cut into 1-inch cubes

2 tablespoons butter

2 tablespoons olive oil

2 ounces pancetta or bacon, diced

1 onion, finely chopped

1 garlic clove, finely chopped

1 celery stalk, finely chopped

1 (14½-ounce) can diced tomatoes

2 tablespoons tomato paste

brown sugar, to taste

1 tablespoon chopped fresh marjoram

½ cup vegetable stock

salt and pepper

**1.** Parboil the potatoes in a saucepan of lightly salted boiling water for 5 minutes. Drain and set aside.

**2.** Melt the butter with the oil in a saucepan. Add the pancetta, onion, garlic, and celery and cook over low heat, stirring occasionally, for 5 minutes, until softened. Stir in the tomatoes, tomato paste, sugar, marjoram, and stock, and season with salt and pepper. Increase the heat to medium and bring to a boil. Gently stir in the potatoes, reduce the heat to low, cover, and simmer, stirring occasionally, for 45–50 minutes, until the potatoes are tender and the sauce has thickened. (Use a fork to stir gently to avoid breaking up the potatoes.)

**3.** Taste and adjust the seasoning, adding salt and pepper, if needed. Transfer the mixture to a serving dish and serve.

SLOW-COOKED
POTATO STEW

# MAPLE-CREAM TART

**SERVES: 6–8  PREP TIME: 15 MIN.  COOK TIME: 55 MIN.**

## INGREDIENTS

1 store-bought rolled dough pie crust, thawed if frozen

½ cup all-purpose flour, plus extra for dusting

3 tablespoons packed light brown sugar

3 cups heavy cream

1 cup pure maple syrup

2 eggs

4 teaspoons lemon juice

½ teaspoon salt

½ teaspoon ground nutmeg

2 tablespoons confectioners' sugar

**1.** Preheat the oven to 400°F. Roll out the pie crust on a lightly floured surface and use to line a 9-inch loose-bottom tart pan. Line the dough with parchment paper and weigh down with pie weights or dried beans. Place on a baking sheet and bake in the preheated oven for 15–20 minutes, until golden at the edges.

**2.** Meanwhile, combine the flour and sugar in a large bowl. Beat 2 cups of the cream in another bowl with the maple syrup, eggs, lemon juice, salt, and nutmeg. Slowly beat this mixture into the flour, beating until no lumps remain.

**3.** When the pie crust is golden, remove the paper and weights and reduce the oven temperature to 350°F. Pour the filling into the pie crust, return to the oven, and cook for 30–35 minutes, until set. Remove the tart from the oven and let cool completely on a wire rack.

**4.** Whip the remaining cream until soft peaks form. Sift over the confectioners' sugar and continue whipping until stiff. Just before serving, spread the whipped cream over the surface of the tart. Cut into slices to serve.

# CHURROS

**SERVES: 4–6  PREP TIME: 15 MIN.  COOK TIME: 15 MIN.**

## INGREDIENTS

1 cup water

6 tablespoons butter or ⅓ cup shortening, diced

2 tablespoons packed light brown sugar

finely grated rind of 1 small orange (optional)

pinch of salt

1⅓ cups all-purpose flour, sifted

1 teaspoon ground cinnamon, plus extra for dusting

1 teaspoon vanilla extract

2 eggs

vegetable oil, for deep-frying

granulated sugar, for dusting

**1.** Heat the water, butter, brown sugar, orange rind, if using, and salt in a heavy saucepan over medium heat until the butter has melted.

**2.** Add all of the flour, the cinnamon, and vanilla extract, then remove the pan from the heat and beat rapidly until the mixture pulls away from the side of the pan. Let cool slightly, then beat in the eggs, one at a time, beating well after each addition, until the mixture is thick and smooth. Spoon into a pastry bag fitted with a wide star tip.

**3.** Heat the oil for deep-frying in a deep-fryer or deep saucepan to 350–375°F, or until a cube of bread browns in 30 seconds. Pipe 5-inch lengths about 3 inches apart into the oil. Deep-fry for 2 minutes on each side, or until golden brown. Remove with a slotted spoon and drain on paper towels.

**4.** Dust the churros with granulated sugar and cinnamon and serve.

MAPLE-CREAM
TART

# REAL HOT CHOCOLATE

**SERVES: 1–2** | **PREP TIME: 5 MIN.** | **COOK TIME: 15 MIN.**

## INGREDIENTS

2 ounces semisweet dark chocolate, broken into pieces

1¼ cups milk

chocolate curls, to decorate

1. Place the chocolate in a heatproof bowl. Place the milk in a heavy saucepan and bring to a boil. Pour about one-quarter of the milk onto the chocolate and let stand until the chocolate has softened.

2. Beat the milk-and-chocolate mixture until smooth. Return the remaining milk to the heat and bring back to a boil, then pour onto the chocolate, beating continuously.

3. Pour into mugs or cups and decorate with chocolate curls.

# CINNAMON MOCHA

**SERVES: 6** | **PREP TIME: 15 MIN.** | **COOK TIME: 10 MIN.**

## INGREDIENTS

8 ounces milk chocolate, broken into pieces

¾ cup light cream

4 cups freshly brewed coffee

1 teaspoon ground cinnamon, plus extra to decorate

whipped cream and marbled chocolate caraque, to decorate

1. Put the chocolate in a large heatproof bowl set over a saucepan of gently simmering water. Add the cream and stir until the chocolate has melted and the mixture is smooth.

2. Pour in the coffee, add the cinnamon, and whisk until foamy. Pour into mugs or cups and decorate with the cream, caraque, and cinnamon. Alternatively, if serving cold, remove the bowl from the heat and let cool. Chill in the refrigerator until required, then decorate with whipped cream, a sprinkling of ground cinnamon, and the caraque.

# RICE PUDDING WITH CINNAMON-POACHED PLUMS

**SERVES: 4**     **PREP TIME: 15 MIN.**     **COOK TIME: 50–55 MIN.**

## INGREDIENTS

½ cup short-grain rice

2 tablespoons sugar

1 tablespoon unsalted butter

2 cups milk

thinly pared strip of orange rind

shreds of orange zest, to decorate

## COMPOTE

8 red plums, halved and pitted

1 cinnamon stick

2 tablespoons sugar

juice of 1 orange

**1.** Put the rice, sugar, and butter into a saucepan and stir in the milk and orange rind. Heat gently, stirring occasionally, until almost boiling.

**2.** Reduce the heat to low, then cover and simmer gently for 40–45 minutes, stirring occasionally, until the rice is tender and most of the liquid has been absorbed.

**3.** Meanwhile, to make the compote, put the plums, cinnamon, sugar, and orange juice into a large saucepan. Heat gently until just boiling, then reduce the heat, cover, and simmer gently for about 10 minutes, or until the plums are tender.

**4.** Remove the plums with a slotted spoon and discard the cinnamon. Serve the rice pudding warm with the compote and sprinkled with orange zest.

# CREAMY TURKEY & BROCCOLI GNOCCHI

SERVES: 4      PREP TIME: **15 MIN.**      COOK TIME: **10 MIN.**

### INGREDIENTS

1 tablespoon sunflower oil

1 pound turkey cutlets,
cut into strips

2 small leeks, sliced diagonally

1 pound store-bought fresh gnocchi

3 cups small broccoli florets

½ cup crème fraîche or
Greek-style yogurt

1 tablespoon whole-grain mustard

3 tablespoons orange juice

3 tablespoons pine nuts

salt and pepper

1. Heat the oil in a wok or large skillet, then add the turkey and leeks and stir-fry over high heat for 5–6 minutes.

2. Meanwhile, bring a saucepan of lightly salted water to a boil. Add the gnocchi and broccoli, then cook for 3–4 minutes.

3. Drain the gnocchi and broccoli and stir into the turkey mixture.

4. Mix together the crème fraîche, mustard, and orange juice in a small bowl. Season with salt and pepper, then stir into the wok.

5. Sprinkle with pine nuts and serve.

# TURKEY SCALLOPS WITH PROSCIUTTO & SAGE

SERVES: 4      PREP TIME: **15 MIN.**      COOK TIME: **2 MIN.**

### INGREDIENTS

2 turkey cutlets

2 slices prosciutto, halved

4 fresh sage leaves

2 tablespoons all-purpose flour

2 tablespoons olive oil

1 tablespoon butter

salt and pepper

lemon wedges, to serve

1. Slice each turkey cutlet in half horizontally into two thinner scallops.

2. Put each scallop between two sheets of plastic wrap and pound lightly with a rolling pin. Season each scallop with salt and pepper.

3. Lay half a slice of prosciutto on each scallop, put a sage leaf on top, and secure with a toothpick.

4. Mix the flour with salt and pepper on a large plate. Dust both sides of each scallop with the seasoned flour.

5. Heat the oil in a large skillet, add the butter, and cook until foaming. Add the scallops and cook over medium heat for 1½ minutes, sage side down.

6. Turn the scallops over and cook for an additional 30 seconds, or until golden brown and cooked through. Serve with lemon wedges.

CREAMY TURKEY &
BROCCOLI GNOCCHI

# FEBRUARY

# DONUTS WITH CINNAMON SUGAR

MAKES: 12–14     PREP TIME: 20 MIN. PLUS RISING TIME     COOK TIME: 10–15 MIN.

## INGREDIENTS

4 cups all-purpose flour, plus extra for dusting

½ cup granulated sugar

½ teaspoon salt

2¼ teaspoons dried yeast

¾ cup lukewarm milk

4 tablespoons unsalted butter, melted

2 eggs, beaten

finely grated rind of 1 lemon

sunflower oil, for deep-frying

## CINNAMON SUGAR

¼ cup granulated sugar

1 teaspoon ground cinnamon

**1.** Sift together the flour, sugar, and salt into a mixing bowl and stir in the yeast. Stir in the milk, butter, eggs, and lemon rind, mixing to a soft, sticky dough.

**2.** Invert the dough onto a lightly floured work surface and knead until smooth. Return to the bowl, cover, and let stand in a warm place for about 1 hour, or until doubled in size.

**3.** Invert the dough onto a lightly floured work surface and knead again for 5 minutes, until smooth and elastic. Roll out to a thickness of ½ inch. Stamp out 3-inch circles with a cutter, then cut a 1-inch circle from the center of each.

**4.** Place the rings on a baking sheet lined with wax paper, cover, and let rise in a warm place for about 1 hour, until doubled in size.

**5.** Heat the oil for deep-frying in a deep-fryer or deep saucepan to 350–375°F, or until a cube of bread browns in 30 seconds. Add the donuts in small batches and cook, turning once, for 3–4 minutes, until golden brown.

**6.** Remove the donuts with a slotted spoon and drain on absorbent paper towels. Mix together the sugar and cinnamon and toss the donuts in the mixture until lightly coated. Serve warm.

# CHICKEN CHOW MEIN

**SERVES: 4**     **PREP TIME: 20 MIN.**     **COOK TIME: 10 MIN.**

## INGREDIENTS

8 ounces dried medium Chinese egg noodles

2 tablespoons sunflower oil

2 cups shredded, cooked chicken breasts

1 garlic clove, finely chopped

1 red bell pepper, thinly sliced

4 ounces shiitake mushrooms, sliced

6 scallions, sliced

1 cup bean sprouts

3 tablespoons soy sauce

1 tablespoon sesame oil

**1.** Cook the noodles according to the package directions and set aside while preparing the other ingredients.

**2.** In a preheated wok or skillet, heat the oil over medium heat. Add the shredded chicken, garlic, red bell pepper, mushrooms, scallions, and bean sprouts to the wok and stir-fry for about 5 minutes.

**3.** Drain the noodles thoroughly, then add them to the wok, toss well, and stir-fry for an additional 5 minutes. Drizzle the soy sauce and sesame oil over the chicken-and-noodles mixture, and toss until thoroughly combined. Transfer to serving bowls and serve.

# BAKED EGGS WITH TOMATO & CORN SAUCE

**SERVES: 4     PREP TIME: 20 MIN.     COOK TIME: 1 HR.**

## INGREDIENTS

2 tablespoons butter

2 tablespoons olive oil

1 onion, finely chopped

2 garlic cloves, finely chopped

1 celery stalk, finely chopped

8 ounces lean bacon, diced

1 red bell pepper, seeded and diced

4 plum tomatoes, peeled, cored, and chopped

2 tablespoons tomato paste

brown sugar, to taste

1 tablespoon chopped fresh parsley

pinch of cayenne pepper

½ cup water

1 (8¾-ounce) can corn kernels, drained

4 extra-large eggs

salt and pepper

1. Melt the butter with the oil in a saucepan. Add the onion, garlic, and celery and cook over low heat, stirring occasionally, for 5 minutes, until softened. Add the bacon and red bell pepper and cook, stirring occasionally, for an additional 10 minutes. Stir in the tomatoes, tomato paste, sugar, parsley, cayenne, and water and season with salt and pepper. Increase the heat to medium and bring to a boil, then reduce the heat and simmer, stirring occasionally, for 15 minutes, until thickened. Meanwhile, preheat the oven to 350°F.

2. Stir the corn kernels into the sauce and transfer the mixture to an ovenproof dish. Make four small hollows with the back of a spoon and break an egg into each. Bake in the preheated oven for 25–30 minutes, until the eggs have set. Serve.

# RICH ORANGE CREPES

SERVES: 4     PREP TIME: 15 MIN.     COOK TIME: 10 MIN.

### INGREDIENTS

**CREPES**

1¼ cups all-purpose flour

1 cup milk

3 tablespoons fresh orange juice

1 extra-large egg

2 tablespoons butter, melted, plus extra for frying

2 oranges, segmented, to serve

**ORANGE BUTTER**

4 tablespoons unsalted butter

finely grated rind and juice of 1 orange

1 tablespoon granulated sugar

**1.** To make the crepes, put all the ingredients (excluding the segmented oranges) into a mixing bowl and beat until smooth. Alternatively, blend in a food processor until smooth.

**2.** Heat a crepe pan or skillet until hot, lightly brush with butter, and pour in a small ladleful of batter, swirling to thinly coat the surface of the pan (these are basically thin pancakes).

**3.** Cook the crepes until golden underneath, then turn and cook the other side. Remove from the pan and keep warm while you cook the remaining batter. Keep warm.

**4.** To make the orange butter, melt the butter in a small saucepan, add the orange rind and juice, and sugar, and stir until the sugar has dissolved. Simmer, stirring, for 30 seconds, then remove from the heat.

**5.** Serve the crepes folded over, with the orange segments and the orange butter poured over.

# BREAD & BUTTER PUDDING

SERVES: 4–6     PREP TIME: 15 MIN. PLUS 15 MIN. STANDING TIME     COOK TIME: 40 MIN.

### INGREDIENTS

6 tablespoons butter, softened

6 slices of thick white bread

⅓ cup mixed dried fruit, such as golden raisins, dried currants, and raisins

2 tablespoons candied peel

3 extra-large eggs

1 ¼ cups milk

⅔ cup heavy cream

¼ cup granulated sugar

whole nutmeg, for grating

1 tablespoon raw brown sugar

cream, to serve (optional)

**1.** Preheat the oven to 350°F.

**2.** Use a little of the butter to grease an 8 x 10-inch baking dish. Butter the slices of bread, cut into quarters, and arrange half of the slices overlapping in the prepared baking dish.

**3.** Sprinkle halve the fruit and the candied peel over the bread, cover with the remaining bread slices, then add the remaining fruit and candied peel.

**4.** In a small bowl, beat the eggs well and mix in the milk, heavy cream, and sugar. Pour the mixture over the bread slices and let stand for 15 minutes so the bread soaks up some of the egg mixture. Tuck in most of the fruit so they don't burn in the oven.

**5.** Grate nutmeg to taste over the top of the dessert, then sprinkle with the raw brown sugar.

**6.** Place the dish on a baking sheet and bake at the top of the preheated oven for 30–40 minutes, until just set and golden brown.

**7.** Remove from the oven and serve warm with a little cream, if using.

RICH ORANGE
CREPES

# 06 FEBRUARY

# CHICKEN CASSEROLE PROVENÇALE

SERVES: 4 · PREP TIME: 15 MIN. · COOK TIME: 1 HR. 10 MIN.

## INGREDIENTS

4 chicken legs

2 tablespoons olive oil

1 large red onion, cut into 8 wedges

1 large green bell pepper, seeded and thickly sliced

1 eggplant, cubed

2 garlic cloves, crushed

1 (14½-ounce) can Italian tomatoes

8 ripe black olives, pitted

salt and pepper

crusty bread or cooked rice, to serve

1. Trim any excess fat from the chicken and season well with salt and pepper. Heat half the oil in a flameproof casserole dish or wide saucepan. Add the chicken and cook over high heat, turning occasionally, for 5–6 minutes, until golden brown. Remove from the casserole dish and keep warm.

2. Add the remaining oil, the onion, green bell pepper, and eggplant to the casserole dish and sauté, stirring frequently, for 4–5 minutes, until lightly browned. Stir in the garlic. Return the chicken to the casserole dish and add the tomatoes and olives.

3. Bring to a boil, then reduce the heat to low, cover, and simmer gently for 45–50 minutes, until a fork can be easily inserted into the thickest part of the meat with ease and the juices run clear. A meat thermometer should read 170°F when inserted into the thickest part of the meat, without touching the bone.

4. Adjust the seasoning and serve the casserole hot, with crusty bread.

# 07 FEBRUARY

# HAM & SPINACH PASTA

SERVES: 4 · PREP TIME: 10 MIN. · COOK TIME: 20 MIN.

## INGREDIENTS

8 ounces dried penne pasta

2 tablespoons olive oil

1 onion, thinly sliced

1 dried red chile, chopped

2 plum tomatoes, diced

8 ounces cooked ham, sliced into strips

1 (8-ounce) package baby spinach leaves

salt and pepper

1. Bring a large, heavy saucepan of lightly salted water to a boil. Add the penne, bring back to a boil, and cook according to the package directions, until just tender but still firm to the bite. Drain.

2. Meanwhile, heat the oil in a large skillet over medium heat, add the onion, and sauté, stirring, for 2–3 minutes, until soft.

3. Add the chile and tomatoes and cook, stirring, for 2 minutes, then add the ham and cook, stirring, for 2–3 minutes, until heated through.

4. Add the spinach and stir until the leaves are just wilted, then stir in the pasta. Season with salt and pepper and serve.

# TAMALE PIE

**SERVES: 6**  **PREP TIME: 15 MIN.**  **COOK TIME: 50 MIN.**

### INGREDIENTS

2 tablespoons corn oil

1 onion, finely chopped

12 ounces ground beef

1½ teaspoons chili powder

1 cup canned diced tomatoes

1 cup drained, canned corn kernels

2 tablespoons chopped, pitted ripe black olives

½ cup sour cream

1 cup cornmeal

½ teaspoon baking powder

4 tablespoons butter, cut into pieces

3 tablespoons milk

about 1 cup hot chicken stock

¾ cup cheddar cheese

salt

**1.** Preheat the oven to 375°. Heat the oil in a large skillet. Add the onion and cook over low heat, stirring occasionally, for 5 minutes, until softened.

**2.** Add the beef, increase the heat to medium, and cook, stirring frequently and breaking it up with a wooden spoon, for 8–10 minutes, until evenly browned. Stir in the chili powder, tomatoes, corn, olives, and sour cream and season with salt. Transfer the mixture to an ovenproof dish.

**3.** Put the cornmeal, baking powder, butter, and milk into a food processor and process until combined. With the motor running, gradually add enough of the hot stock through the feeder tube to make a thick, smooth mixture.

**4.** Pour the cornmeal mixture over the beef mixture and smooth the surface with a spatula. Bake in the preheated oven for 20 minutes, until the topping is just beginning to brown. Sprinkle with the cheese, return to the oven, and bake for an additional 15 minutes, until golden and bubbling. Serve.

# WILD MUSHROOM RISOTTO

SERVES: 6    PREP TIME: 20 MIN. PLUS 30 MIN. SOAKING TIME    COOK TIME: 15–20 MIN.

## INGREDIENTS

2 ounces dried porcini or morel mushrooms

1 pound fresh mixed wild mushrooms, such as porcini, portobello mushrooms, and chanterelles, halved if large

¼ cup olive oil

3–4 garlic cloves, finely chopped

4 tablespoons butter

1 onion, finely chopped

2 cups risotto rice

¼ cup dry white vermouth

5 cups simmering chicken or vegetable stock

1⅓ cups freshly grated Parmesan cheese

¼ cup chopped fresh flat-leaf parsley

salt and pepper

1. Place the dried mushrooms in a heatproof bowl and add boiling water to cover. Set aside to soak for 30 minutes, then carefully lift out and pat dry. Strain the soaking liquid through a strainer lined with paper towels and set aside.

2. Trim the fresh mushrooms and gently brush clean. Heat 3 tablespoons of the oil in a large skillet. Add the fresh mushrooms and stir-fry for 1–2 minutes. Add the garlic and the soaked mushrooms and cook, stirring frequently, for 2 minutes. Transfer to a plate.

3. Heat the remaining oil and half the butter in a large, heavy saucepan. Add the onion and cook over medium heat, stirring occasionally, for 2 minutes, until softened.

4. Reduce the heat, stir in the rice, and cook, stirring continuously, for 2–3 minutes, until the grains are translucent. Add the vermouth and cook, stirring, for 1 minute, until reduced.

5. Gradually add the hot stock, a ladleful at a time, until all the liquid is absorbed and the rice is creamy. Add half the reserved mushroom soaking liquid to the risotto and stir in the mushrooms. Season and add more mushroom liquid, if necessary.

6. Remove the pan from the heat and stir in the remaining butter, grated Parmesan, and chopped parsley. Serve.

# LAMB STEW

SERVES: 4    PREP TIME: 10 MIN.    COOK TIME: 40 MIN.

### INGREDIENTS

1 tablespoon sunflower oil

4 lamb sirloin chops

1 garlic clove, crushed

2 small onions, quartered

10 whole baby carrots

2 small turnips, quartered

1 tablespoon all-purpose flour

1¼ cups lamb stock or beef stock

1 tablespoon whole-grain mustard

salt and pepper

chopped fresh flat-leaf parsley, to garnish

**1.** Heat the oil in a flameproof casserole dish, add the lamb chops, and cook until golden brown, turning once. Remove from the dish and keep warm.

**2.** Add the garlic and onions to the casserole dish and sauté, stirring, for 2–3 minutes. Stir in the carrots and turnips.

**3.** Stir the flour into the vegetables and add the stock. Cook, stirring, until boiling, then add the chops. Season with salt and pepper, then cover and simmer gently for 35 minutes, stirring occasionally.

**4.** Stir in the mustard and adjust the seasoning, if necessary. Sprinkle with the parsley and serve.

# CAULIFLOWER CHEESE GRATIN

SERVES: 4–6    PREP TIME: 15 MIN.    COOK TIME: 10 MIN.

## INGREDIENTS

1 cauliflower, trimmed and cut into florets

3 tablespoons butter

⅓ cup all-purpose flour

2 cups milk

1 cup shredded cheddar cheese

whole nutmeg, for grating

1 tablespoon freshly grated Parmesan cheese

salt and pepper

1. Bring a saucepan of lightly salted water to a boil, add the cauliflower, bring back to a boil, and cook for 4–5 minutes. It should still be firm. Drain, place in a warm 1½-quart gratin dish and keep warm.

2. Melt the butter in the rinsed-out pan over medium heat and stir in the flour. Cook for 1 minute, stirring continuously.

3. Remove the pan from the heat and gradually stir in the milk until you have a smooth consistency.

4. Return the pan to low heat and continue to stir while the sauce comes to a boil and thickens. Reduce the heat and simmer gently, stirring continuously, for about 3 minutes, until the sauce is creamy and smooth.

5. Remove from the heat and stir in the cheddar cheese and a good grating of the nutmeg. Taste and season well with salt and pepper. Meanwhile, preheat the broiler to high.

6. Pour the hot sauce over the cauliflower, top with the Parmesan cheese, and place under the preheated broiler to brown. Serve.

# ROASTED POTATOES

SERVES: 4–6    PREP TIME: 10 MIN.    COOK TIME: 1 HR. 5 MIN.

## INGREDIENTS

6 large russet potatoes (about 3 pounds), peeled and cut into even chunks

3 tablespoons dripping, goose fat, duck fat, or olive oil

salt

1. Preheat the oven to 425°F.

2. Bring a large saucepan of lightly salted water to a boil, add the potatoes, bring back to a boil, and cook for 5–7 minutes. The potatoes should still be firm. Remove from the heat.

3. Meanwhile, add the dripping to a roasting pan and place the pan in the preheated oven.

4. Drain the potatoes well and return them to the saucepan. Cover with the lid and firmly shake the pan so that the surface of the potatoes is roughened to help produce a much crisper texture.

5. Remove the roasting pan from the oven and carefully add the potatoes into the hot oil. Baste them to make sure they are all coated with the oil.

6. Roast at the top of the oven for 45–50 minutes, until they are browned all over and thoroughly crisp. Turn the potatoes and baste again only once during the process, or the crunchy edges will be destroyed.

7. Carefully transfer the potatoes from the roasting pan to a serving dish. Sprinkle with a little salt and serve.

CAULIFLOWER
CHEESE GRATIN

# WALNUT & PECORINO BISCUITS

MAKES: ABOUT 10    PREP TIME: 20 MIN.    COOK TIME: 15 MIN.

## INGREDIENTS

3⅔ cups self-raising flour, plus extra for dusting

1 tablespoon plus 5 teaspoons baking powder

pinch of salt

6 tablespoons butter, diced, plus extra for greasing

¼ cup granulated sugar

½ cup pecorino cheese

100 g/3½ oz walnut pieces

about 1¼ cups milk

1. Preheat the oven to 400°F. Grease a baking sheet.

2. Sift the flour, baking powder, and salt into a large bowl. Add the butter and rub in with your fingertips until the mixture resembles fine bread crumbs. Stir in the sugar, pecorino cheese, and walnuts. Add enough of the milk to bring the mixture together into a soft but not sticky dough.

3. Gently roll the dough out on a lightly floured work surface to a thickness of 1–1¼ inches. Use a 2½-inch round cookie cutter to cut the dough into circles (make the biscuits smaller or larger if you prefer).

4. Put the circles on the prepared baking sheet and bake in the preheated oven for 15 minutes, or until golden and firm. Remove from the oven and let cool on a wire rack.

# BE MY VALENTINE WHOOPIE PIES

**MAKES: 14**     **PREP TIME: 20 MIN.**     **COOK TIME: 30–35 MIN.**

## INGREDIENTS

2 cups all-purpose flour

1 teaspoon baking soda

large pinch of salt

1 stick butter, softened

¾ cup granulated sugar

1 extra-large egg, beaten

1 teaspoon vanilla extract

⅔ cup buttermilk

¼ teaspoon edible red liquid food coloring

2 tablespoons pink heart-shaped sugar sprinkles

## VANILLA BUTTERCREAM

1¼ sticks unsalted butter, softened

1 teaspoon vanilla extract

¼ cup heavy cream

2¼ cups confectioners' sugar, sifted

## ICING

1¼ cups confectioners' sugar

1–2 tablespoons warm water

few drops edible red liquid food coloring

1. Preheat the oven to 350°F. Line two to three large baking sheets with parchment paper. Sift together the all-purpose flour, baking soda, and salt.

2. Place the butter and sugar in a large bowl and beat with an electric mixer until pale and fluffy. Beat in the egg and vanilla extract, followed by half of the flour mixture, then the buttermilk and food coloring. Stir in the rest of the flour mixture and mix until thoroughly incorporated.

3. Pipe or spoon 28 mounds of the batter onto the prepared baking sheets, spaced well apart to allow for spreading. Bake in the preheated oven, one sheet at a time, for 9–11 minutes, until risen and just firm to the touch. Cool for 5 minutes, then, using a spatula, transfer to a wire rack and let cool completely.

4. For the vanilla buttercream, place the butter and vanilla extract in a bowl and beat with an electric mixer for 2–3 minutes, until pale and creamy. Beat in the cream, then gradually beat in the confectioners' sugar and continue beating for 2–3 minutes.

5. For the icing, sift the confectioners' sugar into a bowl and stir in enough water to make a smooth icing that is thick enough to coat the back of a wooden spoon. Beat in a few drops of food coloring to color the icing pale pink.

6. To assemble, spread or pipe the vanilla buttercream on the flat side of half of the cakes. Top with the rest of the cakes. Spoon the icing over the whoopie pies and decorate with the heart-shaped sugar sprinkles. Let set.

# ROASTED SALMON WITH LEMON & HERBS

**SERVES: 4–6   PREP TIME: 20 MIN.   COOK TIME: 15 MIN.**

## INGREDIENTS

⅓ cup extra virgin olive oil

1 onion, sliced

1 leek, trimmed and sliced

juice of ½ lemon

2 tablespoons chopped fresh parsley

2 tablespoons chopped fresh dill

1 pound salmon fillets

salt and pepper

cooked baby spinach leaves and lemon wedges, to serve

**1.** Preheat the oven to 400°F. Heat 1 tablespoon of the oil in a skillet over medium heat. Add the onion and leek and cook, stirring, for about 4 minutes, until slightly soft.

**2.** Meanwhile, put the remaining oil in a small bowl with the lemon juice and herbs and season with salt and pepper. Stir together well. Rinse the fish under cold running water, then pat dry with paper towels. Arrange the fish in an ovenproof dish.

**3.** Remove the skillet from the heat and spread the onion and leek over the fish. Pour the oil mixture over the top, making sure that everything is well coated. Bake in the preheated oven for about 10 minutes, or until the fish is cooked through.

**4.** Arrange the cooked spinach on serving plates. Remove the fish and vegetables from the oven and arrange on top of the spinach. Serve with the lemon wedges.

# CARAMELIZED ONION TART

**SERVES: 4–6   PREP TIME: 10 MIN.   COOK TIME: 1 HR.**

## INGREDIENTS

1 stick unsalted butter

4 onions, thinly sliced

2 eggs

½ cup heavy cream

1 cup grated Swiss cheese

1 (8-inch) prebaked pie crust, thawed, if frozen

1 cup coarsely grated Parmesan cheese,

salt and pepper

**1.** Melt the butter in a heavy skillet over medium heat. Add the onions and cook, stirring frequently to avoid burning, for 30 minutes, or until well-browned and caramelized. Remove the onions from the skillet and set aside.

**2.** Preheat the oven to 375°F. Beat the eggs in a large bowl, stir in the cream, and season with salt and pepper. Add the Swiss cheese and mix well. Stir in the cooked onions.

**3.** Pour the egg-and-onion mixture into the baked pie crust and sprinkle with the Parmesan cheese. Place on a baking sheet and bake in the preheated oven for 15–20 minutes, until the filling has set and is beginning to brown.

**4.** Remove from the oven and let rest for at least 10 minutes. The tart can be served hot or left to cool to room temperature.

# BROCCOLI & BLUE CHEESE SOUP

**SERVES: 4–6     PREP TIME: 15 MIN.     COOK TIME: 35 MIN.**

## INGREDIENTS

3 tablespoons butter

2 onions, chopped

1 large white round or Yukon gold potato, peeled and chopped

1 head of broccoli, trimmed and cut into florets

6½ cups vegetable stock

1 cup diced blue cheese

pinch of ground mace

salt and pepper

croutons, to garnish

**1.** Melt the butter in a large saucepan. Add the onions and potato and stir well. Cover and cook over low heat for 7 minutes. Add the broccoli and stir well, then replace the lid and cook for an additional 5 minutes.

**2.** Increase the heat to medium, pour in the stock, and bring to a boil. Reduce the heat, season with salt and pepper, and replace the lid. Simmer for 15–20 minutes, until the vegetables are tender.

**3.** Remove the pan from the heat, strain into a bowl, reserving the vegetables, and let cool slightly. Put the vegetables into a food processor, add 1 ladleful of the stock, and process to a smooth puree. With the motor running, gradually add the remaining stock.

**4.** Return the soup to the rinsed-out pan and reheat gently, but do not let the soup boil. Remove from the heat and stir in the cheese until melted and thoroughly combined. Stir in the mace, then taste and adjust the seasoning, if necessary. Ladle into serving bowls, sprinkle with the croutons, and serve.

# TILAPIA WITH WHITE WINE, CHILE & TAPENADE

SERVES: 4     PREP TIME: 5 MIN.     COOK TIME: 20 MIN.

### INGREDIENTS

1 tablespoon olive oil

4 tilapia fish fillets or other firm white fish fillets

¼ cup tapenade

1 fresh small red finger chile, finely diced

¼ cup freshly grated Parmesan cheese

¼ cup dry white wine

salt and pepper

cooked rice, to serve

**1.** Preheat the oven to 425°F. Brush a wide, ovenproof dish with the oil.

**2.** Season the fish with salt and pepper and place in the prepared dish in a single layer.

**3.** Mix together the tapenade and chile and spread over the fish, then sprinkle with the cheese.

**4.** Pour the wine around the fish and bake in the preheated oven for about 15 minutes, or until the flesh flakes easily. Serve with rice.

# APPLE SPICED OATMEAL

SERVES: 4    PREP TIME: 5 MIN.    COOK TIME: 10 MIN.

## INGREDIENTS

2½ cups milk or water

1 teaspoon salt

1¼ cups rolled oats

2 large Pippin apples

½ teaspoon ground apple pie spice

honey, to serve (optional)

**1.** Put the milk in a saucepan and bring to a boil. Add the salt and sprinkle in the oats, stirring continuously.

**2.** Place over low heat and let the oats simmer for 10 minutes, stirring occasionally.

**3.** Meanwhile, peel, halve, core, and grate the apples. When the oatmeal is creamy and most of the liquid has evaporated, stir in the grated apple and apple pie spice. Spoon into serving bowls and drizzle with the honey, if using.

# SLOPPY JOES

SERVES: 4    PREP TIME: 15 MIN.    COOK TIME: 40 MIN.

## INGREDIENTS

1 pound chuck ground beef

1 onion, chopped

1 garlic clove, chopped

1 green bell pepper, seeded and chopped

1 tablespoon yellow mustard

¾ cup ketchup

1 teaspoon white vinegar

1 tablespoon packed brown sugar

pinch of chili powder, ground cloves, or paprika (optional)

4 burger buns, halved

salt and pepper

**1.** Put the beef, onion, garlic, and green bell pepper into a nonstick skillet and cook over medium heat, stirring frequently and breaking up the beef with a wooden spoon, for 8–10 minutes, until the beef is evenly browned. Carefully drain off the fat.

**2.** Stir in the mustard, ketchup, vinegar, brown sugar, and chili powder, if using. Season with salt and pepper. Reduce the heat and simmer, stirring occasionally, for 30 minutes.

**3.** Divide the mixture among the burger buns and serve.

APPLE SPICED
OATMEAL

# SPAGHETTI WITH MEAT SAUCE

SERVES: 4    PREP TIME: 25 MIN.    COOK TIME: 1 HR.

### INGREDIENTS

1 tablespoon olive oil

1 onion, finely chopped

2 garlic cloves, chopped

1 carrot, chopped

1 celery stalk, chopped

2 ounces pancetta or bacon, diced

12 ounces ground sirloin beef

1 (14½ -ounce) can diced tomatoes

2 teaspoons dried oregano

½ cup red wine

2 tablespoons tomato paste

12 ounces dried spaghetti

salt and pepper

chopped fresh flat-leaf parsley,
to garnish

**1.** Heat the oil in a large skillet. Add the onion and cook for 3 minutes. Add the garlic, carrot, celery, and pancetta and sauté for 3–4 minutes, or until just beginning to brown.

**2.** Add the beef and cook over high heat for an additional 3 minutes, or until all of the meat is brown. Stir in the tomatoes, oregano, and red wine and bring to a boil. Reduce the heat and let simmer for about 45 minutes.

**3.** Stir in the tomato paste and season with salt and pepper.

**4.** Bring a large, heavy saucepan of lightly salted water to a boil. Add the spaghetti, bring back to a boil, and cook for 8–10 minutes, or until just tender but still firm to the bite. Drain.

**5.** Transfer the spaghetti to serving plates and pour the meat sauce over it. Toss to mix well, garnish with parsley, and serve hot.

# ROASTED CHICKEN

**SERVES: 6**　　**PREP TIME: 10 MIN.**　　**COOK TIME: 2 HR. 10 MIN.**

### INGREDIENTS

5-pound chicken

4 tablespoons butter, softened

2 tablespoons chopped fresh lemon thyme, plus extra sprigs to garnish

1 lemon, quartered

½ cup white wine, plus extra if needed

salt and pepper

1. Preheat the oven to 425°F. Place the chicken in a roasting pan.

2. Place the butter in a bowl, mix in the chopped thyme, and season well with salt and pepper. Butter the chicken all over with the herb butter, inside and out, and place the lemon quarters inside the cavity. Pour the wine over the chicken.

3. Roast the chicken in the center of the preheated oven for 15 minutes. Reduce the temperature to 375°F and continue to roast, basting frequently, for an additional 1¾ hours. Cover with aluminum foil if the skin begins to brown too much. If the pan dries out, add a little more wine or water.

4. Test that the chicken is cooked by inserting a meat thermometer into the thickest part of the meat—in the inner thigh area near the breast—without touching the bone; it should have a reading of 180°F. Or cook until the chicken is tender and the juices run clear when the point of a sharp knife is inserted into the thickest part of the meat. Gently pull the leg away from the body; the leg should give and no traces of pinkness or blood should remain. Remove the chicken from the oven.

5. Remove the chicken from the roasting pan and place on a warm serving plate. Cover with foil and leave to rest for 10 minutes before carving.

6. Place the roasting pan on the top of the stove and simmer the pan juices gently over low heat until they have reduced and are thick and glossy. Season with salt and pepper. Serve the chicken with the pan juices and garnish with thyme sprigs.

# CHICKEN & BROCCOLI CASSEROLE

SERVES: 4     PREP TIME: 10 MIN.     COOK TIME: 35 MIN.

## INGREDIENTS

1 head of broccoli, cut into florets

3 tablespoons butter

1 onion, thinly sliced

2½ cups bite-size cooked chicken chunks

½ cup crème fraîche or sour cream

1 cup chicken stock

½ cup fresh white bread crumbs

½ cup shredded Swiss cheese

salt and pepper

**1.** Preheat the oven to 400°F. Bring a saucepan of lightly salted water to a boil, add the broccoli, and cook for 5 minutes, until tender. Drain well.

**2.** Meanwhile, melt 2 tablespoons of the butter in a skillet, add the onion, and sauté over medium heat, stirring, for 3–4 minutes, until soft.

**3.** Layer the broccoli, onion, and chicken in a 1½-quart casserole dish and season well with salt and pepper. Pour the crème fraîche and stock over the chicken and vegetables.

**4.** Melt the remaining butter in a small saucepan and stir in the bread crumbs. Mix with the cheese and sprinkle the mixture over the dish.

**5.** Place the dish on a baking sheet in the preheated oven and bake for 20–25 minutes, until golden brown and bubbling. Serve hot.

# PAPRIKA TURKEY STRIPS

**SERVES: 4      PREP TIME: 10 MIN.      COOK TIME: 7–10 MIN.**

### INGREDIENTS

1 pound turkey cutlets

1 tablespoon paprika

1 teaspoon crushed coriander seeds

½ teaspoon garlic salt

¼ teaspoon pepper

2 tablespoons olive oil

1 red onion, sliced

3 tablespoons chopped fresh cilantro

cooked rice, to serve

1. Cut the turkey into long strips, about ½-inch thick.

2. Put the paprika, coriander seeds, garlic salt, and pepper into a large bowl and mix together. Stir in 1 tablespoon of the oil. Add the turkey strips and turn to coat evenly in the mixture.

3. Heat the remaining oil in a large skillet or wok, add the onion, and sauté, stirring, for 1 minute. Add the turkey strips and sauté, stirring over high heat for 6–8 minutes, until cooked through.

4. Sprinkle over the chopped cilantro and serve with rice.

# WARM BULGUR WHEAT SALAD

SERVES: 4    PREP TIME: 10 MIN. PLUS 10 MIN. SOAKING TIME    COOK TIME: 2 MIN.

## INGREDIENTS

1½ cups bulgur wheat

4 cups boiling water

¼ cup extra virgin olive oil

1 bunch scallions, sliced

¾ cup chopped dried apricots

½ cup blanched almonds, toasted

2 tablespoons chopped fresh parsley

2 tablespoons chopped fresh cilantro

juice of 1 lime

1 garlic clove, crushed

salt and pepper

1. Place the bulgur wheat in a bowl and pour over the boiling water. Cover and let stand for 10 minutes, or until the grains have swelled and softened. Drain off any excess liquid.

2. Heat 1 tablespoon of the oil in a skillet, add the scallions, and sauté, stirring, for 1 minute, until soft. Add the apricots and almonds and stir for 30 seconds, until heated through.

3. Stir in the bulgar wheat, parsley, and cilantro, then transfer to a large salad bowl.

4. Put the remaining oil, the lime juice, and garlic into a screw-top jar and shake well. Season with salt and pepper.

5. Stir the dressing into the warm salad, tossing to coat all the ingredients evenly. Serve warm or cold.

# PAN-FRIED SHRIMP

SERVES: 4    PREP TIME: 5 MIN.    COOK TIME: 5 MIN.

## INGREDIENTS

4 garlic cloves

20–24 large shrimp, shell on

1 stick butter

¼ cup olive oil

⅓ cup brandy

salt and pepper

chopped fresh parsley, to garnish

lemon wedges, to serve

1. Using a sharp knife, peel and slice the garlic.

2. Wash the shrimp and pat dry with paper towels.

3. Melt the butter with the oil in a large skillet, add the garlic and shrimp, and cook over high heat, stirring, for 3–4 minutes, until the shrimp are pink.

4. Sprinkle with brandy and season with salt and pepper. Sprinkle with parsley and serve with lemon wedges.

# MACARONI & CHEESE

SERVES: 4    PREP TIME: 10 MIN.    COOK TIME: 35 MIN.

## INGREDIENTS

8 ounces dried macaroni pasta

2½ cups milk

½ teaspoon grated nutmeg

4 tablespoons butter, plus extra for cooking the pasta

½ cup all-purpose flour

2 cups shredded cheddar cheese or American cheese

¾ cup freshly grated Parmesan cheese

1 (6-ounce) package baby spinach

salt and pepper

**1.** Preheat the oven to 350°F. Cook the macaroni according to the package directions. Remove from the heat, drain, and add a small pat of butter to keep it soft. Return to the saucepan and cover to keep warm.

**2.** Put the milk and nutmeg into a saucepan over low heat and heat until warm, but do not boil. Put the butter into a heavy saucepan over low heat, melt the butter, add the flour, and stir to make a paste. Cook gently for 2 minutes. Add the milk a little at a time, whisking it into the paste, then cook for about 10–15 minutes to make a sauce.

**3.** Add three-quarters of the cheddar cheese and Parmesan cheese and stir through until they have melted in, then add the spinach, season with salt and pepper, and remove from the heat.

**4.** Put the macaroni into a casserole dish, then pour the sauce over the pasta. Sprinkle the remaining cheese over the top and place the dish in the preheated oven. Bake for about 30 minutes, until the cheese begins to brown, then serve.

# FISH STEW WITH BEER

SERVES: 4          PREP TIME: 25 MIN.          COOK TIME: 35 MIN.

## INGREDIENTS

2 teaspoons butter

1 large leek, thinly sliced

2 shallots, finely chopped

½ cup beer

1¼ cups fish stock

2 white round or Yukon gold potatoes, peeled and diced

1 bay leaf

¼ cup all-purpose flour

1 cup milk

1 cup heavy cream

2 cups choppped fresh sorrel leaves

12 ounces skinless monkfish or cod fillet, cut into 1-inch pieces

salt and pepper

1. Melt the butter in a large saucepan over medium–low heat. Add the leek and shallots and cook for about 5 minutes, stirring frequently, until they start to soften. Add the beer and bring to a boil.

2. Stir in the stock, potatoes, and bay leaf with a large pinch of salt (unless the stock is salty) and bring back to a boil. Reduce the heat, cover, and cook gently for 10 minutes.

3. Put the flour in a small bowl and slowly whisk in a few tablespoons of the milk to make a thick paste. Stir in a little more milk to make a smooth liquid.

4. Adjust the heat so the stew bubbles gently. Stir in the flour-and-milk mixture and cook, stirring frequently, for 5 minutes. Add the remaining milk and half the cream. Continue cooking for about 10 minutes, until the potatoes are tender. Remove and discard the bay leaf.

5. Combine the sorrel with the remaining cream. Stir the sorrel cream into the stew and add the fish. Continue cooking, stirring occasionally, for about 3 minutes, until the monkfish stiffens. Taste the stew and adjust the seasoning, if needed. Ladle into serving bowls and serve.

# PORK CHOPS BRAISED WITH SHALLOTS

SERVES: 4          PREP TIME: 15 MIN.          COOK TIME: 1 HR. 10 MIN.

## INGREDIENTS

2 tablespoons olive oil

4 lean pork chops

12 small shallots, peeled

3 celery stalks, sliced

2 Pippin apples, cored and sliced

1 cup chicken stock

2 tablespoons Worcestershire sauce

1 tablespoon finely chopped fresh rosemary

fresh rosemary sprigs, to garnish

1. Heat the oil in a large, wide saucepan or flameproof casserole dish, add the pork chops, and cook, turning once, for 2–3 minutes, until lightly browned.

2. Add the shallots and celery and cook for an additional 2 minutes, until lightly browned.

3. Stir in the apples, then add the stock, Worcestershire sauce, and chopped rosemary and bring to a boil. Reduce the heat to low, cover, and simmer gently for about 1 hour, until the meat is tender.

4. Garnish with rosemary sprigs and serve.

FISH STEW
WITH BEER

# MARCH

# LEEK & GOAT CHEESE TARTS

SERVES: 4 | PREP TIME: 15 MIN. | COOK TIME: 20 MIN.

## INGREDIENTS

1 (9 x 14-inch) sheet
ready-to-bake puff pastry

3 tablespoons butter

12 ounces baby leeks,
thickly sliced diagonally

1 tablespoon chopped fresh oregano

4 ounces goat cheese,
sliced or crumbled

milk, for brushing

salt and pepper

1. Preheat the oven to 425°F. Cut the pastry into six 4½-inch squares.

2. Place the pastry squares on a baking sheet and use the tip of a sharp knife to score each one about ½-inch from the edge all around.

3. Melt the butter in a skillet, add the leeks, and sauté gently, stirring frequently, for 4–5 minutes, until soft. Add the oregano, season with salt and pepper, and divide the leek mixture among the pastry squares, placing it inside the scored lines.

4. Top each tart with cheese and brush the pastry with milk. Bake in the preheated oven for 12–15 minutes, until risen and golden brown. Serve warm.

# MINI CAKE POPS

MAKES: 24     PREP TIME: 40 MIN. PLUS 1–2 HR. CHILLING TIME     COOK TIME: 10 MIN.

## INGREDIENTS

1 pound store-bought vanilla or almond-flavored sponge cake

⅓ cup mascarpone cheese

½ cup confectioners' sugar

½ teaspoon vanilla or almond extract

## DECORATION

8 ounces milk chocolate, coarsely chopped

24 ice pop sticks

1¼ cups confectioners' sugar

edible pink food coloring

4 teaspoons cold water

24 small candies

sugar sprinkles

**1.** Line a baking sheet with wax paper. Crumble the cake into a mixing bowl. Add the mascarpone cheese, confectioners' sugar, and vanilla extract and mix together until you have a thick paste.

**2.** Roll a piece of the paste into a ball about the size of a walnut. Push this ball into a mini cupcake liner, pressing it down so that when it is removed from the liner, you have a mini cupcake shape. Shape 23 more cake pops in the same way. Place on the baking sheet and chill for 1–2 hours, until firm.

**3.** To make the decoration, put the chocolate in a heatproof bowl. Set the bowl over a saucepan of gently simmering water and heat until melted. Remove from the heat. Push an ice pop stick into each cake pop. Dip a cake pop into the chocolate, turning it until coated. Lift it from the bowl, letting the excess drip back into the bowl, then place it in a cup or glass. Repeat with the remaining cake pops. Chill or let stand in a cool place until the chocolate has set.

**4.** Put the confectioners' sugar in a mixing bowl and beat in a dash of pink food coloring and the water until smooth. The icing should almost hold its shape. Spoon a little onto a cake pop, easing it slightly down the sides with the side of a teaspoon. If the icing is too firm, you might need to add a dash more water. Before the icing sets, place a small candy in the center of each cake pop and sprinkle with sugar sprinkles.

# CHOCOLATE & NUT OAT COOKIES

MAKES: 15     PREP TIME: 5 MIN.     COOK TIME: 15 MIN.

## INGREDIENTS

6 tablespoons unsalted butter, plus extra for greasing

½ cup chocolate-hazelnut spread

2 cups rolled oats

½ cup blanched hazelnuts, chopped

1. Preheat the oven to 400°F. Grease a baking sheet.

2. Place the butter and chocolate-hazelnut spread in a saucepan and heat gently until just melted.

3. Add the rolled oats and hazelnuts to the chocolate mixture and stir to combine thoroughly.

4. Shape the mixture into 15 equal balls, then press onto the prepared baking sheet. Bake in the preheated oven for 10–12 minutes. Remove from the oven and let stand until firm before transferring the cookies to a wire rack to finish cooling.

# 04 MARCH

# SPICY BEEF TACOS

SERVES: 4    PREP TIME: 25 MIN.    COOK TIME: 25 MIN.

## INGREDIENTS

2 tablespoons vegetable oil

1 small onion, finely chopped

2 garlic cloves, finely chopped

1 pound ground sirloin beef

1½ teaspoon hot chili powder

1 teaspoon ground cumin

8 taco shells

1 avocado

2 tablespoons lemon juice

¼ head of lettuce, shredded

4 scallions, thinly sliced

2 tomatoes, peeled and diced

½ cup sour cream

1 cup shredded cheddar cheese

salt and pepper

**1.** Heat the oil in a skillet. Add the onion and garlic and cook over low heat, stirring occasionally, for 5 minutes, until softened. Add the beef, increase the heat to medium, and cook, stirring frequently and breaking it up with a wooden spoon, for 8–10 minutes, until evenly browned. Drain off as much fat as possible.

**2.** Stir in the chili powder and cumin, season with salt and pepper, and cook over low heat, stirring frequently for an additional 8 minutes, then remove from the heat.

**3.** Heat the taco shells according to the package directions. Meanwhile, peel, pit, and slice the avocado and gently toss with the lemon juice in a bowl.

**4.** Divide the lettuce, scallions, tomatoes, and avocado slices among the taco shells. Add a tablespoon of sour cream to each, then divide the beef mixture among them. Sprinkle with the cheese and serve immediately.

# 05 MARCH

# CHILI CON CARNE

SERVES: 4    PREP TIME: 25 MIN.    COOK TIME: 2 HR. 20 MIN.

## INGREDIENTS

1½ pounds beef chuck

2 tablespoons vegetable oil

1 large onion, sliced

2–4 garlic cloves, crushed

1 tablespoon all-purpose flour

2 cups tomato juice

1 (14½-ounce) can diced tomatoes

1–2 tablespoons sweet chili sauce

1 teaspoon ground cumin

1 (15-ounce) can red kidney beans, drained and rinsed

½ teaspoon dried oregano

1–2 tablespoons chopped fresh parsley

salt and pepper

sprigs of fresh herbs, to garnish

cooked rice and tortilla chips, to serve

**1.** Preheat the oven to 325°F. Using a sharp knife, cut the beef into ¾-inch cubes. Heat the vegetable oil in a large, flameproof casserole dish and sauté the beef over medium heat until well sealed on all sides. Remove the beef from the dish with a slotted spoon and reserve until required.

**2.** Add the onion and garlic to the casserole dish and sauté until lightly browned. Stir in the flour and cook for 1–2 minutes.

**3.** Stir in the tomato juice and tomatoes and bring to a boil. Return the beef to the casserole dish, add the chili sauce and cumin, and season with salt and pepper. Cover and cook in the preheated oven for 1½ hours, or until the beef is almost tender.

**4.** Stir in the kidney beans, oregano, and parsley, and adjust the seasoning, if necessary. Cover the casserole dish and return to the oven for 45 minutes. Garnish with sprigs of fresh herbs and serve with rice, accompanied by tortilla chips.

SPICY BEEF
TACOS

# PASTA WITH PESTO

SERVES: 4     PREP TIME: 10 MIN.     COOK TIME: 10 MIN.

## INGREDIENTS

1 pound dried tagliatelle

sprigs of fresh basil, to garnish

## PESTO

2 garlic cloves

3 tablespoons pine nuts

5 cups fresh basil leaves (about 4 ounces)

½ cup olive oil

¾ cup freshly grated Parmesan cheese

salt

1. To make the pesto, put the garlic, pine nuts, and a large pinch of salt into a food processor and process briefly. Add the basil leaves and process to a paste. With the motor still running, gradually add the oil. Scrape into a bowl and beat in the Parmesan cheese. Season with salt.

2. Bring a large saucepan of lightly salted water to a boil. Add the tagliatelle, bring back to a boil, and cook according to the package directions, until tender but still firm to the bite. Drain well, return to the saucepan, and toss with half the pesto, then divide among serving dishes and top with the remaining pesto. Garnish with sprigs of basil and serve.

# CARROT & CILANTRO SOUP

SERVES: 6     PREP TIME: 15 MIN.     COOK TIME: 40 MIN.

## INGREDIENTS

3 tablespoons olive oil

1 red onion, chopped

1 large white round potato, peeled and chopped

1 celery stalk, chopped

8 carrots (about 1 pound), chopped

4 cups vegetable stock

1 tablespoon butter

2 teaspoons coriander seeds, crushed

1½ tablespoons chopped fresh cilantro, plus extra to garnish

1 cup milk

salt and pepper

1. Heat the oil in a large saucepan. Add the onion and cook over low heat, stirring occasionally, for 5 minutes, until softened.

2. Add the potato and celery and cook, stirring occasionally, for 5 minutes, then add the carrots and cook, stirring occasionally, for an additional 5 minutes. Cover the pan, reduce the heat to low, and cook, shaking the pan occasionally, for 10 minutes.

3. Pour in the stock and bring to a boil, then cover and simmer for 10 minutes, until the vegetables are tender.

4. Meanwhile, melt the butter in a skillet. Add the coriander seeds and cook, stirring continuously, for 1 minute. Add the chopped cilantro and cook, stirring continuously, for 1 minute, then remove from the heat.

5. Remove the soup from the heat and let cool slightly. Transfer to a food processor, in batches, if necessary, and process to a puree. Return the soup to the rinsed-out pan, stir in the cilantro mixture and milk, and season with salt and pepper. Reheat gently, then serve, sprinkled with chopped cilantro.

# EGGPLANT CASSEROLE

**SERVES: 4–6     PREP TIME: 25 MIN.     COOK TIME: 1 HR.**

## INGREDIENTS

½ cup all-purpose flour

2 large eggplants, sliced

⅔ cup olive oil

8 ounces mozzarella cheese, thinly sliced

¾ cup freshly grated Parmesan cheese

## TOMATO SAUCE

1 tablespoon butter

1 tablespoon olive oil

1 shallot, finely chopped

1 garlic clove, finely chopped

1 small celery stalk, finely chopped

1 cup canned diced tomatoes

1 tablespoon tomato paste

brown sugar, to taste

½ teaspoon dried oregano

¼ cup water

salt and pepper

1. First, make the tomato sauce. Melt the butter with the oil in a saucepan. Add the shallot, garlic, and celery and cook over low heat, stirring occasionally, for 5 minutes, until softened. Stir in the tomatoes, tomato paste, sugar, oregano, and water and season with salt and pepper. Increase the heat to medium and bring to a boil, then reduce the heat and simmer, stirring occasionally, for 15–20 minutes, until thickened.

2. Meanwhile, preheat the oven to 350°F. Spread out the flour on a shallow dish and season with salt and pepper. Dip the eggplant slices in the flour to coat and shake off any excess. Heat the oil in a skillet, add the eggplant slices, in batches, and cook for 2 minutes on each side, until lightly browned. Remove and drain on paper towels.

3. Make alternating layers of eggplant slices, mozzarella slices, and tomato sauce in an ovenproof dish. Sprinkle with the Parmesan cheese and bake in the preheated oven for 25 minutes, until the topping is golden and bubbling. Serve.

# TURKEY CUTLETS WITH TARRAGON SAUCE

SERVES: 4    PREP TIME: 10 MIN.    COOK TIME: 15–20 MIN.

### INGREDIENTS

1 tablespoon all-purpose flour

4 turkey cutlets

1 tablespoon olive oil

2 tablespoons butter

2 shallots, finely chopped

⅔ cup dry white wine

thinly pared rind and juice of ½ lemon

2 tablespoons chopped fresh tarragon

¼ cup heavy cream

salt and pepper

1. Put the flour into a shallow bowl and season with salt and pepper. Add the turkey cutlets and turn in the flour until lightly coated.

2. Heat the oil with half the butter in a skillet, add the turkey cutlets, and cook over medium heat, turning once, for 8–10 minutes, until golden brown and cooked through. Remove from the skillet and keep warm.

3. Add the remaining butter to the skillet, then add the shallots and sauté, stirring, for 3–4 minutes, until soft. Add the wine, lemon rind and juice, and half the tarragon. Bring to a boil and boil for 2–3 minutes, until reduced by about half.

4. Strain the sauce into a clean saucepan, add the cream and the remaining tarragon, and cook, stirring, until boiling. Adjust the seasoning, then spoon the sauce over the turkey cutlets and serve.

# TURKEY CASSEROLE WITH CABBAGE & DILL

SERVES: 4    PREP TIME: 10 MIN.    COOK TIME: 35 MIN.

### INGREDIENTS

2 tablespoons olive oil

1 pound turkey breast, cubed

1 large onion, thinly sliced

1 garlic clove, chopped

1 cup chicken stock

1 small head of green cabbage, sliced

2 tomatoes, diced

1 tablespoon chopped fresh dill, plus extra to garnish

salt and pepper

1. Heat the oil in a large, flameproof casserole dish, add the turkey, and cook over high heat for 2–3 minutes, until lightly browned.

2. Add the onion and sauté for 2 minutes. Stir in the garlic, then add the stock and bring to a boil. Add the cabbage, tomatoes, and dill and season with salt and pepper.

3. Return to a boil, then reduce the heat, cover, and simmer gently for 20–25 minutes, until tender. Adjust the seasoning, then sprinkle with fresh dill and serve.

# SPRING STEW

**SERVES: 4**    **PREP TIME: 25 MIN.**    **COOK TIME: 35 MIN.**

### INGREDIENTS

2 tablespoons olive oil

4–8 pearl onions, halved

1 celery stalk, sliced

8 ounces baby carrots, scrubbed and halved, if large

8 new potatoes, scrubbed and halved or quartered, if large

3½–5 cups vegetable stock

1 (15-ounce) can navy beans, drained and rinsed

1 fresh bouquet garni, with sprigs of parsley, thyme, and bay leaf tied together

1½–2 tablespoons light soy sauce

8 baby corn

¾ cup shelled fresh or frozen fava beans, thawed, if frozen

½ small head of savoy cabbage or green cabbage

1½ tablespoons cornstarch

2 tablespoons cold water

salt and pepper

freshly grated Parmesan cheese, to serve

**1**. Heat the oil in a large, heavy saucepan with a tight-fitting lid. Add the onions, celery, carrots, and potatoes and cook, stirring frequently, for 5 minutes, or until softened. Add the stock, drained beans, bouquet garni, and soy sauce, then bring to a boil. Reduce the heat, cover, and simmer for 12 minutes.

**2.** Add the baby corn and fava beans and season with salt and pepper. Simmer for an additional 3 minutes.

**3**. Meanwhile, discard the outer leaves and hard core in the center from the cabbage and shred the leaves. Add to the saucepan and simmer for an additional 3–5 minutes, or until all the vegetables are tender.

**4**. Blend the cornstarch with the water, stir into the saucepan, and cook, stirring, for 4–6 minutes, or until the liquid has thickened. Serve with a bowl of Parmesan cheese for stirring into the stew.

# CHOCOLATE FUDGE CAKE

**SERVES: 8**     **PREP TIME: 20 MIN. PLUS 1 HR. COOLING TIME**     **COOK TIME: 40 MIN.**

## INGREDIENTS

1½ sticks unsalted butter, softened, plus extra for greasing

1 cup granulated sugar

3 eggs, beaten

3 tablespoons light corn syrup

½ cup almond meal (ground almonds)

1⅓ cups all-purpose flour

2 teaspoons baking powder

pinch of salt

½ cup unsweetened cocoa powder

## FROSTING

8 ounces semisweet dark chocolate, broken into pieces

¼ cup firmly packed dark brown sugar

2 sticks unsalted butter, diced

⅓ cup evaporated milk

½ teaspoon vanilla extract

1. Preheat the oven to 350°F. Grease and line two 8-inch cake pans.

2. For the frosting, place the ingredients in a heavy saucepan. Heat gently, stirring continuously, until melted.

3. Pour into a bowl and let cool. Cover and chill for 1 hour, or until spreadable.

4. For the cake, place the butter and sugar in a bowl and beat together until light and fluffy. Gradually beat in the eggs. Stir in the corn syrup and almonds.

5. Sift the flour, baking powder, salt, and cocoa powder into a separate bowl, then fold into the butter mixture. Add a little water, if necessary, to make a dropping consistency.

6. Spoon the batter into the prepared pans and bake in the preheated oven for 30–35 minutes, or until springy to the touch and a toothpick inserted in the center comes out clean.

7. Cool in the pans for 5 minutes, then invert onto a wire rack to cool completely.

8. When the cakes are cold, sandwich them together with half the frosting. Spread the remaining frosting over the top and sides of the cake, swirling it to give a decorative appearance.

# KEY LIME PIE

**SERVES: 4–6**     **PREP TIME: 20 MIN. PLUS 2 HR. CHILLING TIME**     **COOK TIME: 20 MIN.**

## INGREDIENTS

### CRUMB CRUST

25 graham crackers or gingersnaps

2 tablespoons granulated sugar

½ teaspoon ground cinnamon

4 tablespoons butter, melted, plus extra for greasing

### FILLING

1 (14-ounce) can condensed milk

½ cup freshly squeezed lime juice

finely grated rind of 3 limes

4 egg yolks

whipped cream, to serve

1. Preheat the oven to 325°F. Lightly grease a 9-inch round tart pan, about 1½ inches deep.

2. To make the crumb crust, put the cookies, sugar, and cinnamon in a food processor and process until fine crumbs form—do not overprocess to a powder. Add the melted butter and process again until moistened.

3. Transfer the crumb mixture to the prepared tart pan and press over the bottom and up the side. Place the tart pan on a baking sheet and bake in the preheated oven for 5 minutes.

4. Meanwhile, to make the filling, beat together the condensed milk, lime juice, lime rind, and egg yolks in a bowl until well blended.

5. Remove the tart pan from the oven, pour the filling into the crumb crust, and spread out to the edges. Return to the oven for an additional 15 minutes, or until the filling is set around the edges but still wobbly in the center.

6. Let cool completely on a wire rack, then cover and chill for at least 2 hours. Spread thickly with whipped cream and serve.

CHOCOLATE
FUDGE CAKE

# RHUBARB & ORANGE CRISP

SERVES: 4 · PREP TIME: 15 MIN. · COOK TIME: 30–35 MIN.

## INGREDIENTS

10 rhubarb stalks, trimmed and cut into 2-inch slices

¼ cup granulated sugar

finely grated rind and juice of 1 orange

whipped cream, to serve

## CRUMB TOPPING

½ cup all-purpose flour

¼ cup firmly packed light brown sugar

4 tablespoons unsalted butter

½ cup rolled oats

½ cup almond meal (ground almonds)

**1.** Preheat the oven to 400°F. Put the rhubarb, sugar, and orange rind and juice into a saucepan and heat until boiling. Reduce the heat, cover, and simmer for about 5 minutes, until the rhubarb is just tender.

**2.** Transfer to a 1½-quart ovenproof dish and place on a baking sheet.

**3.** To make the crumb topping, put the flour and sugar into a bowl and mix together. Add the butter and rub it in with your fingertips to make a crumbly mixture. Stir in the oats and almonds.

**4.** Sprinkle the topping evenly over the fruit and bake in the preheated oven for 25–30 minutes, until golden brown. Serve warm with whipped cream.

# ALL-IN-ONE VANILLA SPONGE CAKE

**SERVES: 8**     **PREP TIME: 20 MIN. PLUS 1 HR COOLING TIME**     **COOK TIME: 20–25 MIN.**

### INGREDIENTS

2¾ cups all-purpose flour

2 teaspoons baking powder

2 sticks unsalted butter, softened, plus extra for greasing

1 cup granulated sugar

4 eggs, beaten

1 teaspoon vanilla extract

### FROSTING

1 stick unsalted butter, softened

1½ cups confectioners' sugar

1 teaspoon vanilla extract

colored flower sprinkles, to decorate

**1.** Preheat the oven to 350°F. Grease and line two 8-inch cake pans.

**2.** Sift together the flour and baking powder into a mixing bowl and add the butter, sugar, eggs, and vanilla extract. Beat with an electric mixer until just smooth.

**3.** Spoon the batter into the prepared pans and level the tops. Bake in the preheated oven for 20–25 minutes, until risen, golden brown, and firm to the touch.

**4.** Let cool in the pans for 5 minutes, then turn out onto a wire rack to cool completely.

**5.** To make the frosting, put the butter, sugar, and vanilla extract into a bowl and beat until smooth and spreadable. Use half the frosting to sandwich together the two cakes.

**6.** Spread the remaining frosting over the top of the cake and decorate with flower sprinkles.

# IRISH STEW

| SERVES: 4 | PREP TIME: 20 MIN. | COOK TIME: 2½ HR. |

## INGREDIENTS

¼ cup all-purpose flour

3 pounds neck of lamb or lamb shanks, trimmed of visible fat

3 large onions, chopped

3 carrots, sliced

4 white round or Yukon gold potatoes, peeled and cut into wedges

½ teaspoon dried thyme

3½ cups hot beef stock

salt and pepper

chopped fresh parsley, to garnish

1. Preheat the oven to 325°F. Spread the flour on a plate and season with salt and pepper. Roll the pieces of lamb in the flour to coat, shaking off any excess, and arrange in the bottom of a casserole dish.

2. Layer the onions, carrots, and potatoes on top of the lamb.

3. Sprinkle in the thyme and pour in the stock, then cover and cook in the preheated oven for 2½ hours. Serve garnished with the parsley.

# MASHED POTATOES WITH SCALLIONS

| SERVES: 4 | PREP TIME: 10 MIN. | COOK TIME: 25 MIN. |

## INGREDIENTS

8 russet potatoes (about 2 pounds)

4 tablespoons butter, plus extra for serving

2 bunches of scallions, cut into ½-inch slices

1 cup milk or light cream

salt and pepper

chopped fresh chives and chopped fresh parsley, to garnish

1. Peel the potatoes and cut into large chunks. Bring a large saucepan of water to a boil, add the potatoes, and cook for 15–20 minutes, until tender.

2. Drain the potatoes well and mash with a potato masher. If you prefer smooth mashed potatoes, press them through a strainer. Keep warm.

3. Melt the butter in medium saucepan and add the scallions. Sauté for 3–4 minutes, until soft. Add the milk and bring to a simmer. Season well and let thicken slightly.

4. Stir the scallion mixture into the warm potatoes and adjust the seasoning, if necessary. Sprinkle with the chopped herbs and serve with extra butter.

# BEEF ENCHILADAS

MAKES: 18     PREP TIME: 35 MINS.     COOK TIME: 1 HR 15 MIN.

## INGREDIENTS

1 tablespoon vegetable oil, plus extra for brushing

1 onion, finely chopped

2 fresh green chiles, seeded and chopped

12 ounce ground sirloin beef

1 cup shredded cheddar cheese

18 tortillas

chopped fresh cilantro, to garnish

## PIQUANT TOMATO SAUCE

2 tablespoons butter

2 tablespoons olive oil

1 onion, finely chopped

2 garlic cloves, finely chopped

1 fresh green chile, seeded and chopped

1 (14½-ounce) can diced tomatoes

2 tablespoons tomato paste

brown sugar, to taste

1 teaspoon dried oregano

½ teaspoon cayenne pepper

½ cup heavy cream

salt and pepper

**1.** Heat the vegetable oil in a skillet. Add the onion and chiles and cook over low heat, stirring occasionally, for 5 minutes. Add the beef, increase the heat to medium, and cook, stirring frequently and breaking it up with the spoon, for 8–10 minutes, until evenly browned. Remove the skillet from the heat and stir in half the cheese.

**2.** To make the piquant tomato sauce, melt the butter with the olive oil in a saucepan. Add the onion, garlic, and chile and cook over medium heat, stirring occasionally, for 5–8 minutes, until the onion is golden brown. Stir in the tomatoes, tomato paste, sugar, oregano, and cayenne pepper and season with salt and pepper. Increase the heat to medium and bring to a boil. Reduce the heat, stir in the cream, and simmer, stirring occasionally, for 15–20 minutes, until thickened. Remove from the heat and let cool slightly.

**3.** Meanwhile, preheat the oven to 350°F. Heat a skillet and brush with vegetable oil. One at a time, dip the tortillas in the sauce, shake off any excess, and cook in the skillet for 30 seconds on each side. Transfer to a large plate, put a tablespoon of the meat mixture in the center, and roll up. Put the filled tortillas, seam side down, in a large ovenproof dish and pour the remaining sauce over them. Sprinkle with the remaining cheese and bake in the preheated oven for 15–20 minutes. Garnish with cilantro and serve.

# CHICKEN FRIED RICE

SERVES: 4     PREP TIME: 25 MIN.     COOK TIME: 10–12 MIN.

## INGREDIENTS

½ tablespoon sesame oil

6 shallots, quartered

3 cups diced, cooked chicken

3 tablespoons soy sauce

2 carrots, diced

1 celery stalk, diced

1 red bell pepper, seeded and diced

1 cup shelled peas

½ cup drained, canned corn kernels

2 cups cold, cooked long-grain rice

2 extra-large eggs, scrambled

1. Heat the oil in a wok or large skillet over medium heat. Add the shallots and cook until soft, then add the chicken and 2 tablespoons of the soy sauce and stir-fry for 5–6 minutes.

2. Stir in the carrots, celery, red bell pepper, peas, and corn and stir-fry for an additional 5 minutes. Add the rice and stir thoroughly.

3. Finally, stir in the scrambled eggs and the remaining soy sauce. Serve.

# PENNE WITH TURKEY MEATBALLS

SERVES: 4     PREP TIME: 25 MIN.     COOK TIME: 1 HR. 10 MIN.

## INGREDIENTS

1 pound fresh ground turkey

1 small garlic clove, finely chopped

2 tablespoons finely chopped fresh parsley

1 egg, lightly beaten

all-purpose flour, for dusting

3 tablespoons olive oil

1 onion, finely chopped

1 celery stalk, finely chopped

1 carrot, finely chopped

1¾ cups tomato puree

1 fresh rosemary sprig

1 bay leaf

1 pound dried penne

salt and pepper

freshly grated Parmesan cheese, to serve

1. Put the turkey, garlic, and parsley in a bowl and mix well. Stir in the egg and season with salt and pepper. Dust your hands lightly with flour and shape the mixture into walnut-size balls between your palms. Lightly dust each meatball with flour.

2. Heat the olive oil in a saucepan. Add the onion, celery, and carrot and cook over low heat, stirring occasionally, for 5 minutes, until softened. Increase the heat to medium, add the meatballs, and cook, turning frequently, for 8–10 minutes, until golden brown all over.

3. Pour in the tomato puree, add the rosemary and bay leaf, season to taste with salt and pepper, and bring to a boil. Lower the heat, cover, and simmer gently, stirring occasionally, for 40–45 minutes. Remove and discard the herbs.

4. Shortly before the meatballs are ready, bring a large saucepan of lightly salted water to a boil. Add the penne, bring back to a boil and cook according to the package directions, until tender but still firm to the bite. Drain and add to the pan with the meatballs. Stir gently and heat through briefly, then spoon into serving dishes. Sprinkle generously with Parmesan cheese and serve.

CHICKEN
FRIED RICE

# SWORDFISH STEAKS WITH LIME BUTTER

SERVES: 4    PREP TIME: 20 MIN. PLUS 30 MIN. MARINATING TIME    COOK TIME: 10 MIN.

## INGREDIENTS

4 swordfish steaks (about 6 ounces each)

3 tablespoons olive oil, plus extra for brushing

⅓ cup lime juice

1 teaspoon sweet paprika

1 stick unsalted butter, cut into pieces

grated rind of 1 lime

1½-inch piece of fresh ginger, chopped

1 tablespoon chopped fresh cilantro

pinch of cayenne pepper

salt and pepper

lime wedges, to serve

1. Place the swordfish steaks in a shallow, nonmetallic dish. Mix together the olive oil, 2 tablespoons of the lime juice, and the paprika in a small bowl and season with salt and pepper. Pour the mixture over the fish and turn to coat. Cover with plastic wrap and set aside in the refrigerator to marinate for 30 minutes.

2. Meanwhile, put the remaining lime juice in a blender with the butter, lime rind, ginger, and cilantro. Season with salt and cayenne pepper. Process until thoroughly combined, scraping down the sides, if necessary.

3. Scrape the lime butter onto a piece of aluminum foil and roll into a log shape. Chill in the refrigerator until ready to serve.

4. Meanwhile, place a ridged, cast-iron skillet over high heat until you can feel the heat rising from the surface. When the fish is thoroughly marinated, lift out of the marinade, place on the hot skillet and chargrill for 4 minutes. Turn the fish over, brush with more marinade, and chargrill on the other side for 4 minutes, or until cooked through.

5. Transfer the swordfish steaks to serving plates. Unwrap the lime butter and cut it into slices. Top each fish with 1–2 slices of the butter and serve with lime wedges.

# TUNA STEAKS WITH SPICY TOMATO SAUCE

SERVES: 4    PREP TIME: 20 MIN.    COOK TIME: ABOUT 30 MIN.

## INGREDIENTS

2 tablespoons olive oil, plus extra for brushing

1 onion, chopped

2 red bell peppers, seeded and chopped

1 fresh red chile, seeded and chopped

1 garlic clove, chopped

1 (14½-ounce) can diced tomatoes

dash of white wine vinegar

½ cup almond meal (ground almonds)

4 tuna steaks (about 4–5 ounces each)

salt and pepper

1. Heat the oil in a nonstick skillet over medium–high heat, add the onion and red bell peppers, and cook, stirring frequently, for 10 minutes, or until soft. Add the chile and garlic and cook, stirring, for 1 minute. Add the tomatoes and their juices, bring to a simmer, and cook for 15 minutes. Stir in the vinegar.

2. Transfer the tomato mixture to a food processor. Add the almonds and process for 20 seconds, or until smooth. Season with salt and pepper, and add a little water if the mixture is too thick to pour.

3. Preheat the broiler to high, or heat a skillet over high heat. Pat dry the tuna steaks with paper towels and lightly brush with oil on both sides. Cook under the preheated broiler or in the hot skillet for 1½ minutes on each side to sear, or until cooked to your liking.

4. Serve the tuna steaks with the sauce spooned around them.

# FRIED CHICKEN WITH TOMATO & BACON SAUCE

SERVES: 4          PREP TIME: 20 MIN.          COOK TIME: 45 MIN.

## INGREDIENTS

2 tablespoons butter

2 tablespoons olive oil

4 skinless, boneless chicken breasts or 8 skinless, boneless chicken thighs

### TOMATO & BACON SAUCE

2 tablespoons butter

2 tablespoons olive oil

1 large onion, finely chopped

2 garlic cloves, finely chopped

1 celery stalk, finely chopped

4 bacon strips, diced

1 (14½-ounce) can diced tomatoes

2 tablespoons tomato paste

brown sugar, to taste

½ cup water

1 tablespoon chopped fresh basil

1 tablespoon chopped fresh flat-leaf parsley, plus extra to garnish

salt and pepper

1. First, make the tomato-and-bacon sauce. Melt the butter with the oil in a large saucepan. Add the onion, garlic, celery, and bacon and cook over low heat, stirring occasionally, for 5 minutes, until softened. Stir in the tomatoes, tomato paste, sugar, and water and season with salt and pepper. Increase the heat to medium and bring to a boil, then reduce the heat and simmer, stirring occasionally, for 15–20 minutes, until thickened.

2. Meanwhile, melt the butter with the oil in a large skillet. Add the chicken and cook over medium–high heat for 4–5 minutes on each side, until evenly browned.

3. Stir the basil and parsley into the sauce. Add the chicken and spoon the sauce over it. Cover and simmer for 10–15 minutes. Check that the chicken is cooked and no longer pink by inserting the tip of a sharp knife into the thickest part of the meat. Garnish with parsley and serve.

# NEW POTATOES WITH GARLIC & CHILE BUTTER

SERVES: 4     PREP TIME: 10 MIN.     COOK TIME: 15 MIN.

## INGREDIENTS

1½ pounds new potatoes

3 tablespoons butter

1 garlic clove, finely chopped

1 fresh red chile, seeded and finely chopped

salt and pepper

chopped fresh cilantro leaves, to garnish (optional)

**1.** Bring a large saucepan of lightly salted water to a boil, add the potatoes, bring back to a boil, and cook for 15 minutes, or until tender. Drain well.

**2.** Melt the butter in a large saucepan, add the garlic and chile, and gently sauté for 30 seconds, without browning.

**3.** Add the potatoes and stir to coat in the butter, then season with salt and pepper. Sprinkle with the cilantro, if using, and serve hot.

# CHICKEN WITH CREAMY PENNE

SERVES: 2     PREP TIME: 5 MIN.     COOK TIME: 15–18 MIN.

## INGREDIENTS

8 ounces dried penne

1 tablespoon olive oil

2 skinless, boneless chicken breasts

¼ cup dry white wine

¾ cup frozen peas

⅓ cup heavy cream

salt

chopped fresh flat-leaf parsley, to garnish

**1.** Bring a large, heavy saucepan of lightly salted water to a boil. Add the penne, bring back to a boil, and cook according to the package directions, until just tender but still firm to the bite.

**2.** Meanwhile, heat the oil in a skillet, add the chicken, and cook over medium heat for about 4 minutes on each side.

**3.** Pour in the wine and cook over high heat until the liquid has almost evaporated.

**4.** Drain the pasta. Add the peas, cream, and pasta to the skillet and stir well. Cover and simmer for 2 minutes. Check that the chicken is cooked and no longer pink by using the tip of a sharp knife to cut into the thickest part of the meat.

**5.** Garnish with parsley and serve.

# CHORIZO & CHICKPEA CASSEROLE

SERVES: 4          PREP TIME: 15 MIN.          COOK TIME: 30 MIN.

## INGREDIENTS

2 tablespoons olive oil

1 onion, sliced

1 large yellow bell pepper, seeded and sliced

1 garlic clove, crushed

1 teaspoon crushed red pepper

8 ounces chorizo sausage

1 (14½-ounce) can diced tomatoes

1 (15-ounce) can chickpeas, drained and rinsed

1 cup long-grain rice

handful of arugula

salt and pepper

chopped fresh basil, to garnish

1. Heat the oil in a flameproof casserole dish and sauté the onion over medium heat, stirring occasionally, for 5 minutes.

2. Add the yellow bell pepper, garlic, and crushed red pepper and cook for 2 minutes, stirring. Chop the chorizo into bite-size chunks and stir into the casserole dish.

3. Add the tomatoes and chickpeas and season with salt and pepper. Bring to a boil, cover, and simmer for 10 minutes.

4. Meanwhile, cook the rice in a saucepan of lightly salted boiling water according to the package directions, until tender. Drain.

5. Stir the arugula into the casserole dish. Serve spooned over the rice, garnished with fresh basil.

# POTATO & BACON CASSEROLE

SERVES: 4    PREP TIME: 10 MIN.    COOK TIME: 45 MIN.

## INGREDIENTS

8 small russet potatoes (about 2 pounds), peeled and sliced

2 tablespoons olive oil

3 garlic cloves, peeled but kept whole

6 ounces bacon, chopped

2½ cups heavy cream

2 tablespoons fresh thyme leaves

8 ounces fontina cheese or any other good melting cheese, sliced

salt

1. Preheat the oven to 350°F.

2. Cook the potato slices in a large saucepan of lightly salted boiling water for 10–15 minutes, until just tender. Drain.

3. Heat the oil in a large skillet over medium heat. Hit the garlic cloves with the back of a sturdy knife to split them and add to the skillet. Add the bacon and cook for 3–4 minutes, until just cooked. Add the potato slices and cook for 3–4 minutes. Pour in the cream, add the thyme leaves, and stir well.

4. Transfer the mixture to a casserole dish and top with the cheese slices. Bake in the preheated oven for 20 minutes, or until golden and bubbling.

# MACARONI & SEAFOOD CASSEROLE

SERVES: 4    PREP TIME: 20 MIN.    COOK TIME: 40 MIN.

## INGREDIENTS

12 ounces dried macaroni

6 tablespoons butter, plus extra for greasing

2 small fennel bulbs, trimmed and thinly sliced

2½ cups thinly sliced white button mushrooms

6 ounces cooked, peeled shrimp

pinch of cayenne pepper

2½ cups store-bought white sauce

¾ cup freshly grated Parmesan cheese

2 large tomatoes, halved and sliced

olive oil, for brushing

1 teaspoon dried oregano

salt

1. Preheat the oven to 350°F. Bring a large saucepan of lightly salted water to a boil. Add the pasta, bring back to a boil, and cook according to the package directions, until just tender but still firm to the bite. Drain and return to the saucepan. Add 2 tablespoons of the butter to the pasta, cover, shake the saucepan, and keep warm.

2. Melt the remaining butter in a separate saucepan. Add the fennel and cook for 3–4 minutes. Stir in the mushrooms and cook for an additional 2 minutes. Stir in the shrimp, then remove the saucepan from the heat. Stir the cooked pasta, cayenne pepper, and shrimp mixture into the white sauce.

3. Grease a large ovenproof dish, then pour the mixture into the dish and spread evenly. Sprinkle with the Parmesan cheese and arrange the tomato slices in a ring around the edge. Brush the tomatoes with oil, then sprinkle with the oregano. Bake in the preheated oven for 25 minutes, or until golden brown. Serve.

POTATO & BACON
CASSEROLE

# BEEF MEDALLIONS WITH ORANGE, LIME & HONEY

SERVES: 4    PREP TIME: 10 MIN. PLUS 20 MIN. STANDING TIME    COOK TIME: 8–10 MIN.

### INGREDIENTS

4 tenderloin steaks

2 oranges

juice of 1 lime

1 tablespoon olive oil

1 tablespoon butter

1 sprig of fresh thyme

2 tablespoons honey

salt and pepper

1. Place the steaks in a wide, nonmetallic dish. Squeeze the juice from one orange and pour it over the steak with the lime juice. Cover and let stand in the refrigerator for 20 minutes. Drain, reserving the juices.

2. Cut all the peel and white pith from the remaining orange and remove the segments, catching any juice in a bowl.

3. Heat a heavy skillet over medium–high heat. Brush the steaks with oil and season with salt and pepper. Place in the hot skillet and cook for 2–2½ minutes on each side, for medium–rare to medium. Remove, cover, and keep warm.

4. Melt the butter in the skillet, then stir in the marinade and reserved citrus juice, thyme, and honey. Bring to a boil and stir for 1 minute. Season with salt and pepper and add the orange segments.

5. Arrange the steaks on serving plates, spoon the juices over them and the orange segments, and serve.

# RASPBERRY CRUMB MUFFINS

MAKES: 12    PREP TIME: 20 MIN.    COOK TIME: 20 MIN.

### INGREDIENTS

oil or melted butter, for greasing (if using)

2¼ cups all-purpose flour

1 tablespoon baking powder

½ teaspoon baking soda

pinch of salt

½ cup granulated sugar

2 eggs

1 cup plain yogurt

6 tablespoons butter, melted and cooled

1 teaspoon vanilla extract

1 cup frozen raspberries

### CRUMB TOPPING

½ cup all-purpose flour

2 tablespoons butter

2 tablespoons granulated sugar

1. Preheat the oven to 400°F. Grease a 12-cup muffin pan or line with 12 muffin cups.

2. To make the crumb topping, sift the flour into a bowl. Cut the butter into small pieces, add to the bowl with the flour, and rub it in with your fingertips until the mixture resembles fine bread crumbs. Stir in the sugar and set aside.

3. To make the muffins, sift together the flour, baking powder, baking soda, and salt into a large bowl. Stir in the sugar.

4. Lightly beat the eggs in a large bowl then beat in the yogurt, butter, and vanilla extract. Make a well in the center of the dry ingredients, pour in the beaten liquid ingredients, and add the raspberries. Stir gently until just combined; do not overmix.

5. Spoon the mixture into the prepared muffin pan. Sprinkle the crumb topping over each muffin and press down lightly. Bake in the preheated oven for about 20 minutes, until well risen, golden brown, and firm to the touch.

6. Let the muffins cool in the pan for 5 minutes, then serve warm or transfer to a wire rack and let cool.

# EASTER CUPCAKES

MAKES: 12    PREP TIME: 20 MIN.    COOK TIME: 20 MIN.

### INGREDIENTS

1 stick butter, softened, plus extra for greasing (if using)

½ cup granulated sugar

2 eggs, lightly beaten

¾ cup all-purpose flour

1 teaspoon baking powder

¼ cup unsweetened cocoa powder

miniature chocolate candy-coated eggs, to decorate

### FROSTING

6 tablespoons butter, softened

1⅔ cups confectioners' sugar

1 tablespoon milk

2–3 drops of vanilla extract

1. Preheat the oven to 350°F. Grease a 12-cup muffin pan or line with 12 muffin cups.

2. Put the butter and sugar in a bowl and beat together until light and fluffy. Gradually add the eggs, beating well after each addition. Sift in the flour, baking powder, and cocoa powder and, using a large metal spoon, fold into the mixture. Spoon the batter into the prepared muffin pan.

3. Bake the cupcakes in the preheated oven for 15–20 minutes, or until well risen and firm to the touch. Transfer to a wire rack and let cool.

4. To make the frosting, put the butter in a bowl and beat until fluffy. Sift in the confectioners' sugar and beat together until well mixed, adding the milk and vanilla extract. Put the frosting in a pastry bag fitted with a large star-shaped tip. When the cupcakes are cold, pipe circles of frosting on top of the cupcakes to form nests. Decorate with chocolate eggs.

RASPBERRY
CRUMB MUFFINS

# MANGO & PASSION FRUIT WHIP

| SERVES: 4 | PREP TIME: **10 MIN.** | COOK TIME: **NO COOKING** |

## INGREDIENTS

1 mango

2 passion fruits

¼ cup granulated sugar

¼ cup sweet white wine

1¼ cups heavy cream

**1.** Halve, pit, and thinly peel the mango. Place the flesh in a food processor or blender and process to a smooth puree.

**2.** Scoop out the flesh from one of the passion fruits and add it to the mango puree.

**3.** Put the sugar, wine, and cream into a bowl and whip until it holds its shape.

**4.** Fold the fruit puree lightly into the cream, then spoon into four serving bowls.

**5.** Spoon the flesh from the remaining passion fruit on top of each and serve.

# DOWN HOME CHERRY PIES

MAKES: 24    PREP TIME: 25 MIN.    COOK TIME: 15 MIN.

### INGREDIENTS

butter, for greasing

2½ cups pitted cherries

2 teaspoons cornstarch

2 tablespoons cherry preserves

grated rind of 2 limes

1 (1-pound) package rolled dough pie crust, chilled

all-purpose flour, for dusting

1 egg yolk mixed with 1 tablespoon water, to glaze

granulated sugar, for sprinkling

### TO SERVE

1 cup heavy cream

grated rind of 2 limes

2 tablespoons confectioners' sugar

**1.** Preheat the oven to 350°F. Grease two 12-cup muffin pans.

**2.** Coarsely chop the cherries. Put them in a mixing bowl and stir in the cornstarch, preserves, and lime rind.

**3.** Roll out half the dough thinly on a lightly floured surface. Using a fluted cookie cutter, stamp out 24 circles, each 2½ inches in diameter. Press these gently into the prepared pans, rerolling the trimmings as needed.

**4.** Brush the top edges of the pie shells with a little of the egg glaze, then spoon in the filling.

**5.** Roll out the reserved dough thinly on a lightly floured surface. Stamp out 24 circles, each 2 inches in diameter, rerolling the trimmings as needed. Attach the circles as lids to the bottom section of the pies with water, pressing together the edges. Use a cookie cutter to cut out miniature hearts from the dough and attach them to the lids with water. Brush egg glaze over the dough and sprinkle with granulated sugar.

**6.** Bake in the preheated oven for 15 minutes, or until golden. Let cool in the pans for 10 minutes, then loosen with a blunt knife and transfer to a wire rack to cool. Whip the cream until it forms soft swirls, then fold in half the lime rind and all the confectioners' sugar. Sprinkle with the rest of the lime rind. Serve spoonfuls of the cream with the pies.

# RISOTTO PRIMAVERA

SERVES: 4     PREP TIME: 25 MIN.     COOK TIME: 20 MIN.

## INGREDIENTS

1½ cups fresh or frozen peas

12 asparagus spears

1 zucchini

2 cups green beans

2 tablespoons olive oil

1 large onion, finely chopped

1½ cups risotto rice

3 cups warm chicken stock

3½ tablespoons Vermouth or white wine

handful chopped fresh flat-leaf parsley

1 tablespoon fresh thyme leaves

4 tablespoons butter

1½ cups freshly grated Parmesan cheese, plus extra to serve

salt and pepper

**1.** Prepare the green vegetables: shell the peas if using fresh ones, chop the asparagus into bite-size portions, cut the zucchini diagonally into finger-thick slices, and trim the beans.

**2.** Bring a large saucepan of lightly salted water to a boil, add the prepared vegetables, and blanch for 1 minute, then remove and drain.

**3.** Place a large, heavy saucepan over medium heat, add the olive oil and onion, and sauté gently for about 10 minutes, until soft. Add the rice and sauté, stirring it into the oil for 2 minutes. Reduce the heat, add a ladleful of stock, and stir it into the rice. Gradually add more stock as each ladleful is absorbed. Check the rice—it should be slightly hard in the middle (you may need a little more or less of the liquid). Add the last ladle of stock, the Vermouth, and herbs, then cook for another 5 minutes.

**4.** Add the butter, Parmesan cheese, and blanched vegetables. Season with salt and pepper and heat through, stirring gently.

**5.** Serve in serving bowls, with Parmesan cheese to sprinkle on top.

# BROILED HALIBUT WITH CARAMELIZED ONION

SERVES: 2     PREP TIME: 20 MIN.     COOK TIME: 25 MIN.

## INGREDIENTS

1 tablespoon vegetable oil

1 small onion, thinly sliced

1 teaspoon balsamic vinegar

2 halibut fillets or steaks (about 4 ounces)

2 tablespoons butter, melted

fresh flat-leaf parsley sprigs, to garnish

cooked new potatoes, to serve

**1.** Heat the oil in a large skillet over medium heat. Add the onion, stir well, and reduce the heat. Cook over low heat, stirring occasionally, for 15–20 minutes, until the onion is soft and brown.

**2.** Add the vinegar to the skillet and cook, stirring continuously to prevent the onions from sticking, for 2 minutes.

**3.** Rinse the fish under cold running water and pat dry with paper towels. Brush the melted butter over the fish.

**4.** Preheat the broiler to hot. Sear the fish, then reduce the heat and cook for about 10 minutes, turning once. The cooking time will depend on the thickness of the fillets, but the fish should be firm and tender when done.

**5.** Remove the fish from the heat, transfer to serving plates, and top with the caramelized onion. Garnish with parsley and serve with new potatoes.

RISOTTO
PRIMAVERA

# DARK CHOCOLATE ROULADE

SERVES: 6–8 | PREP TIME: 45 MIN. | COOK TIME: 15–20 MIN.

## INGREDIENTS

butter, for greasing

6 ounces semisweet dark chocolate, broken into squares

4 extra-large eggs, separated

½ cup granulated sugar

unsweetened cocoa powder, sifted, for dusting

8 ounces white chocolate, broken into squares

1 cup mascarpone cheese or heavy cream

confectioners' sugar, for sprinkling

## RASPBERRY COULIS

2 cups raspberries

2 tablespoons confectioners' sugar

1. Preheat the oven to 350°F. Grease a 13 x 9-inch jelly roll pan and line with parchment paper.

2. Melt the dark chocolate in a heatproof bowl set over a saucepan of simmering water, being careful that the bowl does not touch the water. Remove from the heat and let cool slightly.

3. Put the egg yolks and sugar into a bowl and beat until pale and thick. Beat the egg whites in a separate grease-free bowl until they hold soft peaks. Quickly stir the melted dark chocolate into the egg yolk mixture, then fold in the beatened egg whites.

4. Spread the batter into the prepared pan. Bake in the preheated oven for 15–20 minutes, until risen and firm. Dust a sheet of parchment paper with cocoa powder. Turn out the roulade onto the paper, cover with a clean dish towel, and let cool.

5. Meanwhile, melt the white chocolate in a heatproof bowl set over a saucepan of simmering water, being careful that the bowl does not touch the water. Remove from the heat and let cool slightly. Stir into the mascarpone cheese, mixing until it reaches a spreadable consistency.

6. Uncover the roulade, remove the parchment paper, and spread with the white chocolate cream. Use the paper to roll up the roulade to enclose the filling (do not worry if it cracks).

7. To make the raspberry coulis, put the raspberries and sugar into a food processor and process to a smooth puree. Press through a strainer to remove the seeds.

8. Sprinkle the roulade with confectioners' sugar and serve in slices with the raspberry coulis poured over.

# 06 APRIL

# MUSTARD & HONEY DRUMSTICKS

SERVES: 4    PREP TIME: 10 MIN. PLUS 1 HR. MARINATING TIME    COOK TIME: 30 MIN.

### INGREDIENTS

8 chicken drumsticks

fresh flat-leaf parsley sprigs, to garnish

### GLAZE

½ cup honey

¼ cup Dijon mustard

¼ cup whole-grain mustard

¼ cup white wine vinegar

2 tablespoons sunflower oil

salt and pepper

1. Using a sharp knife, make a few diagonal slashes in the chicken drumsticks and place them in a large, nonmetallic dish.

2. Mix together all the ingredients for the glaze in a small bowl. Pour the glaze over the drumsticks, turning until the drumsticks are well coated. Cover with plastic wrap and let marinate in the refrigerator for at least 1 hour.

3. Preheat the broiler to high. Drain the chicken drumsticks, reserving the marinade. Cook the chicken under the preheated broiler, turning frequently and basting with the reserved marinade, for 25–30 minutes, or until a fork can be inserted into the thickest part of the meat with ease and the juices run clear. A meat thermometer inserted into the thickest part of the meat, without touching the bone, should read 170°F. Transfer to serving plates, garnish with parsley sprigs and serve.

# 07 APRIL

# ASPARAGUS WITH LEMON BUTTER SAUCE

SERVES: 4    PREP TIME: 10 MIN.    COOK TIME: 15 MIN.

### INGREDIENTS

1¾ pounds asparagus, trimmed

1 tablespoon olive oil

salt and pepper

### LEMON BUTTER SAUCE

juice of ½ lemon

2 tablespoons water

6 tablespoons butter, cut into cubes

1. Preheat the oven to 400°F. Lay the asparagus spears out in a single layer on a large baking sheet. Drizzle the oil over the spears and season with salt and pepper. Roast in the preheated oven for 10 minutes, or until just tender.

2. Meanwhile, make the lemon butter sauce. Pour the lemon juice into a saucepan and add the water. Heat for about 1 minute, then slowly add the butter, cube by cube, stirring continuously, until it has all been incorporated. Season with pepper and serve drizzled over the asparagus.

# PEPPERED LAMB

**SERVES: 4**    **PREP TIME: 20 MIN.**    **COOK TIME: 45 MIN.**

## INGREDIENTS

2 pounds lamb fillet

3 tablespoons olive oil

2–3 tablespoons black peppercorns, coarsely ground

cooked broccoli, to serve

## ONION GRATIN

butter, for greasing

6 onions, sliced

3–4 tablespoons dry sherry or white wine

1 tablespoon fresh thyme leaves

3–4 tablespoons mascarpone cheese

1 cup crumbled Gorgonzola cheese or other blue cheese

salt and pepper

1. Preheat the oven to 350°F. Lightly grease a gratin dish.

2. To make the onion gratin, lay out the onions in an even layer in the prepared gratin dish. Pour the sherry over the onions, sprinkle over the thyme leaves, and season with salt and pepper. Add dabs of the mascarpone cheese evenly over the onions and sprinkle with the Gorgonzola cheese.

3. Brush the lamb with 1 tablespoon of the oil and season with salt. Roll in the ground peppercorns. Heat the remaining oil in a skillet over high heat, add the lamb, and cook for 3–4 minutes on each side. Let rest for 5 minutes, then put in a roasting pan.

4. Roast the lamb in the top of the oven for about 25–30 minutes. To test for medium–rare, a meat thermometer should read 145°F before the meat is removed from the oven. For medium, it will read 160°F; well done is 170°F. At the same time, bake the onion gratin in the center of the preheated oven for 30–40 minutes, until the onions are soft and the gratin is golden and bubbling. Slice the lamb and serve immediately with the onion gratin and broccoli.

# POACHED EGGS "FLORENTINE" WITH SPINACH & CHEDDAR

SERVES: 4    PREP TIME: 10 MIN.    COOK TIME: 6–8 MIN.

## INGREDIENTS

1 tablespoon olive oil

1 (6-ounce) package fresh spinach

4 thick slices ciabatta bread

2 tablespoons butter

4 extra-large eggs

1 cup shredded cheddar cheese

salt and pepper

freshly grated nutmeg, to serve

**1.** Preheat the broiler to high. Heat the oil in a large saucepan, add the spinach, and sauté for 2–3 minutes, until the leaves are wilted. Drain in a colander, season with salt and pepper, and keep warm.

**2.** Toast the bread on both sides until golden. Spread one side of each slice with butter and place buttered side up on a baking sheet.

**3.** Bring a small saucepan of lightly salted water to a boil, crack the eggs into the water, and poach for about 3 minutes, until the whites are set but the yolks still runny. Remove from the pan with a draining spoon.

**4.** Arrange the spinach on the toast and top each slice with a poached egg. Sprinkle with the shredded cheese. Cook under the preheated broiler for 1–2 minutes, until the cheese has melted. Sprinkle with nutmeg and serve.

# SNICKERDOODLES

**MAKES: 40** **PREP TIME: 15 MIN. PLUS 1 HR. CHILLING TIME** **COOK TIME: 12 MIN.**

## INGREDIENTS

2 sticks butter, softened

¾ cup granulated sugar

2 extra-large eggs, lightly beaten

1 teaspoon vanilla extract

3¾ cups all-purpose flour

1 teaspoon baking soda

½ teaspoon freshly grated nutmeg

½ cup finely chopped pecans

salt

## CINNAMON COATING

1 tablespoon granulated sugar

2 tablespoons ground cinnamon

**1.** Put the butter and sugar into a bowl and mix well with a wooden spoon, then beat in the eggs and vanilla extract. Sift together the flour, baking soda, nutmeg, and a pinch of salt into the mixture, add the pecans, and stir until thoroughly combined. Shape the dough into a ball, wrap in plastic wrap, and chill in the refrigerator for 30–60 minutes.

**2.** Preheat the oven to 375°F. Line two to three baking sheets with parchment paper.

**3.** For the cinnamon coating, mix together the sugar and cinnamon in a shallow dish. Scoop up tablespoons of the cookie dough and roll into balls. Roll each ball in the cinnamon mixture to coat and place on the prepared baking sheets, spaced well apart.

**4.** Bake in the preheated oven for 10–12 minutes, until golden brown. Let cool on the baking sheets for 5–10 minutes, then using a spatula, carefully transfer to wire racks to cool completely.

# PEPPERONI PASTA

SERVES: 4    PREP TIME: 10 MIN.    COOK TIME: 45 MIN.

## INGREDIENTS

3 tablespoons olive oil

1 onion, chopped

1 red bell pepper, seeded and diced

1 orange bell pepper, seeded and diced

1 (28-ounce) can diced tomatoes

1 tablespoon tomato paste

1 teaspoon paprika

8 ounces pepperoni sausage, sliced

2 tablespoons chopped fresh flat-leaf parsley, plus extra to garnish

1 pound dried penne

salt and pepper

1. Heat 2 tablespoons of the olive oil in a large, heavy skillet. Add the onion and cook over low heat, stirring occasionally, for 5 minutes, or until softened. Add the red and orange bell peppers, tomatoes and their can juices, tomato paste, and paprika and bring to a boil.

2. Add the pepperoni and parsley and season with salt and pepper. Stir well, bring to a boil, then reduce the heat and simmer for 10–15 minutes.

3. Meanwhile, bring a large, heavy saucepan of lightly salted water to a boil. Add the penne, bring back to a boil, and cook according to the package directions, until just tender but still firm to the bite. Drain well and transfer to a serving dish. Add the remaining olive oil and toss. Add the sauce and toss again. Sprinkle with parsley and serve.

# QUICK HAM & PINEAPPLE STIR-FRY

SERVES: 4    PREP TIME: 10 MIN.    COOK TIME: ABOUT 5 MIN.

## INGREDIENTS

2 tablespoons olive oil

1 bunch scallions, cut into ½-inch pieces

1-inch piece fresh ginger, finely chopped

1 pound fully cooked ham, cut into bite-size chunks

1 (8-ounce) can pineapple chunks in natural juice, drained and juice reserved

2 tablespoons chopped fresh mint

2 tablespoons balsamic vinegar

cooked rice or couscous, to serve

1. Heat the oil in a wok or skillet, add the scallions and ginger, and stir-fry for 1 minute.

2. Add the ham and cook, stirring, for an additional 2 minutes. Add the pineapple with 2 tablespoons of the can juices and stir over medium heat for 2–3 minutes.

3. Stir in the mint and vinegar and bring to a boil. Remove from the heat and serve with rice.

# LEMON TURKEY WITH SPINACH

**SERVES: 4**     **PREP TIME: 30 MIN. PLUS 30 MIN. MARINATING TIME**     **COOK TIME: 10 MIN.**

## INGREDIENTS

1 pound turkey cutlets, cut into strips

1 tablespoon vegetable oil

6 scallions, finely sliced

½ lemon, peeled and thinly sliced

1 garlic clove, finely chopped

1 (12-ounce) package fresh spinach, washed, drained, and coarsely chopped

3 tablespoons chopped fresh flat-leaf parsley

sprigs of fresh flat-leaf parsley, to garnish

cooked pasta, such as tagliatelle, to serve

## MARINADE

1 tablespoon soy sauce

1 tablespoon white wine vinegar

1 teaspoon cornstarch

1 teaspoon finely grated lemon zest

½ teaspoon finely ground black pepper

**1.** To make the marinade, put the soy sauce, vinegar, cornstarch, lemon zest, and black pepper in a bowl and mix thoroughly. Add the turkey and stir to coat. Cover with plastic wrap and marinate in the refrigerator for 30 minutes.

**2.** Heat the oil in a large preheated wok or skillet. Add the turkey and marinade and cook over medium heat for 2–3 minutes, or until the turkey is opaque.

**3.** Add the scallions, lemon slices, and garlic and cook for another 2–3 minutes. Stir in the spinach and parsley and cook until the spinach is just wilted.

**4.** Remove from the heat and spoon the mixture over the cooked pasta. Garnish with sprigs of parsley and serve.

# CORN & CHIVE FRITTERS

MAKES: 16    PREP TIME: 10 MIN.    COOK TIME: 6–8 MIN.

### INGREDIENTS

1¼ cups all-purpose flour

1½ teaspoons baking powder

1 cup milk

2 eggs, separated

2 tablespoons melted butter

1⅓ cups canned or frozen corn kernels

2 tablespoons chopped chives, plus extra for sprinkling

oil, for frying

salt and pepper

**1.** Sift together the flour and baking powder into a mixing bowl and season with salt and pepper. Add the milk, egg yolks, and butter and beat to form a smooth batter. Stir in the corn kernels and chives.

**2.** Put the egg whites into a separate grease-free bowl and beat until they hold soft peaks. Fold lightly and evenly into the batter.

**3.** Pour a shallow depth of oil into a large skillet and heat until hot. Drop large spoonfuls of batter into the skillet and cook for 3–4 minutes, turning once, until golden brown. Cook in batches, draining the fritters on paper towels and keeping them warm, until you have made about 16 fritters.

**4.** Serve hot, sprinkled with chives.

# LAMB CASSEROLE WITH DATES

SERVES: 8    PREP TIME: 25 MIN. PLUS 4 HR. MARINATING TIME    COOK TIME: 2½ HR.

### INGREDIENTS

3¼–4½ pounds boned shoulder of lamb, cut into cubes

¼ cup olive oil

1¼ cups pitted dates

2½ cups pitted olives

3 cups red wine

10 whole garlic cloves, peeled

large handful fresh cilantro

cooked couscous, to serve

### DRY MARINADE

2 large onions, grated

4 garlic cloves, crushed

1 fresh red chile, finely chopped

1 teaspoon paprika

2 teaspoons ground cumin

1 teaspoon ground ginger

1 teaspoon pepper

**1.** Combine all the dry marinade ingredients in a flameproof casserole dish, add the cubed lamb, and let marinate in the refrigerator for 4 hours or overnight.

**2.** Preheat the oven to 300°F. Remove the lamb from the refrigerator. Add the oil, dates, olives, wine, and garlic to the casserole dish and cover. Transfer to the preheated oven and cook for 2½ hours, removing the lid for the last 30 minutes. Check that the lamb is meltingly tender, stir in the cilantro, and serve with couscous.

CORN & CHIVE
FRITTERS

# TURBOT STEAKS WITH PARSLEY, LEMON & GARLIC

SERVES: 4    PREP TIME: **10 MIN.**    COOK TIME: **20 MIN.**

## INGREDIENTS

2 tablespoons olive oil, for brushing

4 turbot steaks

juice and finely grated rind of 1 lemon

2 garlic cloves, finely chopped

¼ cup finely chopped fresh flat-leaf parsley

⅓ cup pine nuts, toasted

salt and pepper

cooked seasonal vegetables, to serve

**1.** Preheat the oven to 425°F. Brush a wide, ovenproof dish with oil.

**2.** Place the turbot steaks in the dish, brush with oil, season with salt and pepper, and pour the lemon juice over the fish.

**3.** Mix together the lemon rind, garlic, parsley, and pine nuts and spoon the mixture over the fish. Drizzle with the remaining oil.

**4.** Bake in the preheated oven for 15–20 minutes, until the fish flakes easily with a fork.

**5.** Serve hot with vegetables.

# CHOCOLATE PRETZELS

MAKES: 30     PREP TIME: 30 MIN. PLUS 15 MIN. CHILLING TIME     COOK TIME: 12 MIN.

### INGREDIENTS

1 stick unsalted butter, plus extra for greasing

½ cup granulated sugar

1 egg

1¾ cups all-purpose flour

2 tablespoons unsweetened cocoa powder

### TO DECORATE

1 tablespoon butter

4 ounces semisweet dark chocolate

confectioners' sugar, for dusting

1. Preheat the oven to 375°F. Lightly grease a baking sheet with a little butter. Beat together the butter and sugar in a large mixing bowl until light and fluffy. Beat in the egg, making sure all the ingredients are well combined.

2. Sift together the flour and cocoa powder and gradually beat into the egg mixture to form a soft dough. Use your fingers to incorporate the last of the flour and bring the dough together. Chill in the refrigerator for 15 minutes.

3. Break pieces from the dough and roll into thin log shapes about 4 inches long and ¼ inch thick. Carefully twist into pretzel shapes by making a circle, then twist the ends through each other to form a letter "B."

4. Place the pretzels on the prepared baking sheet, spaced slightly apart to allow for expansion during cooking. Bake in the preheated oven for 8–12 minutes. Let the pretzels cool slightly on the baking sheet, then transfer to a wire rack to cool completely.

5. Melt the butter and chocolate in a bowl set over a saucepan of gently simmering water, stirring. Dip half of each pretzel into the chocolate and let the excess chocolate drip back into the bowl. Place the pretzels on a sheet of wax paper and let set. When set, dust the uncoated side of each pretzel with confectioners' sugar before serving.

# CREAMY MANGO BRÛLÉE

SERVES: 4     PREP TIME: 30 MIN. PLUS 2 HR. CHILLING TIME     COOK TIME: 3 MIN.

### INGREDIENTS

2 mangoes, pitted, peeled, and chopped

1 cup mascarpone cheese

1 cup Greek-style yogurt

1 teaspoon ground ginger

grated rind and juice of 1 lime

2 tablespoons packed light brown sugar

½ cup raw brown sugar

1. Divide the mango among four ramekins (individual ceramic dishes).

2. Beat the mascarpone cheese with the yogurt. Fold in the ginger, lime rind and juice, and light brown sugar. Divide the mixture among the ramekins and level off the tops. Chill in the refrigerator for 2 hours.

3. Preheat the broiler to hot. Sprinkle 2 tablespoons of raw sugar over the top of each dish, covering the creamy mixture. Place under the preheated broiler for 2–3 minutes, until melted and browned. Let cool, then chill until needed.

# LEMON MERINGUE PIE

SERVES: 6–8    PREP TIME: 20 MIN. PLUS 30 MIN. CHILLING TIME    COOK TIME: 1 HR.

## INGREDIENTS

### PASTRY DOUGH

1¼ cups all-purpose flour, plus extra for dusting

6 tablespoons butter, cut into small pieces, plus extra for greasing

¼ cup confectioners' sugar, sifted

finely grated rind of ½ lemon

½ egg yolk, beaten

1½ tablespoons milk

### FILLING

3 tablespoons cornstarch

1¼ cups water

juice and grated rind of 2 lemons

1 cup superfine sugar or granulated sugar

2 eggs, separated

**1.** To make the pastry dough, sift the flour into a bowl. Rub in the butter with your fingertips until the mixture resembles fine bread crumbs. Mix in the remaining ingredients. Invert onto a lightly floured work surface and knead briefly. Wrap in plastic wrap and chill in the refrigerator for 30 minutes. Meanwhile, preheat the oven to 350°F.

**2.** Grease an 8-inch round tart pan. Roll out the dough to a thickness of ¼ inch, then use it to line the bottom and side of the pan. Prick all over with a fork, line with parchment paper, and fill with pie weights or dried beans. Bake in the preheated oven for 15 minutes. Remove the pie crust from the oven and take out the paper and weights. Reduce the oven temperature to 300°F.

**3.** To make the filling, mix the cornstarch with a little of the water to form a paste. Put the remaining water in a saucepan. Stir in the lemon juice, lemon rind, and cornstarch paste. Bring to a boil, stirring. Cook for 2 minutes. Let cool slightly. Stir in ⅓ cup of the sugar and the egg yolks, then pour into the pie crust.

**4.** Beat the egg whites in a clean, grease-free bowl until stiff. Gradually beat in the remaining superfine sugar and spread over the pie. Bake for an additional 40 minutes. Remove from the oven, cool, and serve.

# VEGETABLE COUSCOUS

| SERVES: 4 | PREP TIME: 10 MIN. PLUS 20 MIN. SOAKING TIME | COOK TIME: 25–30 MIN. |
| --- | --- | --- |

## INGREDIENTS

1 red bell pepper, halved and seeded

1 green bell pepper, halved and seeded

1 yellow bell pepper, halved and seeded

1 red onion

1 garlic clove, sliced

2 tablespoons olive oil

2 tomatoes, quartered

1 cup couscous

2 tablespoons lemon juice

⅓ cup toasted cashew nuts

salt and pepper

paprika, to garnish

1. Preheat the oven to 400°F.

2. Cut the red, green, and yellow bell peppers into bite-size chunks and slice the onion into thick wedges. Place the bell peppers, onion, and garlic in a roasting pan, sprinkle with salt and pepper, and drizzle the oil over the vegetables.

3. Bake in the preheated oven for 20 minutes, then add the tomatoes and cook for an additional 5–10 minutes, until tender.

4. Meanwhile, prepare the couscous according to the package directions.

5. Stir in the couscous and lemon juice, add the cashew nuts, and season with salt and pepper. Serve hot, sprinkled with paprika.

# TURKEY CUTLETS WITH LIMA BEANS

| SERVES: 4 | PREP TIME: 10 MIN. | COOK TIME: 20 MIN. |
| --- | --- | --- |

## INGREDIENTS

1 tablespoon all-purpose flour

1 teaspoon dried thyme

4 turkey cutlets

2 tablespoons olive oil

1 red onion, thinly sliced

1 garlic clove, crushed

1 cup drained, rinsed canned lima beans

1 (14½-ounce) can diced tomatoes

salt and pepper

1. Put the flour and thyme into a shallow bowl, season with salt and pepper, and mix. Add the turkey cutlets and turn in the mixture until lightly coated.

2. Heat the oil in a skillet, add the turkey cutlets, and sauté over high heat, turning once, for 2–3 minutes, until golden.

3. Add the onion and garlic and cook for an additional minute, then stir in the beans and tomatoes.

4. Bring to a boil, then reduce the heat, cover the skillet, and simmer gently, stirring occasionally, for 10–15 minutes, until the turkey is tender and no longer pink when cut into with a knife. Season with salt and pepper and serve hot.

# SCALLION & RICOTTA TARTS

MAKES: 12　　PREP TIME: 40 MIN. PLUS 30 MIN. CHILLING TIME　　COOK TIME: 15 MIN.

## INGREDIENTS

### PASTRY DOUGH

1¾ cups all-purpose flour, plus extra for dusting

pinch of salt

1 stick butter, diced, plus extra for greasing

1 egg yolk

### FILLING

1 cup ricotta cheese

1 cup grated pecorino cheese

1 egg, beaten

12 scallions, finely chopped

2 tablespoons shelled fresh peas, lightly cooked and cooled

1 teaspoon green peppercorns in brine, drained

salt and pepper

1. To make the dough, sift together the flour and salt into a bowl, add the butter, and rub in with your fingertips until the mixture resembles fine bread crumbs. Add the egg and enough cold water to form a smooth dough. Cover and chill in the refrigerator for 30 minutes.

2. Preheat the oven to 375°F. Lightly grease a 12-cup muffin pan.

3. Roll out the dough on a floured work surface to a thickness of about ¼ inch. Using a round pastry cutter or a glass, cut out circles large enough to line the cups of the muffin pan. Gently press the pastry shells into the cups. Line each pastry shell with a small piece of parchment paper and fill with pie weights or dried beans.

4. Bake the pastry shells in the preheated oven for 4–5 minutes, until golden and crisp. Remove the paper and weights.

5. Meanwhile, to make the filling, mix together the ricotta and pecorino cheeses in a large bowl. Add the egg, scallions, and peas. Grind the peppercorns finely, then add to the mixture. Season with salt and a good grinding of pepper.

6. Spoon the filling into the pastry shells and bake for 10 minutes, or until golden. Serve warm.

# FISH & FRIES

**SERVES: 2**  **PREP TIME: 20 MIN.**  **COOK TIME: 25 MIN.**

## INGREDIENTS

vegetable oil, for deep-frying

3 large russet potatoes

2 thick cod, tilapia, or flounder fillets, (about 6 ounces each)

1⅓ cups all-purpose flour, plus extra for dusting

2 teaspoons baking powder

1 cup cold beer

salt and pepper

tartar sauce, to serve

**1.** Heat enough oil for deep-frying in a large skillet or deep-fryer to 250°F, checking the temperature with a thermometer.

**2.** Peel the potatoes and cut into even-size sticks. Fry for about 8–10 minutes, depending on size, until soft but not browned. Remove from the oil, drain on paper towels and place in a warm dish in the preheated oven. Increase the temperature of the oil to 350–375°F, or until a cube of bread browns in 30 seconds.

**3.** Meanwhile, season the fish with salt and pepper and dust lightly with flour.

**4.** Make a thick batter by sifting the flour and baking powder into a bowl with a little salt and whisking in most of the beer. Check the consistency of the batter before adding the remaining beer—it should be thick like heavy cream.

**5.** Dip one fillet into the batter and let the batter coat it thickly. Carefully place the fish in the hot oil, then repeat with the other fillets.

**6.** Cook for 8–10 minutes, depending on the thickness of the fish. Turn over the fillets halfway through the cooking time. Remove the fish from the fryer, drain on paper towels, and keep warm.

**7.** Return the potatoes to the fryer at the increased temperature and cook for an additional 2–3 minutes, until they are golden brown and crisp. Drain on paper towels and season with salt and pepper before serving with the battered fish and tartar sauce.

# MINI CHICKEN POT PIES

MAKES: 12     PREP TIME: 30 MIN.     COOK TIME: 45 MIN.

### INGREDIENTS

2 tablespoons butter, plus extra for greasing

1 tablespoon olive oil

1 pound boneless, skinless chicken breasts, cut into ½ inch cubes

1 leek, thinly sliced, white and green slices kept separate

2 tablespoons all-purpose flour, plus extra for dusting

2 cups chicken stock

¼ cup dry white wine

2 tablespoons coarsely chopped fresh tarragon

2 tablespoons coarsely chopped fresh parsley

1 tablespoon chopped capers

1½ pounds rolled dough pie crust, chilled

1 egg yolk mixed with 1 tablespoon water, to glaze

1. Preheat the oven to 350°F. Lightly grease a 12-cup muffin pan.

2. Heat the butter and oil in a skillet over medium heat. Add the chicken and white leek slices and sauté, stirring, for 10 minutes, or until the chicken is golden brown and the leeks are softened. Sprinkle the flour over the top, mix together, then add the stock and wine. Simmer for 5 minutes, stirring from time to time, until the sauce has thickened and the chicken is tender and cooked through. Add the green leek slices and cook for 2 minutes, or until the leeks are just soft. Sprinkle with the tarragon, parsley, and capers and let cool.

3. Roll two-thirds of the dough out thinly on a lightly floured surface. Using a plain cookie cutter, stamp out 12 circles, each 4 inches in diameter. Press these gently into the prepared muffin pan, rerolling the trimmings as needed. Brush the top edges of the pie crusts with a little of the egg glaze, then spoon in the filling.

4. Roll out the reserved dough and any trimmings on a lightly floured surface. Using a plain cookie cutter, stamp out 12 circles, each 2¾ inches in diameter. Arrange these on top of the pies, pressing together the edges well to seal. Brush the pastry with egg glaze; add leaves cut out from rolled pastry trimmings with a sharp knife, then brush these with egg, too.

5. Bake in the preheated oven for 25 minutes, or until golden brown. Let cool in the pan for 5 minutes, then transfer to serving plates. Serve hot or cold.

# CHILI BEEF STIR-FRY SALAD

**SERVES: 4**   **PREP TIME: 30 MIN.**   **COOK TIME: ABOUT 10 MIN.**

### INGREDIENTS

1 pound top sirloin steak, cut into thin strips

1 ripe avocado

2 tablespoons sunflower oil

1 (15-ounce) can red kidney beans, drained and rinsed

10 cherry tomatoes, halved

1 large package tortilla chips

iceberg lettuce, shredded

chopped fresh cilantro, to garnish

### MARINADE

2 garlic cloves, crushed

1 teaspoon chili powder

½ teaspoon salt

1 teaspoon ground coriander

1. To make the marinade, place all the marinade ingredients in a large bowl and stir until well mixed.

2. Add the strips of beef to the marinade and toss thoroughly to coat all over.

3. Using a sharp knife, peel the avocado. Slice the avocado lengthwise in half and remove and discard the pit, then slice crosswise to form small dice.

4. Heat the oil in a large preheated wok. Add the beef and stir-fry for 5 minutes, tossing frequently. Add the kidney beans, tomatoes, and avocado and cook for 2 minutes.

5. Arrange the tortilla chips and iceberg lettuce around the edge of a serving plate and spoon the beef into the center. Alternatively, serve the tortilla chips and lettuce separately. Garnish with fresh cilantro and serve immediately.

# SPAGHETTI WITH MEATBALLS

**SERVES: 6**   **PREP TIME: 10 MIN.**   **COOK TIME: 45 MIN.**

### INGREDIENTS

1 white round potato, peeled and diced

1 pound ground sirloin beef

1 onion, finely chopped

1 egg

¼ cup chopped fresh flat-leaf parsley

all-purpose flour, for dusting

⅓ cup olive oil

1¾ cups tomato puree

2 tablespoons tomato paste

1 pound dried spaghetti

salt and pepper

1. Place the potato in a small saucepan, add cold water to cover and a pinch of salt, and bring to a boil. Cook for 10–15 minutes, until tender, then drain. Either mash thoroughly with a potato masher or fork or pass through a potato ricer.

2. Combine the potato, beef, onion, egg, and parsley in a bowl and season with salt and pepper. Spread out the flour on a plate. With dampened hands, shape the meat mixture into walnut-size balls and roll in the flour. Shake off any excess.

3. Heat the oil in a heavy skillet, add the meatballs, and cook over medium heat, stirring and turning frequently, for 8–10 minutes, until golden all over.

4. Add the tomato puree and tomato paste and cook for an additional 10 minutes, until the sauce is reduced and thickened.

5. Meanwhile, bring a large saucepan of lightly salted water to a boil. Add the spaghetti, bring back to a boil, and cook according to the package directions, until just tender but still firm to the bite.

6. Drain well and add to the meatball sauce, tossing well to coat. Serve.

CHILI BEEF
STIR-FRY SALAD

# COOKIES & CREAM SANDWICHES

SERVES: 4 | PREP TIME: 20 MIN. PLUS 2 HR. CHILLING TIME | COOK TIME: 20 MIN.

## INGREDIENTS

1 stick butter, softened

75 g/2¾ oz confectioners' sugar

1 cup all-purpose flour

½ cup, unsweetened cocoa powder

½ teaspoon ground cinnamon

## FILLING

4 ounces semisweet dark chocolate, broken into pieces

¼ cup heavy cream

1. Preheat the oven to 325°F. Line a baking sheet with parchment paper. Place the butter and sugar in a large bowl and beat together until light and fluffy. Sift the flour, cocoa, and ground cinnamon into the bowl and mix to form a dough.

2. Place the dough between 2 sheets of parchment paper and roll out to ⅛-inch thick. Cut out 2½-inch circles and place on the prepared baking sheet. Bake in the preheated oven for 15 minutes, or until firm to the touch. Let cool for 2 minutes, then transfer to wire racks to cool completely.

3. Meanwhile, make the filling. Place the chocolate and cream in a saucepan and heat gently until the chocolate has melted. Stir until smooth. Let cool, then leave to chill in the refrigerator for 2 hours, or until firm. Sandwich the cookies together in pairs with a spoonful of chocolate cream and serve.

# QUICK TIRAMISU

SERVES: 4 | PREP TIME: 30 MIN. | COOK TIME: NO COOKING

## INGREDIENTS

1 cup mascarpone or cream cheese

1 egg, separated

2 tablespoons plain yogurt

2 tablespoons superfine sugar or granulated sugar

2 tablespoons dark rum

2 tablespoons strong black coffee

8 ladyfingers

1. Put the mascarpone cheese in a large bowl, add the egg yolk and yogurt, and beat until smooth.

2. Beat the egg white until stiff but not dry, then beat in the sugar and fold into the mascarpone mixture. Spoon half of the mixture into 4 glasses.

3. Mix together the rum and coffee in a shallow dish. Dip the ladyfingers into the rum mixture, break them in half, or into smaller pieces, if necessary, and divide among the glasses.

4. Stir any remaining coffee mixture into the remaining cheese and spoon over the ladyfingers. Serve.

# NEW YORK CHEESECAKE

**SERVES: 4** | **PREP TIME: 20 MIN. PLUS 2 HR. COOLING TIME** | **COOK TIME: 55 MIN.**

## INGREDIENTS

1 stick butter,
plus extra for greasing

1½ cups finely crushed
graham crackers

1¼ cups plus 1 tablespoon
granulated sugar

4 cups cream cheese

2 tablespoons all-purpose flour

1 teaspoon vanilla extract

finely grated zest of 1 orange

finely grated zest of 1 lemon

3 eggs

2 egg yolks

1¼ cups heavy cream

**1.** Preheat the oven to 350°F. Place a small saucepan over low heat, add the butter and heat until it melts. Remove from the heat, stir in the crushed crackers and 1 tablespoon of the sugar and mix.

**2.** Press the mixture tightly into the bottom of a 9-inch springform cake pan. Place in the preheated oven and bake for 10 minutes. Remove from the oven and let cool on a wire rack.

**3.** Increase the oven temperature to 400°F. Use an electric mixer to beat the cheese until creamy, then gradually add the sugar and flour and beat until smooth. Increase the speed and beat in the vanilla extract, orange zest, and lemon zest, then beat in the eggs and egg yolks, one at a time. Finally, beat in the cream. Scrape any excess from the sides and beaters of the mixture into the batter. It should be light and fluffy—beat on a faster setting if you need to.

**4.** Grease the side of the cake pan and pour in the filling. Smooth the top, transfer to the oven, and bake for 15 minutes. Reduce the temperature to 225°F and bake for an additional 30 minutes. Turn off the oven and let the cheesecake cool and set in the oven for 2 hours. Cover and chill in the refrigerator overnight.

**5.** Slide a knife around the edge of the cake, then unfasten the pan, cut the cheesecake into slices, and serve.

# DEVILED CRAB RAMEKINS

SERVES: 4     PREP TIME: 10 MIN.     COOK TIME: 15 MIN.

## INGREDIENTS

melted butter, for greasing

6 ounces crabmeat, light and dark meat

1 extra-large egg, beaten

¼ cup crème fraîche or sour cream

juice of 1 lime

1 teaspoon hot chili sauce

2 cups fresh white bread crumbs

¼ cup Parmesan cheese, finely grated

salt and pepper

paprika, to garnish

## TO SERVE

lime wedges

salad greens

toasted whole wheat bread

**1.** Preheat the oven to 400°F. Brush four ⅔ cup ramekins (individual ceramic dishes) with butter and place on a baking sheet.

**2.** Mix the crabmeat with the egg, crème fraîche, lime juice, and chili sauce. Stir in the bread crumbs and season with salt and pepper.

**3.** Spoon the mixture into the prepared ramekins and sprinkle with the cheese. Bake in the preheated oven for about 15 minutes, until golden and bubbling.

**4.** Sprinkle with paprika and serve hot, with lime wedges, salad greens, and toast.

# MAY

# MINI PEACH CHEESECAKE CRISPS

**SERVES: 4     PREP TIME: 15 MIN. PLUS AT LEAST 1 HR. CHILLING TIME     COOK TIME: NO COOKING**

## INGREDIENTS

3 ripe peaches, halved and pitted

3 tablespoons peach liqueur or orange juice

1 cup mascarpone cheese

¼ cup granulated sugar

½ teaspoon almond extract

⅓ cup crushed graham crackers

½ cup almond meal (ground almonds)

2 tablespoons unsalted butter, melted

**1.** Reserve eight small slices of peach and coarsely chop the remainder. Divide among four ⅔-cup ramekins (individual ceramic dishes) and spoon the liqueur over them.

**2.** Put the mascarpone cheese, sugar, and almond extract into a bowl and beat together. Spoon the mixture over the peaches, covering completely.

**3.** Mix together the cookie crumbs and almond meal, then stir in the butter. Spoon the cookie mixture over the mascarpone mixture and top with the reserved peach slices. Chill in the refrigerator for at least 1 hour before serving.

# FUSILLI WITH ZUCCHINI & LEMON

**SERVES: 4      PREP TIME: 20 MIN.      COOK TIME: 30 MIN.**

## INGREDIENTS

⅓ cup olive oil

1 small onion, thinly sliced

2 garlic cloves, finely chopped

2 tablespoons chopped fresh rosemary

1 tablespoon chopped fresh flat-leaf parsley

4 small zucchini, cut into 1½-inch strips

finely grated rind of 1 lemon

1 pound dried fusilli

salt and pepper

freshly grated Parmesan cheese, to serve

**1.** Heat the oil in a large skillet over medium–low heat. Add the onion and cook gently, stirring occasionally, for about 10 minutes, until golden.

**2.** Increase the heat to medium–high. Add the garlic, rosemary, and parsley. Cook for a few seconds, stirring.

**3.** Add the zucchini and lemon rind. Cook for 5–7 minutes, stirring occasionally, until just tender. Season with salt and pepper. Remove from the heat.

**4.** Bring a large saucepan of lightly salted water to a boil. Add the fusilli, bring back to a boil, and cook according to the package directions, until just tender but still firm to the bite.

**5.** Drain the pasta and transfer to a serving dish.

**6.** Briefly reheat the zucchini sauce. Pour over the pasta and toss together well to mix.

**7.** Sprinkle with the Parmesan cheese and serve.

# FISH STICKS WITH CHILI MAYONNAISE

SERVES: 4     PREP TIME: 20 MIN.     COOK TIME: 15 MIN.

## INGREDIENTS

1⅔ cups all-purpose flour

3 eggs

1¼ cups matzo meal

1 pound firm white fish fillets, such as halibut, cod, or tilapia, cut into strips

sunflower oil or peanut oil, for pan-frying

salt and pepper

## CHILI MAYONNAISE

2 tablespoons sweet chili sauce

¼–⅓ cup mayonnaise

1. Mix the flour with plenty of salt and pepper on a large flat plate.

2. Beat the eggs in a bowl.

3. Spread out the matzo meal on another flat plate.

4. Dip the fish pieces into the seasoned flour, then into the beaten egg, then into the matzo meal, making sure there is a generous coating.

5. Pour the oil into a nonstick skillet to a depth of ½ inch and heat. Cook the fish pieces, in batches, for a few minutes, turning once, until golden and cooked through.

6. To make the chili mayonnaise, put the chili sauce and mayonnaise in a bowl and beat together until combined.

7. Transfer the fish to serving plates and serve with the chili mayonnaise on the side.

# 04 MAY

# ASPARAGUS & TOMATO TART

SERVES: 4    PREP TIME: 35 MIN.    COOK TIME: 1 HR. 10 MIN.

## INGREDIENTS

butter, for greasing

1 sheet rolled dough pie crust, thawed, if frozen

1 bunch thin asparagus spears

2 (5-ounce) packages spinach

3 extra-large eggs, beaten

⅔ cup heavy cream

1 garlic clove, crushed

10 small cherry tomatoes, halved

handful fresh basil, chopped

¼ cup freshly grated Parmesan cheese

salt and pepper

1. Preheat the oven to 375°F. Grease a 9-inch tart pan with butter, then roll out the dough and use to line the pan.

2. Cut off any excess dough and prick the bottom with a fork. Cover with a sheet of parchment paper and fill with pie weights or dried beans. Bake the pie crust in the preheated oven for 20–30 minutes, until lightly browned. Remove from the oven and take out the paper and weights. Reduce the oven temperature to 350°F.

3. Meanwhile, bend the asparagus spears until they snap, and discard the woody ends. Bring a large saucepan of lightly salted water to a boil. Add the asparagus and blanch for 1 minute, then remove and drain. Add the spinach to the boiling water, then remove immediately and drain well.

4. Mix together the eggs, cream, and garlic and season with salt and pepper. Lay the blanched spinach at the bottom of the pie crust. Add the asparagus and tomatoes, cut side up, in any arrangement you prefer. Sprinkle with the basil, then pour the egg mixture on top.

5. Transfer to the oven and bake for about 35 minutes, or until the filling has set. Sprinkle the cheese on top and let cool to room temperature before serving.

# 05 MAY

# TOMATO & MOZZARELLA STACKS

SERVES: 4    PREP TIME: 25 MIN.    COOK TIME: 10 MIN.

## INGREDIENTS

4 large tomatoes

8 ounces mozzarella cheese

24 fresh basil leaves

olive oil, for brushing

salt and pepper

1. Preheat the barbecue. Using a sharp serrated knife, cut a thin slice from the top and bottom of each tomato, and discard the ends. Slice the rest of the tomato horizontally into three. Slice the mozzarella into thin circles. Slice the basil leaves into thin ribbons, reserving a few whole leaves.

2. Brush a double-thickness piece of aluminum foil with oil. Place a tomato slice on the foil, brush with oil, and season with salt and pepper. Add a few shreds of basil and a slice of cheese. Continue layering, using the second and third tomato slices, seasoning each layer, and finishing with a layer of mozzarella. Top each stack with the reserved basil leaves. Fold up the edges of the foil to make a bowl shape. Repeat with the three remaining tomatoes and mozzarella.

3. Arrange on the grill rack and cook over medium–hot coals, covered, for 8–10 minutes, until the top tomato slice is heated through and the mozzarella is melted. Transfer to serving plates and serve.

ASPARAGUS &
TOMATO TART

# SALAD NIÇOISE

SERVES: 4–6    PREP TIME: 35 MIN.    COOK TIME: 10 MIN.

### INGREDIENTS

2 tuna steaks, about ¾ inch thick

olive oil, for brushing

2¼ cups trimmed green beans

store-bought garlic vinaigrette, to taste

2 hearts of lettuce, leaves separated

3 extra-large hard-boiled eggs, halved

2 tomatoes, cut into wedges

1 (2-ounce) can anchovy fillets in oil, drained

½ cup Niçoise olives or Kalmata olives

salt and pepper

1. Heat a ridged, cast-iron grill pan over high heat. Brush the tuna steaks with oil on one side, place oiled side down on the hot pan, and chargrill for 2 minutes.

2. Lightly brush the top side of the tuna steaks with a little more oil. Turn the tuna steaks over, then season with salt and pepper. Continue chargrilling for an additional 2 minutes for rare or up to 4 minutes for well done. Let cool.

3. Meanwhile, bring a saucepan of lightly salted water to a boil. Add the beans to the pan and bring back to a boil, then boil for 3 minutes. Drain the beans and immediately transfer to a large bowl. Pour the garlic vinaigrette over the beans and stir together.

4. To serve, line a serving dish with lettuce leaves. Lift the beans out of the bowl, leaving the excess dressing behind, and pile them in the center of the dish. Break the tuna into large flakes and arrange it over the beans.

5. Arrange the hard-boiled eggs, tomatoes, anchovy fillets, and olives on the dish. Drizzle with more vinaigrette, if required, and serve.

# CALAMARI WITH SHRIMP & FAVA BEANS

SERVES: 4–6    PREP TIME: 10 MIN.    COOK TIME: 20 MIN.

### INGREDIENTS

2 tablespoons olive oil

4 scallions, thinly sliced

2 garlic cloves, finely chopped

1 pound cleaned squid bodies, thickly sliced

½ cup dry white wine

1½ cups fresh or frozen fava beans

8 ounces jumbo shrimp, peeled and deveined

¼ cup chopped fresh flat-leaf parsley

salt and pepper

crusty bread, to serve

1. Heat the oil in a large skillet with a lid, add the scallions, and cook over medium heat, stirring occasionally, for 4–5 minutes, until soft.

2. Add the garlic and cook, stirring, for 30 seconds, until soft.

3. Add the squid and cook over high heat, stirring occasionally, for 2 minutes, or until golden brown.

4. Stir in the wine and bring to a boil. Add the beans, reduce the heat, cover, and simmer for 5–8 minutes, if using fresh beans, or 4–5 minutes, if using frozen beans, until tender.

5. Add the shrimp, replace the lid, and simmer for an additional 2–3 minutes, until the shrimp turn pink and start to curl.

6. Stir in the parsley and season with salt and pepper. Serve with crusty bread.

# TUNA & CHEESE QUICHE

**SERVES: 4** **PREP TIME: 25 MIN.** **COOK TIME: ABOUT 1 HR.**

## INGREDIENTS

### POTATO DOUGH

4 russet potatoes, diced

2 tablespoons butter

⅓ cup all-purpose flour, plus extra for dusting

### FILLING

1 tablespoon vegetable oil

1 shallot, chopped

1 garlic clove, crushed

1 red bell pepper, seeded and diced

1 (5-ounce) can chunk light tuna in oil, drained

⅓ cup drained, canned corn kernels

⅔ cup skim milk

3 eggs, beaten

1 tablespoon chopped fresh dill

½ cup shredded cheddar cheese,

salt and pepper

1. Preheat the oven to 400°F. Cook the potatoes in a saucepan of lightly salted boiling water for 10 minutes, or until tender. Drain and mash the potatoes. Add the butter and flour and mix to form a dough.

2. Knead the potato dough on a lightly floured surface and press the mixture into an 8-inch tart pan. Prick the bottom with a fork, cover with a sheet of parchment paper, and fill with pie weights or dried beans. Bake the tart shell in the preheated oven for 20–30 minutes, until lightly browned. Remove from the oven and remove the paper and weights.

3. Heat the oil in a skillet. Cook the shallot, garlic, and red bell pepper for 5 minutes. Spoon the mixture into the tart shell. Flake the tuna and arrange it on top with the corn.

4. In a bowl, combine the milk, eggs, and dill and season with salt and pepper. Pour the mixture into the tart shell and sprinkle the shredded cheese on top. Bake in the preheated oven for 20 minutes, until the filling has set. Serve.

# SCALLOPS IN BLACK BEAN SAUCE

SERVES: 4    PREP TIME: 10 MIN.    COOK TIME: 5 MIN.

## INGREDIENTS

2 tablespoons vegetable oil or peanut oil

1 teaspoon finely chopped garlic

1 teaspoon finely chopped fresh ginger

1 tablespoon fermented black beans, rinsed and lightly mashed

1 pound scallops

½ teaspoon light soy sauce

1 teaspoon Chinese rice wine

1 teaspoon sugar

3–4 fresh red Thai chiles, finely chopped

1–2 tablespoons chicken stock

1 tablespoon finely chopped scallion

1. Heat the oil in a preheated wok or large skillet. Add the garlic and stir, then add the ginger and stir-fry for about 1 minute, until fragrant.

2. Mix in the black beans, add the scallops, and stir-fry for 1 minute. Add the light soy sauce, rice wine, sugar and chiles.

3. Lower the heat and simmer for 2 minutes, then add the stock. Finally, add the scallion, stir, and serve.

# NACHOS

SERVES: 6    PREP TIME: 20 MIN.    COOK TIME: 8 MIN.

## INGREDIENTS

6 ounces of tortilla chips

1 (16-ounce) can refried beans, warmed

2 tablespoons of finely chopped canned jalapeño peppers

1 (7-ounce) can or jar of pimientos or roasted bell peppers, drained and finely sliced

1 cup shredded Monterey Jack cheese

1 cup shredded cheddar cheese

salt and pepper

1. Preheat the oven to 400°F. Spread the tortilla chips out over the bottom of a large, shallow, ovenproof dish. Cover with the warm refried beans. Sprinkle with the peppers and pimientos and season with salt and pepper.

2. Mix together the cheeses in a bowl and sprinkle on top.

3. Bake in the preheated oven for 5–8 minutes, or until the cheese is bubbling and melted. Serve.

# FRESH POTATO SALAD

SERVES: 4–6    PREP TIME: 20 MIN.    COOK TIME: 12 MIN.

## INGREDIENTS

2 pounds small red-skinned new potatoes, unpeeled

16–18 cornichons or sweet gerkins, halved diagonally, or dill pickle slices

2 tablespoons finely chopped red onion

3 tablespoons snipped chives

¼ teaspoon pepper

salt

## MUSTARD VINAIGRETTE

2 teaspoons Dijon mustard

1 tablespoon red wine vinegar

¼ teaspoon pepper

¼ cup extra virgin olive oil

sea salt flakes

**1.** Put the potatoes in a saucepan of lightly salted water and bring to a boil. Reduce the heat to medium and cook for 10–12 minutes, until tender. Drain, then return to the pan and let stand for a few minutes.

**2.** To make the mustard vinaigrette, combine the mustard, vinegar, pepper, and a pinch of sea salt flakes in a bowl, mixing well. Add the olive oil and beat until smooth and thickened.

**3.** Put the potatoes in a serving bowl and pour the dressing over them. Add the remaining ingredients and toss gently to mix. Let stand at room temperature for at least 30 minutes before serving.

# SPICY CHICKEN DRUMSTICKS

**SERVES: 4–6      PREP TIME: 15 MIN.      COOK TIME: 25 MIN.**

### INGREDIENTS

8 chicken drumsticks

1½ teaspoons crushed red pepper

2 garlic cloves, crushed

1 teaspoon dried oregano

2 teaspoons smoked paprika

juice of ½ lemon

salt and pepper

### TO SERVE

lemon wedges

mixed salad greens

tortillas

1. Preheat the oven to 425°F. Cut deep slashes into the thickest parts of the meat.

2. Place the crushed red pepper, garlic, oregano, paprika, and lemon juice in a large mixing bowl. Season with salt and pepper and mix together. Add the chicken and turn to coat evenly.

3. Arrange the chicken in a single layer in a large, shallow roasting pan. Bake in the preheated oven for 20–25 minutes, turning occasionally, until a fork can be inserted into the thickest part of the meat with ease and the juices run clear. A meat thermometer inserted into the thickest part of the meat, without touching the bone, should read 170°F.

4. Transfer to serving plates. Serve with lemon wedges, mixed salad greens, and tortillas.

# PIZZA MARGHERITA

**MAKES: 2      PREP TIME: 40 MIN. PLUS 1 HR. RISING TIME      COOK TIME: 20 MIN.**

### INGREDIENTS

**PIZZA DOUGH**

1¾ cups all-purpose flour, plus extra for dusting

1 teaspoon salt

1 teaspoon active dry yeast

1 tablespoon olive oil, plus extra for brushing

⅔ cup lukewarm water

**TOPPING**

6 tomatoes, thinly sliced

6 ounces mozzarella cheese, sliced

2 tablespoons shredded fresh basil

2 tablespoons olive oil

salt and pepper

1. To make the pizza dough, sift the flour and salt into a bowl and stir in the yeast. Make a well in the center and pour in the oil and water. Gradually incorporate the dry ingredients into the liquid, using a wooden spoon or floured hands.

2. Invert the dough onto a lightly floured surface and knead well for 5 minutes, or until smooth and elastic. Return to the clean bowl, cover with lightly oiled plastic wrap, and set aside to rise in a warm place for 1 hour, or until doubled in size.

3. Preheat the oven to 450°F. Invert the dough onto a lightly floured surface and punch down to knock out the air. Knead briefly, then cut it in half and roll out each piece into a circle about ¼ inch thick. Transfer to a lightly oiled baking sheet and push up the edges with your fingers to form a small rim.

4. To make the topping, arrange the tomato and mozzarella slices alternately over the pizza crusts. Season with salt and pepper, sprinkle with the basil, and drizzle with the olive oil.

5. Bake in the preheated oven for 15–20 minutes, or until the crusts are crisp and the cheese has melted. Serve.

SPICY CHICKEN
DRUMSTICKS

# CHICKEN BREASTS BRAISED WITH BABY VEGETABLES

SERVES: 4    PREP TIME: 10 MIN.    COOK TIME: 25–30 MIN.

## INGREDIENTS

4 skinless chicken breasts

1 tablespoon butter

1 tablespoon olive oil

8 shallots

1 cup chicken stock

12 baby carrots

8 baby turnips

2 bay leaves

1 cup fresh or frozen peas

salt and pepper

boiled new potatoes, to serve

**1.** Cut deep slashes through the chicken at intervals and sprinkle with salt and pepper.

**2.** Heat the butter and oil in a large flameproof casserole dish or saucepan, add the chicken breasts and shallots, and cook, turning, for 3–4 minutes, until golden brown.

**3.** Add the stock and bring to a boil, then add the carrots, turnips, and bay leaves. Reduce the heat, cover, and simmer gently for 20 minutes.

**4.** Stir in the peas and cook for an additional 5 minutes. Check the vegetables are tender. The chicken is cooked when a fork can be inserted into the thickest part of the meat with ease and the juices run clear. A meat thermometer inserted into the thickest part of the meat, without touching the bone, should read 170°F.

**5.** Remove and discard the bay leaves. Season with salt and pepper and serve with new potatoes.

# ROASTED BELL PEPPER & GARLIC FOCACCIA

SERVES: 6–8    PREP TIME: 30 MIN. PLUS 1½ HR. RISING TIME    COOK TIME: 45 MIN.

### INGREDIENTS

3¾ cups white bread flour, plus extra for dusting

1½ teaspoons salt

2¼ teaspoons active dry yeast

1½ cups lukewarm water

¼ cup olive oil, plus extra for greasing

1 red bell pepper, halved and seeded

3 garlic cloves

1. Preheat the oven to 475°F. Grease a baking sheet.

2. Put the flour and salt into a mixing bowl and stir in the yeast. Add the water and 3 tablespoons of the oil and mix to a soft dough.

3. Invert the dough onto a lightly floured work surface and knead until smooth. Return to the bowl, cover, and let rest in a warm place for 30 minutes.

4. Meanwhile, place the red bell pepper cut side down on a baking sheet, add the unpeeled garlic cloves, and roast in the preheated oven for 20 minutes, until the skins are charred. Remove from the oven (do not turn off the oven), peel the bell pepper and cut it into strips, then squeeze the flesh from the garlic and chop.

5. Invert the dough onto a lightly floured work surface and lightly knead the dough until smooth. Roll out to a rectangle and press into the prepared sheet with your knuckles. Sprinkle the bell pepper and garlic over the dough, pressing them into the dough.

6. Cover and let rise in a warm place for about 1 hour, until doubled in size.

7. Drizzle the remaining oil over the dough and bake for 20–25 minutes, until golden brown and firm. Invert and let cool on a wire rack.

# RASPBERRY MACARON BOMBE

**SERVES: 6**    **PREP TIME: 30 MIN. PLUS SOAKING AND FREEZING TIME**    **COOK TIME: NO COOKING**

## INGREDIENTS

4 ounces of amaretti cookies

2 tablespoons cherry brandy

2½ cups fresh raspberries

¼ cup granulated sugar

1¼ cups heavy cream

⅔ cup light cream

3 tablespoons unsweetened cocoa powder

2 tablespoons confectioners' sugar

1. Put the cookies into a food processor and process to form coarse crumbs. Alternatively, put the cookies in a strong plastic food bag and crush with a rolling pin. Put the crumbs in a bowl, add the cherry brandy, and let soak for 30 minutes.

2. Meanwhile, put the raspberries into a food processor and process to form a puree. Add the sugar and mix well together. Pour the raspberry mixture into a bowl.

3. Pour the heavy cream and light cream into a large bowl and whip together until the mixture holds its shape. Add one-third of the whipped cream to the cookie mixture and fold in until well blended. Add another third of the cream to the raspberry mixture and fold in. Sift the cocoa powder and confectioners' sugar over the remaining third of the cream, then fold into the cream until thoroughly incorporated.

4. Put the macaron mixture in the bottom of a deep 1½-quart bowl. Add the chocolate cream and spread over to form a layer, then add the raspberry mixture. Cover the bowl and freeze for 5 hours, or until firm or required.

5. Take the ice cream out of the freezer about 30 minutes before you are ready to serve it. Uncover, place a serving plate over the bowl, invert it, and let stand at room temperature.

# RED VELVET CAKE

**SERVES: 12**    **PREP TIME: 20 MIN.**    **COOK TIME: 30 MIN.**

## INGREDIENTS

2 sticks unsalted butter, plus extra for greasing

¼ cup water

½ cup unsweetened cocoa powder

3 eggs

1 cup buttermilk

2 teaspoons vanilla extract

2 tablespoons red food coloring

2¼ cups all-purpose flour

½ cup cornstarch

1½ teaspoons baking powder

1½ cups granulated sugar

## FROSTING

1 cup cream cheese

3 tablespoons unsalted butter

3 tablespoons granulated sugar

1 teaspoon vanilla extract

1. Preheat the oven to 375°F. Grease two 9-inch cake pans and line the bottoms with parchment paper.

2. Place the butter, water, and cocoa powder in a small saucepan and heat gently, without boiling, stirring until melted and smooth. Remove from the heat and let cool slightly.

3. Beat together the eggs, buttermilk, vanilla extract, and food coloring until frothy. Beat in the butter mixture. Sift in the flour, cornstarch, and baking powder, then stir quickly and evenly into the mixture with the granulated sugar.

4. Divide the batter between the prepared pans and bake in the preheated oven for 25–30 minutes, or until risen and firm to the touch. Let cool in the pans for 3–4 minutes, then invert and finish cooling on a wire rack.

5. To make the frosting, beat together all the ingredients until smooth. Use about half of the frosting to sandwich together the cakes, then spread the remainder over the top, swirling with a spatula.

# APRICOT ALMOND TART

**SERVES: 6–8**   **PREP TIME: 30 MIN.**   **COOK TIME: 45–50 MIN.**

### INGREDIENTS

6 tablespoons unsalted butter, softened

⅓ cup granulated sugar

1 extra-large egg, beaten

1½ cups almond meal (ground almonds)

⅓ cup all-purpose flour

½ teaspoon almond extract

10–12 apricots, pitted and quartered

¼ cup apricot preserves

1 tablespoon water

### PASTRY DOUGH

1⅓ cups all-purpose flour, plus extra for dusting

6 tablespoons cold unsalted butter

2 tablespoons confectioners' sugar

1 egg yolk

2 tablespoons orange juice

**1.** Preheat the oven to 375°F. To make the pastry dough, put the flour, butter, and confectioners' sugar into a food processor and process to fine crumbs. Mix the egg yolk and orange juice and stir into the flour mixture to make a soft dough.

**2.** Turn out the dough onto a lightly floured work surface and roll out to a circle large enough to line a 9-inch loose-bottom tart pan. Prick the bottom with a fork, cover with a sheet of parchment paper, and fill with pie weights or dried beans. Bake the tart shell in the preheated oven for 10 minutes. Remove from the oven and take out the paper and weights.

**3.** For the filling, put the butter, sugar, egg, almonds, flour, and almond extract into a food processor and process to a smooth paste.

**4.** Spread the almond filling over the bottom of the pastry shell and arrange the apricots, cut side up, on top.

**5.** Reduce the oven temperature to 350°F and bake the tart for 35–40 minutes, until the filling is set and golden brown.

**6.** Put the apricot preserves into a small saucepan with the water and heat gently until melted. Brush over the apricots and serve.

## 19 MAY

# SPAGHETTI WITH FRESH PEA PESTO

**SERVES: 4**     **PREP TIME: 10 MIN.**     **COOK TIME: ABOUT 15 MIN.**

### INGREDIENTS

1½ cups shelled fava beans

1 pound dried spaghetti

### PEA PESTO

2 cups shelled fresh peas

⅓ cup extra virgin olive oil

2 garlic cloves, crushed

1 cup freshly grated Parmesan cheese, plus extra, shaved, to serve

¾ cup blanched almonds, chopped

pinch of sugar

salt and pepper

1. To make the pea pesto, cook the peas in a saucepan of boiling water for 2–3 minutes, until just tender. Drain and transfer to a food processor. Add the oil, garlic, and grated Parmesan cheese and process to a coarse paste. Add the almonds and process again. Add the sugar and season with salt and pepper. Set aside.

2. Blanch the fava beans in a saucepan of lightly salted boiling water until just tender. Drain and let cool. Peel off the dull skins.

3. Bring a large, heavy saucepan of lightly salted water to a boil. Add the spaghetti, bring back to a boil, and cook according to the package directions, until just tender but still firm to the bite. Drain, stir in the fava beans, and toss with the pesto. Add a good coarse grinding of pepper and serve with Parmesan cheese shavings.

## 20 MAY

# QUICK CHICKEN STEW

**SERVES: 4**     **PREP TIME: 10 MIN.**     **COOK TIME: ABOUT 20 MIN.**

### INGREDIENTS

3½ cups canned coconut milk

1 cup chicken stock

2–3 tablespoons laksa paste or Thai curry paste (from Asian grocery stores)

3 skinless, boneless chicken breasts (about 6 ounces each), sliced into strips

8 ounces dried rice noodles

15 cherry tomatoes, halved

3 cups diagonally halved sugar snap peas

1 bunch fresh cilantro, coarsely chopped

1. Pour the coconut milk and stock into a saucepan and stir in the laksa paste. Add the chicken strips and simmer for 10–15 minutes over low heat. Cut a piece of chicken to check that it is tender and cooked through, with no signs of pinkness.

2. Meanwhile, prepare the noodles according to the package directions, then drain.

3. Stir in the tomatoes, sugar snap peas, and noodles into the chicken mixture. Simmer for an additional 2–3 minutes. Stir in the cilantro and serve.

**SPAGHETTI WITH FRESH PEA PESTO**

# RED SALAD WITH BEETS & RADISH

SERVES: 4    PREP TIME: 10 MIN.    COOK TIME: NO COOKING

### INGREDIENTS

8 small cooked beets, quartered

1 small red onion, cut into thin wedges

1 bunch radishes, sliced

2 tablespoons chopped fresh mint

flatbread, to serve

### DRESSING

⅓ cup extra virgin olive oil

1 tablespoon whole-grain mustard

1 tablespoon balsamic vinegar

1 tablespoon lemon juice

2 teaspoons honey

salt and pepper

1. Toss together the beets, onion, and radishes and stir in half the mint. Arrange on four serving plates.

2. To make the dressing, put the oil, mustard, vinegar, lemon juice, and honey into a screw-top jar and shake well to mix. Season with salt and pepper.

3. Spoon the dressing over the salad and sprinkle the remaining mint on top. Serve immediately with flatbread.

# CHICKEN SATAY SKEWERS WITH PEANUT SAUCE

SERVES: 4–6    PREP TIME: 35 MIN. PLUS 2 HR. MARINATING TIME    COOK TIME: 20 MIN.

### INGREDIENTS

4 skinless, boneless chicken breasts (about 4 ounces each), cut into ¾-inch cubes

¼ cup soy sauce

1 tablespoon cornstarch

2 garlic cloves, finely chopped

1-inch piece fresh ginger, peeled and finely chopped

cucumber cubes, to serve

### PEANUT SAUCE

2 tablespoons peanut oil or vegetable oil

½ onion, finely chopped

1 garlic clove, finely chopped

¼ cup chunky peanut butter

¼–⅓ cup water

½ teaspoon chili powder

1. Put the chicken in a shallow dish. Mix together the soy sauce, cornstarch, garlic, and ginger in a small bowl and pour it over the chicken. Cover and let marinate in the refrigerator for at least 2 hours. Meanwhile, presoak 8–12 wooden skewers, if using, for 30 minutes to prevent them for charring.

2. Preheat the oven to 375°F. Divide the chicken cubes among the presoaked wooden skewers or metal skewers. Heat a ridged grill pan until hot, add the skewers, and cook over high heat for 3–4 minutes, turning occasionally, until browned all over. Transfer the skewers to a baking sheet and cook in the preheated oven for 5–8 minutes, until cooked through.

3. Meanwhile, to make the peanut sauce, heat the oil in a saucepan, add the onion and garlic, and cook over medium heat, stirring frequently, for 3–4 minutes, until softened. Add the peanut butter, water, and chili powder and simmer for 2–3 minutes, until softened and thinned.

4. Serve the skewers with the peanut sauce and the cucumber.

# HONEY & MUSTARD CHICKEN PASTA SALAD

**SERVES: 4** **PREP TIME: 25 MIN.** **COOK TIME: 20 MIN.**

## INGREDIENTS

8 ounces dried fusilli

2 tablespoons olive oil

1 onion, thinly sliced

1 garlic clove, crushed

4 skinless, boneless chicken breasts (about 4 ounces each), thinly sliced

2 tablespoons whole-grain mustard

2 tablespoons honey

10 cherry tomatoes, halved

handful of mizuna or arugula leaves

fresh thyme leaves, to garnish

## DRESSING

3 tablespoons olive oil

1 tablespoon sherry vinegar

2 teaspoons honey

1 tablespoon fresh thyme leaves

salt and pepper

1. To make the dressing, place all the ingredients, including salt and pepper to taste, in a small bowl and whisk together until well blended.

2. Bring a large, heavy saucepan of lightly salted water to a boil. Add the fusilli, bring back to a boil, and cook according to the package directions, until just tender but still firm to the bite.

3. Meanwhile, heat the oil in a large skillet. Add the onion and garlic and sauté for 5 minutes. Add the chicken and cook, stirring frequently, for 3–4 minutes. Stir the mustard and honey into the skillet and cook for an additional 2–3 minutes, until the chicken and onion are golden brown and sticky. Check the chicken is tender and cooked through—when cut through with a knife, there should be no signs of pinkness.

4. Drain the pasta and transfer to a serving bowl. Pour the dressing over the pasta and toss well. Stir in the chicken and onion and let cool.

5. Gently stir the tomatoes and mizuna into the pasta. Serve garnished with thyme leaves.

# BROILED MONKISH WITH HERB POLENTA SLICES

SERVES: 4     PREP TIME: 10 MIN. PLUS CHILLING TIME     COOK TIME: 12–15 MIN.

### INGREDIENTS

4 cups boiling water

1½ cups instant polenta

2 tablespoons butter

2 tablespoons finely chopped fresh parsley

2 teaspoons chopped fresh dill

4 monkfish fillets (about 6 ounces each)

1 tablespoon olive oil, plus extra for greasing

salt and pepper

lemon wedges, to serve

1. Lightly grease a rectangular baking dish. Pour the water into a large saucepan, bring to a boil, and stir in the polenta. Cook over medium heat, stirring, for 5 minutes, or until thickened and starting to come away from the sides of the pan.

2. Remove from the heat, stir in the butter, parsley, and dill, and season with salt and pepper. Spread evenly in the prepared dish and let cool. Chill in the refrigerator until set.

3. Preheat the broiler to high. Brush the monkfish with the oil and sprinkle with salt and pepper. Cook in the preheated broiler for 6–8 minutes, turning once, until cooked through.

4. Meanwhile, invert the polenta and cut into slices. Add to the broiler rack about halfway through the fish cooking time and cook until golden, turning once.

5. Slice the monkfish and arrange on the polenta slices. Serve hot, with lemon wedges for squeezing over.

# GARLIC & HERB BREAD SPIRAL

SERVES: 6–8    PREP TIME: 30 MIN. PLUS ABOUT 2 HR. RISING TIME    COOK TIME: 25 MIN.

### INGREDIENTS

3¾ cups white bread flour, plus extra for dusting

2¼ teaspoons active dry yeast

1½ teaspoons salt

1½ cups lukewarm water

2 tablespoons oil, plus extra for greasing

6 tablespoons butter, melted and cooled

3 garlic cloves, crushed

2 tablespoons chopped fresh parsley

2 tablespoons snipped fresh chives

beaten egg, for glazing

sea salt flakes, for sprinkling

1. Brush a large baking sheet with oil. Combine the flour, yeast, and salt in a mixing bowl. Stir in the water and half the oil, mixing to a soft, sticky dough.

2. Invert the dough onto a lightly floured work surface and knead until smooth and no longer sticky. Return to the bowl, cover, and let stand in a warm place for about 1 hour, until doubled in size.

3. Meanwhile, preheat the oven to 475°F. Mix together the butter, garlic, herbs, and remaining oil. Roll out the dough to a 13 x 9-inch rectangle and spread the herb mix evenly over the dough to within ½-inch of the edge.

4. Roll up the dough from one long side and place on the work surface, seam underneath. Cut into 12 thick slices and arrange, cut side down, on the baking sheet about ¾ inch apart.

5. Cover and let rise in a warm place until doubled in size and springy to the touch. Brush with egg and sprinkle with sea salt flakes. Bake in the preheated oven for 20–25 minutes, until golden brown and firm. Let cool on a wire rack.

# TOASTED MUFFINS WITH BLUEBERRIES & BACON

SERVES: 2    PREP TIME: 10 MIN.    COOK TIME: 5 MIN.

### INGREDIENTS

2 muffins

2 lean bacon strips

¾ cup fresh blueberries

2 teaspoons maple syrup (optional)

1. Preheat the broiler to medium–high. Slice the muffins horizontally and place them, cut sides down, on the rack in the broiler pan.

2. Lay the bacon strips on the rack and cook until the tops of the muffins are toasted and the bacon is lightly cooked on one side.

3. Turn the muffins and divide the blueberries between the bottom halves. Invert the bacon onto the blueberries, covering them completely. Cook for an additional 2 minutes, removing the top halves as soon as they are toasted and the bottoms when the bacon is browned and crisp.

4. Place the muffin bottoms on serving plates, drizzle with maple syrup, if using, and add the muffin tops. Serve.

GARLIC & HERB
BREAD SPIRAL

# 27 MAY

# RUSTIC FISH CASSEROLE

SERVES: 4     PREP TIME: **15 MIN.**     COOK TIME: **15 MIN.**

### INGREDIENTS

1 pound clams, scrubbed

2 tablespoons olive oil

1 large onion, chopped

2 garlic cloves, crushed

2 celery stalks, sliced

1 pound firm white fish fillets, such as halibut, red snapper, or Alaskan pollock

8 ounces prepared squid rings

1¾ cups fish stock

6 plum tomatoes, chopped

small bunch of fresh thyme

salt and pepper

crusty bread, to serve

1. Clean the clams under cold running water, scrubbing the shells. Discard any with broken shells and any that refuse to close when tapped.

2. Heat the oil in a large skillet and sauté the onion, garlic, and celery for 3–4 minutes, until softened but not browned. Meanwhile, cut the fish into chunks.

3. Stir the fish and squid into the skillet, then sauté gently for 2 minutes.

4. Stir in the stock, tomatoes, and thyme and season with salt and pepper. Cover and simmer gently for 3–4 minutes.

5. Add the clams, cover, and cook over high heat for an additional 2 minutes, or until the shells open. Discard any that remain closed.

6. Serve the casserole with crusty bread.

# 28 MAY

# BAKED CHILE CHEESE SANDWICHES

MAKES: 4     PREP TIME: **10 MIN.**     COOK TIME: **10 MIN.**

### INGREDIENTS

3 cups shredded cheese, such as American, Monterey Jack, Swiss, or cheddar

1 stick butter, softened, plus extra to finish

4 fresh green chiles, seeded and chopped

½ teaspoon ground cumin

8 thick slices bread

1. Preheat the oven to 375°F. Mix together the cheese and butter in a bowl until creamy, then add the chiles and cumin.

2. Spread this mixture over four slices of bread and top with the remaining slices. Place on a baking sheet.

3. Spread the outside of the sandwiches with extra butter and bake for 8–10 minutes, until crisp. Serve.

# BEEF, SCALLION & BOK CHOY STIR-FRY

**SERVES: 4**   **PREP TIME: 10 MIN.**   **COOK TIME: 8–10 MIN.**

### INGREDIENTS

1 tablespoon peanut oil

2 garlic cloves, crushed

1-inch piece fresh ginger, chopped

1 pound ground sirloin beef

1 bunch scallions, diagonally sliced

4 cups thickly sliced bok choy

2 cups bean sprouts

2 tablespoons lime juice

2 tablespoons ketchup

2 tablespoons soy sauce

cooked egg noodles or rice, to serve

**1.** Heat the oil in a wok or large skillet, add the garlic and ginger, and stir-fry over medium heat for a few seconds, without browning.

**2.** Increase the heat to high, stir in the beef, and stir-fry for 4–5 minutes. Add the scallions and bok choy and stir-fry for 2 minutes.

**3.** Add the bean sprouts and stir-fry for 1–2 minutes, until soft.

**4.** Stir in the lime juice, ketchup, and soy sauce, then heat until bubbling. Serve with noodles.

# MIXED BERRY MINI TARTS

**MAKES: 12**     **PREP TIME: 30 MIN. PLUS 30 MIN. CHILLING TIME**     **COOK TIME: ABOUT 20 MIN.**

### INGREDIENTS

1⅔ cups all-purpose flour, plus extra
for dusting

¾ cup confectioners' sugar, sifted

½ cup almond meal
(ground almonds)

1 stick butter

1 egg yolk

1 tablespoon milk

### FILLING

1 cup cream cheese

confectioners' sugar, to taste, plus
extra, sifted, for dusting

3 cups fresh berries, such as
strawberries, cut into quarters,
raspberries, and blueberries

1. Sift the flour and confectioners' sugar into a bowl. Stir in the almonds. Add the butter, rubbing in until the mixture resembles bread crumbs. Add the egg yolk and milk and work in until the dough binds together. Wrap in plastic wrap and chill for 30 minutes. Meanwhile, preheat the oven to 400°F.

2. Roll out the dough on a lightly floured surface and use it to line 12 deep mini tart pans. Prick the bottoms and press a piece of aluminum foil into each.

3. Bake in the preheated oven for 10–15 minutes, or until light golden brown. Remove the foil and bake for an additional 2–3 minutes. Transfer to a wire rack to cool.

4. To make the filling, place the cream cheese and confectioners' sugar in a bowl and mix together. Place a spoonful of filling in each mini tart and arrange the berries on top.

5. Dust with sifted confectioners' sugar and serve.

# CHOCOLATE CHIP COOKIES

**MAKES: 10–12**    **PREP TIME: 10 MIN.**    **COOK TIME: ABOUT 15 MIN.**

### INGREDIENTS

unsalted butter, melted, for greasing

1½ cups all-purpose flour, sifted

1 teaspoon baking powder

1 stick margarine, melted

⅓ cup firmly packed light brown sugar

¼ cup granulated sugar

½ teaspoon vanilla extract

1 egg

1 cup semisweet chocolate chips

**1**. Preheat the oven to 375°F. Line and lightly grease two baking sheets.

**2**. Place all of the ingredients in a large mixing bowl and beat until well combined.

**3**. Place tablespoonfuls of the mixture onto the prepared baking sheets, spaced well apart.

**4**. Bake in the preheated oven for 10–12 minutes, or until golden brown. Transfer to a wire rack and let cool.

**5**. Serve or store in an airtight container.

# JUNE

# MÂCHE & CUCUMBER SALAD WITH FIGS

| SERVES: 4 | PREP TIME: 5 MIN. | COOK TIME: NO COOKING |
|---|---|---|

### INGREDIENTS

3½ cups mâche, mizuna, arugula, or other salad greens

½ cucumber, diced

4 ripe figs

### DRESSING

1 small shallot, finely chopped

¼ cup walnut oil

2 tablespoons extra virgin olive oil

2 tablespoons cider vinegar

½ teaspoon honey

salt and pepper

**1.** Place all the dressing ingredients in a screw-top jar, season with salt and pepper, and shake well to mix.

**2.** Put the mâche and cucumber into a bowl and pour half the dressing over them. Toss well to coat evenly, then divide among four serving plates.

**3.** Cut the figs into quarters and arrange four quarters on top of each plate. Drizzle over the remaining dressing and serve immediately.

# BROILED SALMON WITH CITRUS SALSA

SERVES: 4 · PREP TIME: 10 MIN. · COOK TIME: 10 MIN.

## INGREDIENTS

4 salmon fillets

1 tablespoon olive oil

1 tablespoon light soy sauce

## CITRUS SALSA

1 large orange

1 lime

2 tomatoes, peeled and diced

2 tablespoons extra virgin olive oil

2 tablespoons chopped fresh cilantro

¼ teaspoon granulated sugar

salt and pepper

1. Preheat the broiler to high. To make the salsa, cut all the peel and white pith from the orange and lime and remove the segments, discarding the membranes and reserving the juices.

2. Chop the segments and mix with the reserved juice, the tomatoes, oil, and cilantro. Add the sugar and season with salt and pepper.

3. Place the salmon fillets on the broiler rack. Mix together the oil and soy sauce, brush over the salmon, and season with pepper. Place under the preheated broiler and cook, turning once, for 8–10 minutes, until the fish is firm and flakes easily.

4. Serve the salmon with a spoonful of citrus salsa on the side.

# SWORDFISH WITH COCONUT GLAZE

SERVES: 4     PREP TIME: 30 MIN. PLUS 1 HR. MARINATING TIME     COOK TIME: 25 MIN.

## INGREDIENTS

4 swordfish steaks (about 6 ounces each), ¾ inch thick

sea salt flakes

2 tablespoons olive oil, plus extra for oiling

chopped fresh cilantro, to garnish

## COCONUT GLAZE

2 cups coconut milk

½ cup rum

¼ cup soy sauce

1 tablespoon black peppercorns, cracked

2-inch piece cinnamon stick, broken

1. Put the swordfish steaks in a shallow dish in which they sit snugly in a single layer. Rub with sea salt flakes and olive oil.

2. Put the coconut glaze ingredients in a small saucepan and bring to a boil, stirring. Boil for 12–15 minutes, until reduced by half. Strain, pour into a shallow dish, and let stand until completely cold.

3. Pour the glaze over the swordfish, turning to coat and making sure the steaks are completely covered with the glaze. Cover with plastic wrap and let marinate in the refrigerator for 30–60 minutes.

4. Preheat the barbecue. Oil a hinged wire grill basket, using a wad of oil-soaked paper towels, or broiler rack. Drain the steaks, reserving the marinade. Brush the steaks with oil on both sides, and arrange in the basket. Cook over medium–hot coals, covered, for 5–6 minutes, until blackened. Turn and cook the other side for 1 minute, or until the flesh is no longer opaque.

5. Meanwhile, pour the marinade into a small saucepan. Bring to a boil and boil for 3 minutes. Pour into a small serving boat.

6. Carefully remove the steaks from the basket. Arrange in a serving dish, sprinkle with the cilantro, and serve with the coconut glaze.

# ROSEMARY POTATOES

SERVES: 5–6     PREP TIME: 15 MIN.     COOK TIME: 45 MIN.

## INGREDIENTS

5–6 potatoes, unpeeled and scrubbed

2 sticks unsalted butter

2 tablespoons chopped fresh rosemary leaves

salt and pepper

1. Preheat the barbecue. Slice the potatoes ⅛ inch thick. Plunge into a large bowl of water to wash off the starch. Drain and blot dry with paper towels.

2. Take a large sheet of double-thickness aluminum foil and smear butter over an area in the middle measuring about 12 x 8 inches. Arrange a single layer of potatoes on the greased area. Sprinkle with some of the rosemary, season with salt and pepper, and dab generously with butter. Repeat until all the potato slices are used—there should be three layers. Fold over the foil to make a flat package, sealing and crimping the edges well. Wrap the package in two more large pieces of foil, sealing well.

3. Cook for 45 minutes over hot coals, turning every 10 minutes, or until the potatoes are tender. Serve straight from the package.

SWORDFISH WITH
COCONUT GLAZE

# CRABMEAT & DILL TART

SERVES: 4–6     PREP TIME: 30 MIN. PLUS 15 MIN. CHILLING TIME     COOK TIME: 45–50 MIN.

## INGREDIENTS

### PASTRY DOUGH

1⅔ cups all-purpose flour, plus extra for dusting

1 tablespoon chopped fresh dill

1 stick butter

2–3 tablespoons cold water

### FILLING

1 bunch scallions, chopped

6 ounces crabmeat, light and dark meat

2 tablespoons chopped fresh dill

1 extra-large egg, beaten

¾ cup light cream

¼ cup finely grated Parmesan cheese

salt and pepper

1. Sift the flour into a bowl, add the dill, and rub in the butter with your fingertips until the mixture resembles fine bread crumbs. Stir in just enough water to make a soft dough.

2. Invert the dough onto a lightly floured work surface and roll out until it is big enough to line a 9-inch tart pan. Press the dough into the edges of the pan, trim the excess, and prick the bottom with a fork. Chill in the refrigerator for 15 minutes. Preheat the oven to 400°F.

3. Line the tart shell with a piece of parchment paper and fill with pie weights or dried beans, then bake the bottom in the preheated oven for 10 minutes. Remove from the oven, take out the paper and weights, and bake for an additional 10 minutes.

4. To make the filling, put the onions, crabmeat, and dill into a bowl and mix together. Stir in the egg and cream. Season well with salt and pepper, then spoon into the tart shell and sprinkle with the cheese.

5. Reduce the oven temperature to 375°F. Bake the tart in the oven for 25–30 minutes, until the filling is just set. Serve warm or cold.

# 06 JUNE

# NO-BAKE CHOCOLATE CAKE

SERVES: 6–8 · PREP TIME: 10 MIN. PLUS 1–2 HR. SETTING TIME · COOK TIME: 5 MIN.

## INGREDIENTS

8 ounces semisweet dark chocolate

2 sticks unsalted butter, plus extra for greasing

3 tablespoons black coffee

¼ cup firmly packed light brown sugar

few drops of vanilla extract

2 cups crushed graham crackers

½ cup raisins

¾ cup chopped walnuts

1. Grease and line an 8½-inch loaf pan with parchment paper.

2. Place the chocolate, butter, coffee, sugar, and vanilla extract in a saucepan over low heat. Stir until the chocolate and butter have melted, the sugar has dissolved, and the mixture is well combined.

3. Stir in the crushed cookies, raisins, and walnuts and stir well.

4. Spoon the mixture into the prepared loaf pan. Let set for 1–2 hours in the refrigerator, then turn out and cut into thin slices to serve.

# 07 JUNE

# ALMOND & RASPBERRY COOKIES

MAKES: 25 · PREP TIME: 25 MIN. · COOK TIME: 15 MIN.

## INGREDIENTS

2 sticks butter, softened

¾ cup granulated sugar

1 egg yolk, lightly beaten

2 teaspoon almond extract

2¼ cups all-purpose flour

⅓ cup almonds, toasted and chopped

¼ cup chopped candied peel

¼ cup raspberry preserves

salt

1. Preheat the oven to 375°F. Line two baking sheets with parchment paper.

2. Put the butter and sugar into a bowl and mix well with a wooden spoon, then beat in the egg yolk and almond extract. Sift together the flour and a pinch of salt into the mixture, add the almonds and candied peel, and stir until thoroughly combined.

3. Scoop out tablespoons of the dough and shape into balls with your hands, then put them on to the prepared baking sheets, spaced well apart. Use the dampened handle of a wooden spoon to make a hollow in the center of each cookie and fill the hollows with raspberry preserves.

4. Bake for 12–15 minutes, until golden brown. Let cool on the baking sheets for 5–10 minutes, then using a spatula, carefully transfer the cookies to wire racks to cool completely.

# BANANA PANCAKES WITH WHIPPED MAPLE BUTTER

**SERVES: 4**   **PREP TIME: 15 MIN.**   **COOK TIME: 10 MIN.**

### INGREDIENTS

1¼ cups all-purpose flour

1½ teaspoons baking powder

1 tablespoon granulated sugar

pinch of salt

1 cup buttermilk

1 extra-large egg

2 tablespoons melted butter, plus extra for greasing

3 ripe bananas

finely grated rind of 1 small orange

### MAPLE BUTTER

6 tablespoons butter

¼ cup maple syrup

**1.** Sift the flour, baking powder, sugar, and salt into a bowl. Add the buttermilk, egg, and butter and beat to a smooth batter. Mash two bananas and mix thoroughly into the batter with the orange rind. Let stand for 5 minutes.

**2.** Lightly grease a griddle pan or skillet and heat over medium heat. Spoon tablespoons of batter into the pan and cook until bubbles appear on the surface.

**3.** Turn over with a spatula and cook the other side until golden brown. Repeat this process using the remaining batter, while keeping the cooked pancakes warm.

**4.** For the maple butter, beat together the butter and maple syrup, beating until light and fluffy.

**5.** Slice the remaining banana and serve with the pancakes, with the maple butter spooned over the pancakes.

# TURKEY TERIYAKI

SERVES: 4    PREP TIME: 20 MIN. PLUS 30 MIN. MARINATING TIME    COOK TIME: 10 MIN.

## INGREDIENTS

1 pound turkey cutlets, cut into strips

3 tablespoons peanut oil

1 small yellow bell pepper, seeded and sliced into thin strips

8 scallions, green part included, diagonally sliced into 1-inch pieces

cooked rice, to serve

## TERIYAKI GLAZE

⅓ cup shoyu (Japanese soy sauce)

⅓ cup mirin

2 tablespoons honey

1 teaspoon finely chopped fresh ginger

**1.** Mix the teriyaki glaze ingredients in a small saucepan over medium–low heat. Stir until the honey has melted, then remove from the heat and let cool.

**2.** Put the turkey in a large shallow dish. Pour the glaze over the turkey, turning the strips so they are well coated. Let marinate for 30 minutes or overnight in the refrigerator.

**3.** Using a slotted spoon, remove the turkey from the marinade, shaking off the excess liquid. Reserve the marinade.

**4.** Heat a wok or skillet over medium–high heat, then add the oil. Add the turkey and stir-fry for 2 minutes. Add the yellow bell pepper and scallions, and stir-fry for 1 minute. Pour in the reserved marinade. Bring to a boil, then reduce the heat slightly and cook for 3–4 minutes, until the turkey is cooked through.

**5.** Transfer the turkey and vegetables to a serving dish. Boil the liquid remaining in the wok until syrupy, then pour over the turkey. Serve with rice.

# CAJUN CHICKEN

**SERVES: 4**    **PREP TIME: 10 MIN.**    **COOK TIME: 30 MIN.**

## INGREDIENTS

4 chicken drumsticks

4 chicken thighs

2 fresh ears of corn, husks and silks removed

6 tablespoons butter, melted

oil, for oiling

## SPICE MIXTURE

2 teaspoons onion powder

2 teaspoons paprika

1½ teaspoons salt

1 teaspoon garlic powder

1 teaspoon dried thyme

1 teaspoon cayenne pepper

1 teaspoon ground black pepper

½ teaspoon ground white pepper

¼ teaspoon ground cumin

**1.** Preheat the barbecue. Using a sharp knife, make two to three diagonal slashes in the chicken drumsticks and thighs, then place them in a large dish. Add the ears of corn. Mix together all the ingredients for the spice mixture in a small bowl.

**2.** Brush the chicken and corn with the melted butter and sprinkle with the spice mixture. Toss to coat well.

**3.** Oil the grill rack. Cook the chicken over medium–hot coals, turning occasionally, for 15 minutes, then add the corn and cook, turning occasionally, for an additional 10–15 minutes, or until beginning to blacken slightly at the edges. The chicken is cooked when a fork can be inserted into the thickest part of the meat with ease and the juices run clear. A meat thermometer inserted into the thickest part of the meat, without touching the bone, should read 170°F. Transfer to a serving plate and serve.

# 11 JUNE

## PASTA WITH ARUGULA & MOZZARELLA

SERVES: 4    PREP TIME: 15 MIN.    COOK TIME: 15 MIN.

### INGREDIENTS

1 pound dried pappardelle

2 tablespoons olive oil

1 garlic clove, chopped

2 cups halved cherry tomatoes,

3 cups arugula leaves

10 ounces mozzarella cheese, chopped

salt and pepper

Parmesan cheese shavings, to serve

1. Bring a large, heavy saucepan of lightly salted water to a boil. Add the pappardelle, bring back to a boil, and cook according to the package directions, until just tender but still firm to the bite.

2. Meanwhile, heat the oil in a skillet over medium heat and sauté the garlic, stirring, for 1 minute, without browning.

3. Add the tomatoes, season well with salt and pepper, and cook gently for 2–3 minutes, until softened.

4. Drain the pasta and stir into the skillet. Add the arugula and mozzarella, then stir until the arugula wilts.

5. Serve the pasta with Parmesan cheese.

# 12 JUNE

## TEQUILA-MARINATED TENDERLOIN STEAKS

SERVES: 4    PREP TIME: 10 MIN. PLUS 2 HR. CHILLING TIME    COOK TIME: ABOUT 10 MIN.

### INGREDIENTS

2 tablespoons olive oil

3 tablespoons tequila

3 tablespoons freshly squeezed orange juice

1 tablespoon freshly squeezed lime juice

3 garlic cloves, crushed

2 teaspoon chili powder

2 teaspoon ground cumin

1 teaspoon dried oregano

4 tenderloin steaks

oil, for oiling

salt and pepper

1. Place the oil, tequila, orange juice, lime juice, garlic, chili powder, cumin, and oregano in a large, shallow, nonmetallic dish, season with salt and pepper, and mix together. Add the steaks and turn to coat in the marinade. Cover and chill in the refrigerator for at least 2 hours or overnight, turning occasionally.

2. Preheat the barbecue. Let the steaks return to room temperature, then remove from the marinade. Oil the grill rack. Cook over hot coals for 3–4 minutes on each side for medium, or longer according to taste, basting frequently with the marinade. Serve.

# SEAFOOD RISOTTO

SERVES: 4     PREP TIME: 20 MIN.     COOK TIME: 25 MIN.

## INGREDIENTS

⅔ cup dry white wine

4 baby squid, cleaned and sliced

8 ounces shrimp, peeled and deveined

8 ounces mussels, scrubbed and debearded

2 tablespoons olive oil

4 tablespoons butter

1 onion, finely chopped

2 garlic cloves, finely chopped

2 bay leaves

2 cups risotto rice

about 6½ cups hot fish stock

salt and pepper

chopped fresh flat-leaf parsley, to garnish

**1.** Heat the wine in a saucepan until boiling. Add the squid and shrimp, cover, and cook for 2 minutes. Remove the squid and shrimp with a slotted spoon and set aside.

**2.** Discard any mussels with broken shells and any that refuse to close when tapped. Add to the cooking liquid.

**3.** Heat the oil and butter in a deep saucepan. Add the onion and cook, stirring frequently, for 3–4 minutes, until softened.

**4.** Add the garlic, bay leaves, and rice, and mix to coat in the butter and oil. Cook, stirring continuously, for 2–3 minutes, until the grains are translucent.

**5.** Stir in the cooking juices from the mussels, then gradually add the hot stock, a ladleful at a time. Cook, stirring, for 15 minutes, until the liquid is absorbed and the rice is creamy.

**6.** Stir in the cooked seafood, cover, and cook for an additional 2 minutes to heat through. Remove the bay leaves. Season with salt and pepper.

**7.** Serve garnished with parsley.

## 14 JUNE

# TUNA & TOMATO PITA POCKETS

SERVES: 4    PREP TIME: 10 MIN.    COOK TIME: NO COOKING

### INGREDIENTS

4 pita breads

1 butterhead lettuce, coarsely shredded

8 cherry tomatoes, halved

1 (12-ounce) can chunk light tuna in oil, drained and flaked

½ cup mayonnaise

1 teaspoon finely grated lemon rind

2 tablespoons lemon juice

3 tablespoons chopped fresh chives

salt and pepper

1. Cut the pita breads in half and open them out to make a pocket.

2. Divide the lettuce among the pitas, then add the tomatoes and tuna.

3. Put the mayonnaise, lemon rind, lemon juice, and chives into a bowl and mix together. Season with salt and pepper and spoon over the pita filling to serve.

## 15 JUNE

# BARBECUED TUNA WITH CHILE & GINGER SAUCE

SERVES: 4–6    PREP TIME: 20 MIN. PLUS 30–60 MIN. MARINATING TIME    COOK TIME: 15 MIN.

### INGREDIENTS

4 tuna steaks (about 6 ounces each), ¾ inch thick

2 tablespoons olive oil, plus extra for oiling

salt

lime wedges, to serve

### CHILE & GINGER SAUCE

½ cup firmly packed brown sugar

½ cup water

1-inch piece fresh ginger, finely shredded

1 fresh green chile, seeded and finely chopped

1 large garlic clove, crushed

juice of ½ lime

1. Put the tuna steaks in a shallow dish in which they sit snugly in a single layer. Rub with salt and the olive oil.

2. To make the chile-and-ginger sauce, put the sugar and water in a small saucepan and bring to a boil. Boil for 7–8 minutes, until syrupy. Add the ginger, chile, garlic, and lime, and boil for an additional minute. Pour into a bowl and let stand until completely cold.

3. Pour the cold sauce over the tuna steaks, turning to coat. Cover with plastic wrap and let marinate in the refrigerator for 30–60 minutes, turning occasionally. Meanwhile, preheat the barbecue.

4. Oil a hinged wire grill basket. Place the tuna steaks in the basket, reserving the marinade. Cook over hot coals for 2 minutes. Turn and cook the other side for 1 minute. Remove from the basket and keep warm.

5. Pour the reserved marinade into a small saucepan. Bring to a boil and boil for 2 minutes. Pour into a small serving boat. Transfer the steaks to serving plates and serve with the hot marinade and lime wedges.

TUNA & TOMATO
PITA POCKETS

# PEPPERED TENDERLOIN STEAK WITH BRANDY & CREAM SAUCE

**SERVES: 4**     **PREP TIME: 10 MIN.**     **COOK TIME: ABOUT 20 MIN.**

## INGREDIENTS

2 tablespoons black peppercorns, coarsely crushed

4 tenderloin steaks, about ¾ inch thick

cooked baked potatoes and green salad, to serve

### BRANDY & CREAM SAUCE

2 tablespoons butter

1 tablespoon olive oil, plus extra for oiling

1 small onion, finely chopped

3 tablespoons brandy

1 cup heavy cream

2 teaspoon Dijon mustard

1. Preheat the barbecue. To make the brandy-and-cream sauce, melt the butter and oil in a saucepan, add the onion, and sauté, stirring, for 4–5 minutes, until tender and golden.

2. Add the brandy and boil for 30 seconds, then stir in the cream and mustard. Cook over moderate heat, stirring, for 2 minutes, then remove from the heat and keep warm.

3. Spread the crushed peppercorns on a plate and press the steaks into them, turning to coat on both sides and pressing firmly so the peppercorns stick to the meat.

4. Oil the grill rack. Cook the steaks, turning once, for 5 minutes for rare, 9–10 minutes for medium and 12–14 minutes for well done. Remove from the heat and let rest for 5 minutes before serving with the sauce spooned over the steaks, accompanied by baked potatoes and salad.

# SPICED FISH SKEWERS ON TOMATO SALAD

SERVES: 4    PREP TIME: 20 MIN. PLUS 1 HR. MARINATING TIME    COOK TIME: 10 MIN.

## INGREDIENTS

1 pound cod loin or monkfish, cut into 1-inch cubes

3 tablespoons lime juice

¼ cup sunflower oil

2 teaspoon mild chili powder

1 teaspoon dried oregano

1 lime, cut into 8 wedges

12 cherry tomatoes, halved

12 yellow cherry tomatoes, halved

½ small onion, thinly sliced

2 tablespoons coarsely chopped fresh cilantro

½ teaspoon sugar

1 teaspoon yellow mustard

salt and pepper

1. Place the fish cubes in a shallow bowl. Mix together 2 tablespoons of the lime juice and 2 tablespoons of the oil with the chili powder and oregano. Season with salt and pepper and pour the marinade over the fish. Cover and let marinate for 1 hour. Meanwhile, presoak eight wooden skewers, if using, for 30 minutes to prevent them for charring.

2. Preheat the broiler to medium. Thread the fish and lime wedges onto the presoaked wooden skewers or metal skewers. Cook the fish skewers under the preheated broiler for 8–10 minutes, turning occasionally, until just cooked.

3. Mix together the tomatoes, onion, and cilantro in a bowl. Beat together the remaining lime juice and oil with the sugar and mustard. Pour the dressing over the tomatoes and toss well to mix. Season with salt and pepper.

4. Divide the tomato salad among four serving dishes and top each with two fish skewers.

# CHEESE & CORN FRITTERS

MAKES: 8–10    PREP TIME: 10 MIN.    COOK TIME: ABOUT 5 MIN.

## INGREDIENTS

1 egg

1 cup milk

¾ cup all-purpose flour

½ teaspoon baking powder

½ cup canned corn kernels, drained

¼ cup shredded Monterey Jack cheese, American cheese, or cheddar cheese

1 teaspoon snipped fresh chives

2 teaspoons sunflower oil

1. Put the egg and milk into a small bowl and beat with a fork. Add the flour and baking powder and beat until smooth. Stir in the corn kernels, cheese, and chives. Heat the sunflower oil in a nonstick skillet. Drop in even tablespoonfuls of the batter. Cook for 1–2 minutes on each side, until the fritters are puffed up and golden.

2. Drain on paper towels and serve.

# BROILED PEACHES WITH RICOTTA

**SERVES: 4**   **PREP TIME: 10 MIN.**   **COOK TIME: ABOUT 5 MIN.**

### INGREDIENTS

4 peaches or nectarines, halved and pitted

1 tablespoon unsalted butter, melted, for greasing

⅓ cup ricotta cheese

½ teaspoon vanilla extract

¼ cup raw brown sugar

1 teaspoon allspice

**1**. Preheat the broiler to high and brush a baking pan with the melted butter. Place the peach halves, cut side up, in the prepared baking pan.

**2**. Mix the ricotta cheese with the vanilla extract and spoon into the peach cavities.

**3**. Mix together the sugar and spice, then sprinkle over the peaches.

**4**. Place under the preheated broiler for 3–4 minutes, until bubbling and golden brown. Serve warm.

## 20 JUNE

# HONEY & LEMON TART

**SERVES: 4–6**     **PREP TIME: 35 MIN. PLUS 30 MIN. CHILLING TIME**     **COOK TIME: 50 MIN.**

### INGREDIENTS

1⅓ cups cottage cheese, cream cheese, or ricotta cheese

⅓ cup Greek honey

3 eggs, beaten

½ teaspoon cinnamon

grated rind and juice of 1 lemon

### PASTRY DOUGH

1¾ cups all-purpose flour, plus extra for dusting

pinch of salt

1½ teaspoons granulated sugar

1¼ sticks butter, diced

3–4 tablespoons cold water

1. To make the pastry dough, put the flour, salt, sugar, and butter into a food processor. Mix in short bursts until the mixture resembles fine bread crumbs. Sprinkle the water over the crumbs and mix until a smooth dough forms. Alternatively, make the pastry dough in a bowl and rub in with your hands. The dough can be used right away, but it is better to first let it rest in the refrigerator, wrapped in wax paper, for about 30 minutes.

2. If using cottage cheese for the filling, push the cheese through a strainer into a bowl. Add the honey to the cheese and beat until smooth. Add the eggs, cinnamon, lemon rind, and lemon juice, and mix together well.

3. Preheat the oven to 400°F. Roll out the dough on a lightly floured surface and use to line a 9-inch tart pan. Prick the bottom with a fork, cover with a sheet of parchment paper, and fill with pie weights or dried beans, then bake the bottom in the preheated oven for 15 minutes. Remove from the oven and remove the paper and weights. Bake for an additional 5 minutes, until the bottom is firm but not brown.

4. Reduce the oven temperature to 350°F. Pour the filling into the pastry shell and bake in the oven for about 30 minutes, until set. Serve cold.

## 21 JUNE

# SHRIMP NOODLE SOUP

**SERVES: 4**     **PREP TIME: 10 MIN.**     **COOK TIME: 10 MIN.**

### INGREDIENTS

1 bunch scallions

2 celery stalks

1 red bell pepper

8 ounces vermicelli rice noodles

2 tablespoons peanut oil

⅓ cup unsalted peanuts

1 fresh Thai chile, sliced

1 lemongrass stalk, crushed

1¾ cups fish stock or chicken stock

1 cup coconut milk

2 teaspoons Thai fish sauce

12 ounces cooked, peeled jumbo shrimp

salt and pepper

chopped fresh cilantro, to garnish

1. Trim the scallions and celery and thinly slice diagonally. Seed and thinly slice the red bell pepper.

2. Prepare the noodles according to the package directions, until tender. Drain. Heat the oil in a wok, add the peanuts, and stir-fry for 1–2 minutes, until golden. Lift out with a slotted spoon. Add the sliced vegetables to the wok and stir-fry over high heat for 1–2 minutes. Add the chile, lemongrass, stock, coconut milk, and fish sauce and bring to a boil.

3. Stir in the shrimp and bring back to a boil, stirring. Season with salt and pepper, then add the noodles. Serve in bowls, sprinkled with fresh cilantro.

# STRAWBERRIES WITH VANILLA CREAM

SERVES: 4     PREP TIME: 10 MIN.     COOK TIME: NO COOKING

### INGREDIENTS

1 pound strawberries, hulled

3 tablespoons confectioners' sugar

1 tablespoon lemon juice

1 vanilla bean

1 cup heavy cream

1. Halve the strawberries, place in a bowl, and sprinkle with 1 tablespoon of the confectioners' sugar and the lemon juice. Let stand for a few minutes.

2. Cut the vanilla bean in half lengthwise and scrape out the seeds. Put the cream in a bowl and add the vanilla seeds and the remaining confectioners' sugar.

3. Beat the cream-and-vanilla mixture until it just holds its shape.

4. Divide the strawberries among four serving dishes, top with the vanilla cream, and serve.

# VEGETARIAN CHILE BURGERS

**SERVES: 4–6**    **PREP TIME: 25 MIN. PLUS 1 HR. CHILLING TIME**    **COOK TIME: 20 MIN.**

## INGREDIENTS

½ cup bulgur wheat

1 cup drained, rinsed canned red kidney beans

1 cup drained, rinsed canned cannellini beans

1–2 fresh red jalapeño chiles, seeded and coarsely chopped

2–3 garlic cloves

6 scallions, coarsely chopped

1 yellow bell pepper, seeded, peeled and chopped

1 tablespoon chopped fresh cilantro

1 cup shredded cheddar cheese or Monterey Jack cheese

2 tablespoons whole-wheat flour

1–2 tablespoons sunflower oil

1 large tomato, sliced

salt and pepper

whole wheat buns, to serve

1. Place the bulgur wheat in a strainer and rinse under cold running water. Cook the bulgur wheat in a saucepan of lightly salted water according to the package directions, until tender. Drain and reserve.

2. Place the beans in a food processor with the chiles, garlic, scallions, yellow bell pepper, cilantro, and half the cheese. Using the pulse button, chop finely. Add to the cooked bulgur wheat and season with salt and pepper. Mix well, then shape into four to six equal burgers. Cover and let chill for 1 hour. Coat the burgers in the flour.

3. Preheat the broiler to medium. Heat a heavy skillet and add the oil. When hot, add the burgers and cook over medium heat for 5–6 minutes on each side, or until piping hot.

4. Place one to two slices of tomato on top of each burger and sprinkle with the remaining cheese. Cook under the hot broiler for 2–3 minutes, or until the cheese begins to melt. Serve in whole wheat buns.

# VEGETARIAN HOT DOGS

**SERVES: 4**     **PREP TIME: 25 MIN. PLUS 30 MIN. CHILLING TIME**     **COOK TIME: 20 MIN.**

### INGREDIENTS

1 tablespoon sunflower oil, plus extra for oiling

1 small onion, finely chopped

¾ cup finely chopped white button mushrooms

½ red bell pepper, seeded and finely chopped

1 (15-ounce) can cannellini beans, drained and rinsed

2 cups fresh bread crumbs

1 cup shredded American cheese or Swiss cheese

1 teaspoon dried mixed herbs

1 egg yolk

seasoned all-purpose flour

### TO SERVE

small bread rolls

fried onion slices

tomato chutney or ketchup

**1.** Heat the sunflower oil in a saucepan. Add the onion, mushrooms, and bell pepper and sauté until softened.

**2.** Mash the cannellini beans in a large bowl. Add the vegetable mixture, bread crumbs, cheese, herbs, and egg yolk and mix well. Press together the mixture with your fingers and shape into eight log shapes. Roll each frankfurter in the seasoned flour. Let chill in the refrigerator for at least 30 minutes.

**3.** Preheat the barbecue. Brush a double-thickness sheet of aluminum foil with oil and cook the frankfurters over medium–hot coals for 15–20 minutes, turning and basting frequently with oil, until golden. Slice bread rolls down the center and insert a layer of fried onions. Place the frankfurters in the rolls and serve with tomato chutney.

# SLICED STEAKS WITH PARMESAN

SERVES: 4    PREP TIME: 10 MIN. PLUS 30 MIN. STANDING TIME    COOK TIME: ABOUT 5 MIN.

### INGREDIENTS

4 tenderloin steaks, about 1¼ inches thick

olive oil, for oiling

3½ cups arugula

Parmesan cheese shavings

balsamic vinegar, for drizzling

salt and pepper

1. Snip the fat on the steaks at ½-inch intervals to stop it from curling and shrinking. Sprinkle both sides with salt and pepper. Cover and let stand at room temperature for 30 minutes.

2. Meanwhile, preheat the barbecue. Pile some of the coals on one side, leaving a slightly cooler zone with a single layer of coals.

3. Oil the grill rack. Cook the steaks on the hottest part of the rack for 2–3 minutes on each side until brown. Move to the cooler part and cook the steak to your liking. Transfer to a board and let rest for 5 minutes.

4. Carve each steak diagonally into ¾-inch slices. Place the arugula on top of the steak, and sprinkle with Parmesan cheese shavings and more pepper. Drizzle a little balsamic vinegar over the steak and serve.

# MEXICAN TURKEY BURGERS

SERVES: 4    PREP TIME: 15 MIN. PLUS 1 HR. CHILLING TIME    COOK TIME: 12 MIN.

### INGREDIENTS

1 pound fresh ground turkey

1 cup canned refried beans

2–4 garlic cloves, crushed

1–2 fresh jalapeño chiles, seeded and finely chopped

2 tablespoons tomato paste

1 tablespoon chopped fresh cilantro

olive oil, for oiling

salt and pepper

### TO SERVE

burger buns

lettuce leaves

tomato slices

tomato salsa

1. Place the ground turkey in a bowl and break up any large lumps. Beat the refried beans until smooth, then add to the turkey in the bowl.

2. Add the garlic, chiles, tomato paste, and cilantro, season with salt and pepper, and mix together. Shape into four equal burgers, then cover and let chill for 1 hour. Meanwhile, preheat the barbecue.

3. Oil the grill rack. Cook the burgers over medium–hot coals for 5–6 minutes on each side, or until thoroughly cooked. Transfer to serving plates and serve in the burger buns with the lettuce, tomato slices, and salsa.

SLICED STEAKS
WITH PARMESAN

# 27 JUNE

## CHICKEN WITH GOAT CHEESE

**SERVES: 4–6**  **PREP TIME: 10 MIN.**  **COOK TIME: 20 MIN.**

### INGREDIENTS

4 skinless, boneless chicken breasts

4 ounces soft goat cheese

small bunch fresh basil

2 tablespoons olive oil

salt and pepper

**1.** Using a sharp knife, slit along one long edge of each chicken breast, then carefully open out each breast to make a small pocket. Divide the cheese equally among the pockets and tuck three to four basil leaves in each. Close the openings and season the breasts with salt and pepper.

**2.** Heat the oil in a skillet, add the chicken breasts, and sauté gently for 15–20 minutes, turning several times. Check the chicken is cooked and no longer pink by cutting through thickest part of the meat. Serve warm.

# 28 JUNE

## TURKEY SALAD PITA

**MAKES: 1**  **PREP TIME: 10 MIN.**  **COOK TIME: 2 MIN.**

### INGREDIENTS

small handful baby leaf spinach, rinsed, patted dry, and shredded

½ red bell pepper, seeded and thinly sliced

½ carrot, peeled and coarsely grated

¼ cup hummus

½ cup thinly sliced boneless, skinless cooked turkey

½ tablespoon toasted sunflower seeds

1 whole-wheat pita bread

salt and pepper

**1.** Preheat the broiler to high.

**2.** Put the spinach leaves, red bell pepper, carrot, and hummus into a large bowl, then stir together so all the salad ingredients are coated with the hummus. Stir in the turkey and sunflower seeds and season with salt and pepper.

**3.** Put the pita bread under the broiler for about 1 minute on each side to warm through, but do not brown. Cut it in half to make two pockets of bread.

**4.** Divide the salad between the bread pockets and serve.

# TOFU POCKETS

**SERVES: 4**  **PREP TIME: 10 MIN.**  **COOK TIME: 15 MIN.**

## INGREDIENTS

2 tablespoons olive oil, plus extra for brushing

1 garlic clove, crushed

8 ounces firm tofu, cut into chunks

15 cherry tomatoes, halved

1 small red onion, thinly sliced

handful of fresh basil leaves

salt and pepper

crusty bread, to serve

**1.** Preheat the oven to 425°F. Brush four double-thickness, 12-inch squares of aluminum foil with the oil. Mix the remaining oil with the garlic.

**2.** Divide the tofu, tomatoes, onion, and basil among the foil squares, sprinkle with salt and pepper, and spoon the garlic-flavored oil over the filling.

**3.** Fold over the foil to enclose the filling and seal firmly. Place on a baking sheet in the preheated oven and cook for 10–15 minutes, until heated through.

**4.** Carefully open the pockets and serve with crusty bread to mop up the juices.

# STRAWBERRY MERINGUE

SERVES: 6–8     PREP TIME: 20 MIN.     COOK TIME: 1 HR. 20 MIN.

## INGREDIENTS

3 egg whites

¼ cup superfine sugar

1 teaspoon cornstarch

1 teaspoon white wine vinegar

1 teaspoon vanilla extract

⅔ cup heavy cream

⅔ cup Greek-style yogurt

8 ounces strawberries, hulled and halved

fresh mint sprigs, to decorate

**1.** Preheat the oven to 250°F. Line a baking sheet with parchment paper.

**2.** Put the egg whites into a grease-free bowl and whisk until stiff, then gradually add the sugar, whisking between each addition. Whisk in the cornstarch, vinegar, and vanilla extract.

**3.** Spoon the mixture onto the parchment paper in a 9-inch circle, making an indentation in the center.

**4.** Bake in the preheated oven for 1 hour–1 hour 20 minutes, until the surface is dry but the center is still soft. Remove from the oven and let cool.

**5.** Pour the cream into a bowl and whip until it holds stiff peaks, then stir in the yogurt. Chop half the strawberries into slightly smaller pieces and stir into the cream, then spoon into the meringue.

**6.** Decorate with the remaining strawberries, top with mint sprigs, and serve chilled.

# BLUEBERRY & CRANBERRY SQUARES

**MAKES: 12**    **PREP TIME: 20 MIN.**    **COOK TIME: 30 MIN.**

## INGREDIENTS

1½ sticks unsalted butter, softened, plus extra for greasing

1 cup granulated sugar

1 teaspoon vanilla extract

3 eggs, beaten

1⅓ cup all-purpose flour

2 teaspoons baking powder

⅓ cup dried cranberries

1¼ cups blueberries

## FROSTING

1 cup mascarpone cheese or cream cheese

¾ cup confectioners' sugar

1. Preheat the oven to 350°F. Grease a shallow 7 x 11-inch rectangular cake pan and line with parchment paper.

2. Put the butter, sugar, and vanilla extract into a bowl and cream together until pale and fluffy. Add the eggs gradually, beating hard after each addition.

3. Fold in the flour and baking powder with a metal spoon, then stir in the cranberries and ⅔ cup of the blueberries.

4. Spoon the batter into the prepared pan and spread evenly over the bottom. Bake in the preheated oven for 25–30 minutes, or until risen, firm, and golden brown. Let cool in the pan for 15 minutes, then turn out and transfer to a wire rack to cool completely.

5. To make the frosting, beat together the mascarpone cheese and sugar until smooth, then spread over the cake with a spatula.

6. Sprinkle the remaining blueberries over the cake and cut into 12 squares to serve.

# MIXED BERRY PANCAKE STACK

SERVES: 4 　　 PREP TIME: 10 MIN. 　　 COOK TIME: 10 MIN.

### INGREDIENTS

1 cup all-purpose flour

1½ teaspoons baking powder

pinch of salt

1 tablespoon granulated sugar

1 cup milk

1 extra-large egg

2 tablespoons butter, melted

2 tablespoons finely chopped fresh mint

sunflower oil, for greasing

fresh mint sprigs, to decorate

### TO SERVE

1 cup Greek-style plain yogurt

3 cups mixed berries, such as blackberries, raspberries, and blueberries

confectioners' sugar, for dusting

**1.** Sift the flour, baking powder, salt, and sugar into a bowl. Add the milk, egg, butter, and mint and beat to form a smooth batter. Let stand for 5 minutes.

**2.** Lightly grease a griddle pan or skillet and heat over medium heat. Spoon tablespoons of batter into the pan and cook until bubbles appear on the surface.

**3.** Turn over with a spatula and cook the other side until golden brown. Repeat this process using the remaining batter, while keeping the cooked pancakes warm.

**4.** To serve, stack the pancakes with the yogurt and berries, dust with confectioners' sugar, and decorate with mint sprigs.

# CAESAR SALAD

**SERVES: 4**      **PREP TIME: 20 MIN.**      **COOK TIME: ABOUT 5 MIN.**

## INGREDIENTS

1 extra-large egg

2 heads of romaine lettuce or 3 heads of Boston or butterhead lettuce

⅓ cup olive oil

2 tablespoons lemon juice

8 canned anchovy fillets, drained and coarsely chopped

salt and pepper

Parmesan cheese shavings, to garnish

### GARLIC CROUTONS

¼ cup olive oil

2 garlic cloves

5 slices white bread, crusts removed, cut into ½-inch cubes

**1.** Bring a small, heavy saucepan of water to a boil.

**2.** Meanwhile, make the garlic croutons. Heat the oil in a heavy skillet. Add the garlic and diced bread and cook, stirring and tossing frequently, for 4–5 minutes, or until the bread is crispy and golden all over. Remove from the pan with a slotted spoon and drain on paper towels.

**3.** While the bread is cooking, add the egg to the boiling water and cook for 1 minute, then remove from the pan and reserve.

**4.** Arrange the lettuce leaves in a salad bowl. Mix together the oil and lemon juice, then season with salt and pepper. Crack the egg into the dressing and beat to blend. Pour the dressing over the lettuce leaves, toss well, then add the croutons and anchovies and toss the salad again. Sprinkle with Parmesan cheese shavings and serve.

# BACON CHEESEBURGERS

SERVES: 4    PREP TIME: 10 MIN.    COOK TIME: 15 MIN.

### INGREDIENTS

1½ pounds ground chuck beef

2 tablespoons grated onion

1 teaspoon Worcestershire sauce

olive oil, for brushing and oiling

4 bacon strips

4 American cheese, Swiss cheese, or cheddar cheese slices

salt and pepper

burger buns and toppings of your choice, to serve

1. Preheat the barbecue. Using a fork, lightly mix the beef with the onion, Worcestershire sauce, salt, and pepper. Divide the mixture into four balls and flatten into patties about 1 inch thick. Season the outside with salt and pepper, and lightly brush with oil.

2. Oil the grill rack. Cook the bacon for 3–4 minutes, turning once. Set aside and keep warm. Cook the patties for 5 minutes, then turn and place the cheese slices on top. Cook for an additional 3–4 minutes. Brush the inside of the buns with oil and toast over the barbecue, cut side down, for 1–2 minutes. Serve in burger buns with toppings of your choice.

# WINE-STEAMED MUSSELS

SERVES: 4    PREP TIME: 15 MIN.    COOK TIME: 10 MIN.

### INGREDIENTS

1 stick butter

1 shallot, chopped

3 garlic cloves, finely chopped

4½ pounds mussels, scrubbed and debearded

1 cup dry white wine

¼ cup chopped fresh parsley

salt and pepper

crusty bread, to serve

1. Place half the butter in a large saucepan and melt over low heat. Add the shallot and garlic and cook for 2 minutes.

2. Discard any mussels with broken shells and any that refuse to close when tapped. Add the mussels and wine to the pan and season with salt and pepper. Cover and bring to a boil, then cook for 3 minutes, shaking the pan from time to time.

3. Remove the mussels from the pan with a slotted spoon and place in serving bowls. Discard any mussels that remain closed.

4. Stir the remaining butter and the parsley into the cooking juices in the pan. Bring to a boil, then pour the juices over the mussels.

5. Serve with crusty bread for mopping up the juices.

BACON
CHEESEBURGERS

# BROILED TENDERLOIN STEAKS

SERVES: 4–6 · PREP TIME: 10 MIN. PLUS 30 MIN. MARINATING TIME · COOK TIME: 15 MIN.

## INGREDIENTS

2 tablespoons olive oil

3 tablespoons raspberry vinegar

1 tablespoon granulated sugar

1 tablespoon finely chopped fresh rosemary

4 tenderloin steaks

1 small red onion, finely chopped

½ cup red wine

2 cups raspberries

salt and pepper

1. Put the oil, vinegar, sugar, and rosemary into a small bowl and mix together. Place the steaks in a nonmetallic dish and pour the vinegar mixture over the steaks. Cover and let marinate for 30 minutes.

2. Preheat the broiler to high. Drain the meat well, season with salt and pepper, place on the broiler rack, and cook under the preheated broiler, turning once, for 2 minutes on each side for medium–rare, and for 2½ minutes on each side for medium. Remove from the rack and let stand for 5 minutes.

3. Meanwhile, put the marinade into a saucepan with the onion and bring to a boil, then cook over moderate heat, stirring, for 3–4 minutes, until the onion is soft. Add the wine, bring to a boil, and boil for 2–3 minutes, until the liquid is reduced by half. Add the raspberries and cook, stirring, for 1 minute.

4. Season the raspberry sauce with salt and pepper, spoon it over the steaks, and serve immediately.

# ROASTED SUMMER VEGETABLES

SERVES: 4 · PREP TIME: 25 MIN. · COOK TIME: 25 MIN.

## INGREDIENTS

⅔ cup olive oil, plus extra for brushing

1 fennel bulb, cut into wedges

2 red onions, cut into wedges

2 beefsteak tomatoes, cut into wedges

1 eggplant, thickly sliced

2 zucchini, thickly sliced

1 yellow bell pepper, seeded and cut into chunks

1 red bell pepper, seeded and cut into chunks

1 orange bell pepper, seeded and cut into chunks

4 garlic cloves

4 fresh rosemary sprigs

pepper

crusty bread, to serve

1. Preheat the oven to 400°F. Brush a large ovenproof dish with a little of the oil. Arrange the prepared vegetables in the dish and tuck the garlic cloves and rosemary sprigs among them. Drizzle with the remaining oil and season with plenty of pepper.

2. Roast the vegetables in the preheated oven for 20–25 minutes, turning once, until they are tender and beginning to turn golden brown.

3. Serve the vegetables with crusty bread.

# SHRIMP TACOS WITH CHILI SAUCE

SERVES: 4–6     PREP TIME: 15 MIN.     COOK TIME: 40 MIN.

## INGREDIENTS

1¼ pounds shrimp, shelled and deveined

2 tablespoons chopped fresh flat-leaf parsley

12 tortilla shells

scallions, chopped, to garnish

sour cream and lemon wedges, to serve

## CHILI SAUCE

1 tablespoon olive oil

1 onion, finely chopped

1 green bell pepper, seeded and diced

1–2 fresh hot green chiles, such as jalapeño, seeded and finely chopped

3 garlic cloves, crushed

1 teaspoon ground cumin

1 teaspoon ground coriander

1 teaspoon packed brown sugar

4 ripe tomatoes, peeled and coarsely chopped

juice of ½ lemon

salt and pepper

**1.** To make the chili sauce, heat the oil in a deep skillet over medium heat. Add the onion and cook for 5 minutes, or until softened. Add the bell pepper and chiles and cook for 5 minutes. Add the garlic, cumin, coriander, and sugar and cook for an additional 2 minutes, stirring.

**2.** Preheat the oven to 350°F. Add the tomatoes and lemon juice to the sauce and season with salt and pepper. Bring to a boil, then reduce the heat and simmer for 10 minutes. Stir in the shrimp and parsley, cover, and cook gently for 5–8 minutes, or until the shrimp are pink and tender.

**3.** Meanwhile, place the tortilla shells, open side down, on a baking sheet. Warm in the preheated oven for 2–3 minutes. To serve, spoon the shrimp mixture into the tortilla shells, garnish with scallions, and serve with sour cream and lemon wedges.

# SEARED SESAME SALMON WITH BOK CHOY

SERVES: 4     PREP TIME: 25 MIN.     COOK TIME: 10 MIN.

## INGREDIENTS

1-inch piece fresh ginger

1 tablespoon soy sauce

1 teaspoon sesame oil

4 skinless salmon fillets

2 tablespoons sesame seeds

lime wedges, to serve

## STIR-FRY

1 tablespoon sunflower oil

1 teaspoon sesame oil

2 small bok choy, cut lengthwise into quarters

1 bunch scallions, cut diagonally into thick slices

salt and pepper

1. Peel and finely grate the ginger and mix with the soy sauce and sesame oil in a shallow dish. Add the salmon fillets, turning to coat evenly on both sides.

2. Sprinkle the salmon on one side with half the sesame seeds, then turn and sprinkle the other side with the remaining sesame seeds.

3. Preheat a heavy skillet. Add the salmon and cook for 3–4 minutes. Turn and cook for an additional 3–4 minutes.

4. Meanwhile, heat the sunflower oil and sesame oil in a wok, add the bok choy and scallions, and stir-fry for 2–3 minutes. Season with salt and pepper.

5. Divide the vegetables among serving plates and place the salmon on top.

6. Serve with lime wedges for squeezing over.

# SCRAMBLED EGGS WITH SMOKED SALMON

SERVES: 4    PREP TIME: 10 MIN.    COOK TIME: 10 MIN.

### INGREDIENTS

8 eggs

⅓ cup light cream

2 tablespoons chopped fresh dill, plus extra to garnish

4 ounces smoked salmon, cut into small pieces

2 tablespoons butter

8 slices sourdough bread or white bread, toasted

salt and pepper

1. Break the eggs into a large bowl and beat together with the cream and dill. Season with salt and pepper. Add the smoked salmon and mix to combine.

2. Melt the butter in a large nonstick skillet and pour in the egg-and-smoked salmon mixture. Gently scrape the egg away from the sides of the skillet as it begins to set and swirl the skillet slightly to let the uncooked egg fill the surface. When the eggs are almost cooked but still creamy, remove from the heat and spoon onto the prepared toast. Garnish with dill and serve.

# FRUIT & NUT GRANOLA

MAKES: ABOUT 20 SERVINGS    PREP TIME: 5 MIN. PLUS 12 HR. SOAKING TIME    COOK TIME: NO COOKING

### INGREDIENTS

1½ cups rolled oats

4 cups wheat flakes

1½ cups rice flakes

½ cup rye flakes

⅔ cup raisins

1 cup chopped dried banana chips

½ cup toasted hazelnuts

⅓ cup sunflower seeds or flaxseeds

½ cup wheat germ

milk, for soaking

1. Put all the dried ingredients into a large jar with an airtight seal. Seal the jar and shake to mix together. Make sure that the ingredients are well distributed.

2. To serve, put the desired number of servings of granola into a bowl, pour enough milk over it to cover, and let soak overnight. The dry granola will keep for at least a month in a well-sealed jar.

# BARBECUED CHICKEN WITH TARRAGON BUTTER

SERVES: 4    PREP TIME: 10 MIN. PLUS 30 MIN. MARINATING TIME    COOK TIME: 10 MIN.

## INGREDIENTS

4 skinless, boneless chicken breasts (about 8 ounces each)

oil, for brushing and oiling

### TARRAGON BUTTER

1 stick unsalted butter, at room temperature

½ cup chopped fresh tarragon

1 shallot, finely chopped

salt and pepper

### MARINADE

1½ tablespoons lemon juice

2 tablespoons water

1 teaspoon sugar

1 teaspoon salt

½ teaspoon pepper

3 tablespoons olive oil

**1.** To make the tarragon butter, mash the butter with a fork until soft, then add the remaining ingredients, including salt and pepper to taste, mixing well. Scrape the mixture onto a piece of plastic wrap and form into a log. Wrap tightly and chill in the refrigerator.

**2.** Slice the chicken breasts lengthwise to make eight portions. Trim any excess fat. Place in a single layer in a shallow dish. Beat together the marinade ingredients and pour the marinade over the chicken. Cover with plastic wrap and marinate for 30 minutes, turning halfway through. Meanwhile, preheat the barbecue.

**3.** Drain the chicken and discard the marinade. Pat dry and lightly brush with oil. Oil the grill rack. Place the chicken on the rack, and cover with a disposable foil pan. Grill over medium–hot coals for 5–6 minutes, until the underside is striped with grill marks and is no longer translucent. Using tongs, turn and cook the other side for 4–5 minutes. Check that the chicken is cooked and no longer pink by cutting through the thickest part of the meat.

**4.** Place in a warm dish, cover with aluminum foil, and let rest in a warm place for 5 minutes. Serve with slices of tarragon butter.

# STRAWBERRY SHORTCAKE

SERVES: 6–8    PREP TIME: 25 MIN.    COOK TIME: 20 MIN.

## INGREDIENTS

2 cups all-purpose flour

1 tablespoon baking powder

4 tablespoons butter, diced, plus extra for greasing

¼ cup superfine or granulated sugar

¼–⅓ cup milk

fresh mint leaves, to garnish

## TOPPING

¼ cup milk

2 cups mascarpone cheese

⅓ cup superfine or granulated sugar

1 pound strawberries, hulled and quartered

finely grated rind of 1 orange

1. Preheat the oven to 400°F. Lightly grease an 8-inch loose-bottom cake pan.

2. Sift the flour and baking powder into a large bowl, add the butter, and rub in with your fingertips until the mixture resembles fine bread crumbs. Add the sugar. Stir in enough of the milk to form a soft but smooth batter. Gently push the batter evenly into the prepared cake pan. Bake in the preheated oven for 15–20 minutes, until risen, firm to the touch, and golden brown. Let cool for 5 minutes in the pan, then turn out onto a wire rack and let cool completely.

3. To make the topping, beat together the milk and mascarpone cheese with 3 tablespoons of the sugar in a bowl until smooth and fluffy. Put the strawberries in a separate bowl and sprinkle with the remaining sugar and the orange rind.

4. Spread the mascarpone mixture over the cake and pile the strawberries on top. Spoon any leftover juices from the strawberries over the top, sprinkle with mint leaves, and serve.

# BLUEBERRY FROZEN YOGURT

SERVES: 6–8    PREP TIME: 10 MIN. PLUS 6 HR. FREEZING TIME    COOK TIME: NO COOKING

## INGREDIENTS

1¼ cups fresh blueberries

finely grated rind and juice of 1 orange

3 tablespoons maple syrup

2 cups plain low-fat yogurt

1. Put the blueberries and orange juice into a food processor and process to a puree. Strain through a nylon strainer into a bowl.

2. Stir together the maple syrup and yogurt in a large mixing bowl, then fold in the fruit puree.

3. Churn the mixture in an ice cream machine, following the manufacturer's directions, then freeze for 5–6 hours. If you don't have an ice cream machine, transfer the mixture to a freezer-proof container and freeze for 2 hours. Remove from the freezer, invert into a bowl, and beat until smooth. Return to the freezer and freeze until firm. When ready to serve, decorate with the orange rind.

STRAWBERRY
SHORTCAKE

# AVOCADO, FETA & ARUGULA SALAD

**SERVES: 4     PREP TIME: 10 MIN.     COOK TIME: 5 MIN.**

### INGREDIENTS

2 ripe avocados

4 cups arugula

1⅓ cups crumbled feta cheese

### DRESSING

⅓ cup olive oil

2 tablespoons white wine vinegar

1 shallot, finely chopped

2 large ripe tomatoes, seeded and diced

1 tablespoon lemon juice

1 teaspoon granulated sugar

salt and pepper

**1.** Halve, pit, peel, and slice the avocados and arrange on a serving dish with the arugula. Top with the cheese.

**2.** To make the dressing, put the oil and vinegar into a saucepan and gently heat, then add the shallot and cook, stirring, for 2–3 minutes, until soft. Add the tomatoes, lemon juice, and sugar and gently heat, stirring, for 30 seconds.

**3.** Season the dressing with salt and pepper, then spoon it over the salad and serve immediately.

# GAZPACHO

SERVES: 4　　PREP TIME: 25 MIN. PLUS 2 HR. COOLING TIME　　COOK TIME: **NO COOKING**

### INGREDIENTS

1 red bell pepper, seeded and chopped

9 ripe tomatoes (about 2¼ pounds), peeled, seeded, and chopped

2 tablespoons minced onion

3 garlic cloves, crushed

1 cucumber, peeled and chopped

3½ slices stale bread, crumbled

3 tablespoons red wine vinegar or sherry vinegar

¼ cup olive oil, plus extra for drizzling

1 cup ice cubes (optional)

salt and pepper

**1.** Set aside a handful of the red bell pepper, a handful of the tomatoes, and half the chopped onion in the refrigerator. Put the rest in a food processor with the garlic and cucumber and puree until smooth. Add the bread, vinegar, and oil and process again. Season with salt and pepper. If the soup is too thick, add the ice, then place in the refrigerator for 2 hours.

**2.** When ready to serve, check the vinegar and seasoning and ladle into bowls. Sprinkle with the reserved red bell pepper, tomatoes, and onions, then drizzle a swirl of olive oil over the top and serve.

# CRAB CAKES WITH TARTAR SAUCE

**MAKES: 6**    **PREP TIME: 25 MIN. PLUS 2 HR. CHILLING TIME**    **COOK TIME: ABOUT 10 MIN.**

### INGREDIENTS

1 extra-large egg, beaten

2 tablespoons mayonnaise

½ teaspoon Dijon mustard

¼ teaspoon Worcestershire sauce

½ teaspoon celery salt

¼ teaspoon salt

10 water crackers, finely crushed

1 pound fresh crabmeat

2–3 cups fresh bread crumbs

2 tablespoons unsalted butter

1 tablespoon vegetable oil

salad greens and lemon wedges, to serve

### TARTAR SAUCE

1 cup mayonnaise

¼ cup sweet pickle relish

1 tablespoon minced chopped onion

1 tablespoon chopped capers

1½ tablespoons freshly squeezed lemon juice

dash of Worcestershire sauce

salt and pepper

1. To make the crab cakes, beat together the egg, mayonnaise, mustard, Worcestershire sauce, celery salt, and salt in a large bowl until combined. Stir in the cracker crumbs with a spatula, then let stand for 5 minutes.

2. Pick over the crabmeat to remove any pieces of shell or cartilage, then gently fold into the mixture, trying to avoid breaking it up too much. Cover the bowl with plastic wrap and chill in the refrigerator for at least 1 hour.

3. Meanwhile, make the tartar sauce. Mix together all the ingredients in a bowl and season with salt and pepper. Cover and chill in the refrigerator for at least 1 hour before serving.

4. Sprinkle the bread crumbs over a large plate until lightly covered. Shape the crab mixture into six even cakes, about 1 inch thick, placing them on the plate as they are formed. Dust the tops of each crab cake lightly with more bread crumbs.

5. Melt the butter with the oil in a large skillet over medium–high heat. Carefully transfer each crab cake from the plate to the skillet, using a metal spatula.

6. Cook the crab cakes for 4 minutes on each side, until golden brown. Remove from the skillet and drain on paper towels. Serve with the tartar sauce, salad greens, and lemon wedges.

# LAMB KOFTAS WITH THYME & LEMON DIP

SERVES: 4    PREP TIME: **20 MIN.**    COOK TIME: **ABOUT 10 MIN.**

## INGREDIENTS

1 pound ground lamb

½ cup fresh white bread crumbs

1 onion, grated

1 garlic clove, crushed

1 teaspoon ground coriander

1 teaspoon ground cumin

2 tablespoons chopped fresh mint

olive oil, for brushing

salt and pepper

lemon wedges, to serve

## THYME & LEMON DIP

⅔ cup plain yogurt

finely grated rind and
juice of ½ lemon

1 tablespoon chopped fresh thyme

1. Preheat the barbecue and soak eight wooden skewers, if using, in water for 30 minutes to prevent them from charring. Put the ground lamb, bread crumbs, onion, garlic, coriander, cumin, and mint into a bowl and mix together. Season well with salt and pepper.

2. Divide the mixture into eight equal portions and press evenly onto eight presoaked wooden skewers or metal skewers.

3. To make the thyme-and-lemon dip, put the yogurt, lemon rind, and lemon juice into a bowl and mix together. Stir in the thyme and season with salt and pepper.

4. Brush the koftas with oil, place on the grill rack, and cook, turning occasionally, for 10–12 minutes, until golden brown and cooked through. Serve with the thyme-and-lemon dip and with lemon wedges.

# 19 JULY

# MEXICAN TURKEY CUTLETS

SERVES: 4–6     PREP TIME: 20 MIN. PLUS AT LEAST 4 HR. MARINATING TIME     COOK TIME: 5 MIN.

### INGREDIENTS

4 turkey cutlets

olive oil, for brushing and oiling

avocado salsa and warm tortillas, to serve

### MARINADE

juice of 1 orange

juice of 2 limes

2 garlic cloves, crushed

1 teaspoon paprika

½ teaspoon salt

½ teaspoon chili powder

½ teaspoon cumin seeds, crushed

¼ teaspoon pepper

¼ cup olive oil

1. Halve the turkey cutlets horizontally to make eight thinner pieces. Place between two sheets of plastic wrap and pound with a meat mallet until flattened to ½ inch thick. Slice into strips about 1½ inches wide and 2½ inches long. Place in a single layer in a shallow dish.

2. Beat together the marinade ingredients and pour the marinade over the turkey. Cover with plastic wrap and let marinate in the refrigerator for at least 4 hours or overnight. Let reach room temperature before cooking. When ready to cook, preheat the barbecue and soak four to six wooden skewers, if using, in water to prevent them from charring.

3. Drain the turkey, discarding the marinade. Lightly brush with oil and thread concertina-style onto the presoaked wooden skewers or metal skewers. Oil the grill rack. Grill for 2–2½ minutes on each side over hot coals until no longer pink when cut into with a small knife. Remove from the skewers and serve with the avocado salsa and warm tortillas.

# 20 JULY

# SPICY TURKEY & SAUSAGE KABOBS

SERVES: 8     PREP TIME: 15 MIN. PLUS 1 HR. STANDING TIME     COOK TIME: 15 MIN.

### INGREDIENTS

⅓ cup olive oil, plus extra for oiling

2 garlic cloves, crushed

1 fresh red chile, seeded and chopped

12 ounces turkey cutlets

8 ounces chorizo sausage

1 Golden Delicious or Pippin apple

1 tablespoon lemon juice

8 bay leaves

salt and pepper

1. Place the olive oil, garlic, and chile in a small screw-top jar, season with salt and pepper, and shake well to combine. Let stand for 1 hour for the garlic and chile to flavor the oil.

2. Preheat the barbecue and soak eight wooden skewers, if using, in water for 30 minutes to prevent charring. Using a sharp knife, cut the turkey into 1-inch pieces. Cut the sausage into 1-inch lengths. Cut the apple into chunks and remove the core. Toss the apple in the lemon juice to prevent discoloration.

3. Thread the turkey and sausage pieces onto the presoaked wooden skewers or metal skewers, alternating with the apple chunks and bay leaves.

4. Oil the grill rack. Cook the kabobs over hot coals for 15 minutes, or until the turkey is cooked through. Turn and baste the kabobs frequently with the flavored oil.

5. Transfer the kabobs to warm serving plates and serve immediately. Do not eat the bay leaves.

MEXICAN TURKEY
CUTLETS

# MIXED VEGETABLE BRUSCHETTA

SERVES: 4    PREP TIME: 15 MIN.    COOK TIME: 10 MIN.

### INGREDIENTS

olive oil, for greasing and drizzling

1 large red bell pepper, halved and seeded

1 large orange bell pepper, halved and seeded

4 thick slices baguette or ciabatta

1 fennel bulb, sliced

1 red onion, sliced

2 zucchini, sliced diagonally

2 garlic cloves, halved

1 tomato, halved

salt and pepper

1. Preheat the barbecue. Oil the grill rack. Cut each bell pepper half lengthwise into four strips. Toast the bread on both sides in a toaster or under a broiler.

2. Cook the bell pepper strips and fennel over medium–hot coals for 4 minutes, then add the onion and zucchini and cook for an additional 5 minutes, until all the vegetables are tender but still firm to the bite.

3. Meanwhile, rub the garlic halves over the toasted bread, then rub with the tomato halves. Place on serving plates. Pile the chargrilled vegetables on top, drizzle with oil, and season with salt and pepper. Serve.

# ROMAINE, BACON & BLUE CHEESE SALAD

SERVES: 4    PREP TIME: 10 MIN.    COOK TIME: 5 MIN.

### INGREDIENTS

4 bacon strips

1 small head of romaine lettuce

4 ounces blue cheese, such as Roquefort or Gorgonzola cheese

### DRESSING

finely grated rind and juice of ½ lemon

3 tablespoons olive oil

2 teaspoons poppy seeds

½ teaspoon granulated sugar

salt and pepper

1. Preheat the broiler to high. Place the bacon on the broiler rack and cook under the preheated broiler, turning once, for 4–5 minutes, until golden brown and crisp. Place on absorbent paper towels and let cool.

2. Tear or cut the lettuce into bite-size pieces and place in a large bowl. Crumble the cheese over the leaves. Chop the bacon and sprinkle it over the salad.

3. To make the dressing, put the lemon rind, lemon juice, oil, poppy seeds, and sugar into a screw-top jar and shake well to mix. Season with salt and pepper, then pour the dressing over the salad, lightly toss, and serve.

# POTATO KABOBS WITH FETA

**SERVES: 4–6    PREP TIME: 25 MIN.    COOK TIME: ABOUT 20 MIN.**

## INGREDIENTS

4 large garlic cloves, peeled

1 teaspoon sea salt flakes

1 tablespoon finely chopped fresh rosemary

½ teaspoon pepper

¼ cup olive oil, plus extra for oiling

2 pounds red-skinned new potatoes, about 2 inches long

⅓ cup crumbled feta cheese

1 tablespoon chopped fresh flat-leaf parsley

**1.** Preheat the barbecue. and soak six wooden skewers, if using, in water for 30 minutes to prevent them from charring. Using a mortar and pestle, crush the garlic cloves with the sea salt until smooth and creamy. If necessary, push through a strainer to remove any fibrous shreds, which could burn. Add the rosemary and pepper, and pound to a paste. Beat in the olive oil, then pour the mixture into a large bowl and let stand.

**2.** Scrub the potatoes and slice in half widthwise. Steam over boiling water for 7 minutes, until only just tender. Spread out on a clean dish towel to dry. Add to the garlic mixture in the bowl and toss to coat.

**3.** Arrange the potatoes cut side down on a cutting board, reserving the remaining garlic mixture in the bowl. Thread onto the six presoaked wooden skewers or metal skewers, piercing the potato halves through the middle so that the cut sides remain facing downward.

**4.** Pile some of the coals to one side, leaving a slightly cooler zone with a single layer of coals. Oil the grill rack. Cook the kabobs over hot coals, cut side down, for 3–4 minutes, turning when each side is striped from the grill. Brush the upper surface with the garlic oil as you turn. Move to the cooler zone and cook for an additional 5–7 minutes, turning and brushing, until tender when pierced with the tip of a knife.

**5.** Arrange the kabobs on a serving platter, and sprinkle with the feta cheese and parsley. Serve while still hot.

# ITALIAN-STYLE SAUSAGES WITH SALSA

SERVES: 4     PREP TIME: 10 MIN. PLUS AT LEAST 1 HR. CHILLING TIME     COOK TIME: 15 MIN.

### INGREDIENTS

8 Italian-style sausages

oil, for brushing

crusty bread rolls, to serve

### SALSA

1 red bell pepper,
seeded and finely diced

2 tomatoes, finely diced

1 fresh red finger chile,
finely chopped

2 jalapeño chiles, finely chopped

2 tablespoons extra virgin olive oil

1 tablespoon balsamic vinegar

salt and pepper

1. To make the salsa, put the red bell pepper, tomatoes, and chiles into a bowl and mix together. Stir in the oil and vinegar, then season with salt and pepper. Cover and chill in the refrigerator for at least 1 hour, or until required.

2. Preheat the broiler to medium. Arrange the sausages on the broiler rack and brush lightly with oil. Cook under the preheated broiler, turning occasionally, for 12–15 minutes, until golden and thoroughly cooked.

3. Serve the sausages hot, with a large spoonful of salsa on the side, accompanied by bread rolls.

# PEA & MINT RISOTTO

SERVES: 4      PREP TIME: 10 MIN.      COOK TIME: 20 MIN.

## INGREDIENTS

2 tablespoons olive oil

3 tablespoons butter

1 onion, finely chopped

1 garlic clove, crushed

2 cups risotto rice

⅓ cup dry white wine

6½ cups boiling chicken stock or vegetable stock

3 cups fresh or frozen peas

2 tablespoons chopped fresh mint

salt and pepper

1. Heat the oil with 1 tablespoon of the butter in a large, heavy saucepan. Add the onion and sauté gently over medium heat, stirring, for 4–5 minutes, until soft but not brown.

2. Add the garlic and rice and cook, stirring, for 1–2 minutes. Stir in the wine, bring to a boil, and cook, stirring, for about 1 minute.

3. Gradually add the stock, stirring until each addition is absorbed before adding the next. Stir in the peas and half the mint with the final addition of stock.

4. Continue stirring until most of the liquid has been absorbed and the rice is almost tender, with a slight firmness in the center. Stir in the remaining butter.

5. Season with salt and pepper, stir in the remaining mint, and serve.

# SPAGHETTI WITH TOMATOES & BLACK OLIVES

SERVES: 4      PREP TIME: 10 MIN.      COOK TIME: 40 MIN.

## INGREDIENTS

1 tablespoon olive oil

1 garlic clove, finely chopped

2 teaspoons, drained, rinsed, and chopped capers

12 ripe black olives, pitted and chopped

½ crushed red pepper

1 (28-ounce) can diced tomatoes

1 tablespoon chopped fresh parsley, plus extra to garnish

1 pound dried spaghetti

2 tablespoons freshly grated Parmesan cheese

salt

1. Heat the olive oil in a large, heavy skillet. Add the garlic and cook over low heat for 30 seconds. Add the capers, olives, crushed red pepper, and tomatoes and season with salt. Partly cover the skillet and simmer gently for 20 minutes.

2. Stir in the parsley, partly cover the skillet again, and simmer for an additional 10 minutes.

3. Meanwhile, bring a large, heavy saucepan of lightly salted water to a boil. Add the spaghetti, bring back to a boil, and cook according to the package directions, until just tender but still firm to the bite. Drain and transfer to a serving dish. Add the tomato and olive sauce and toss well. Sprinkle the Parmesan cheese over the pasta and garnish with chopped parsley. Serve.

# SHRIMP & MUSSEL PAELLA

**SERVES: 6–8**     **PREP TIME: 25 MIN. PLUS 10 MIN. SOAKING TIME**     **COOK TIME: 35–40 MIN.**

### INGREDIENTS

16 mussels

½ teaspoon saffron threads

2 tablespoons hot water

1¾ cups paella rice or risotto rice

⅓ cup olive oil

6–8 boned chicken thighs

5 ounces Spanish chorizo sausage, sliced

2 large onions, chopped

4 large garlic cloves, crushed

1 teaspoon mild or hot Spanish paprika

1 cup chopped green beans

1 cup frozen peas

5½ cups fish stock

16 shrimp, peeled and deveined

2 red bell peppers, halved and seeded, then broiled, peeled, and sliced

salt and pepper

chopped fresh flat-leaf parsley, to garnish

1. Soak the mussels in lightly salted water for 10 minutes. Put the saffron threads and hot water in a small bowl and let steep for a few minutes. Meanwhile, put the rice in a strainer and rinse in cold water until the water runs clear. Set aside.

2. Heat 3 tablespoons of the oil in a 12-inch paella pan or flameproof dish. Cook the chicken thighs over medium–high heat, turning frequently, for 5 minutes, or until golden and crispy. Using a slotted spoon, transfer to a bowl. Add the chorizo to the pan and cook, stirring, for 1 minute, or until beginning to crisp. Add to the chicken.

3. Heat the remaining oil in the pan and cook the onions, stirring frequently, for 2 minutes. Add the garlic and paprika and cook for an additional 3 minutes, or until the onions are soft but not browned.

4. Add the drained rice, beans, and peas and stir until coated in oil. Return the chicken, chorizo, and any accumulated juices to the pan. Stir in the stock and saffron and its soaking liquid, season with salt and pepper, and bring to a boil, stirring continuously. Reduce the heat to low and simmer, uncovered and without stirring, for 15 minutes, or until the rice is almost tender.

5. Discard any mussels with broken shells and any that refuse to close when tapped. Arrange the mussels, shrimp, and red bell peppers on top, then cover and simmer, without stirring, for an additional 5 minutes, or until the shrimp turn pink and the mussels open. Discard any mussels that remain closed. Check that the chicken is cooked and no longer pink by cutting through the thickest part of the meat. Taste and adjust the seasoning, if necessary. Sprinkle with the parsley and serve.

# RASPBERRY RIPPLE ICE CREAM

SERVES: 6–8    PREP TIME: 20 MIN. PLUS 30 MIN. STEEPING TIME, PLUS 2–3 HR. FREEZING TIME    COOK TIME: 25 MIN.

## INGREDIENTS

1¼ cups milk

1 vanilla bean

1 cup superfine sugar or granulated sugar

3 egg yolks

2½ cups fresh raspberries

⅓ cup water

1¼ cups heavy whipping cream

**1.** Pour the milk into a heavy saucepan, add the vanilla bean and bring almost to a boil. Remove from the heat and let steep for 30 minutes. Put ⅓ cup of the sugar and the egg yolks in a large bowl and beat together until pale and the mixture leaves a trail when the beaters are lifted. Remove the vanilla bean from the milk, then slowly add the milk to the sugar mixture, stirring all the time with a wooden spoon.

**2.** Strain the mixture into the rinsed-out saucepan or a double boiler and cook over low heat for 10–15 minutes, stirring all the time, until the mixture thickens enough to coat the back of the wooden spoon. Do not let the mixture boil or it will curdle. Remove the custard from the heat and let cool for at least 1 hour, stirring from time to time to prevent a skin from forming.

**3.** Meanwhile, put the raspberries in a heavy saucepan with the remaining sugar and the water. Heat gently, stirring, until the sugar has dissolved, then simmer gently for 5 minutes, or until the raspberries are soft. Push the raspberries through a nylon strainer into a bowl to remove the seeds, then let the puree cool. Meanwhile, whip the cream until it holds its shape. Keep in the refrigerator until ready to use.

**4.** If using an ice cream machine, fold the whipped cream into the cold custard, then churn the mixture in the machine following the manufacturer's directions. Just before the ice cream freezes, spread half into a freezer-proof container. Pour over half the raspberry puree then repeat the layers. Freeze for 1–2 hours, or until firm or required. Alternatively, fold the whipped cream into the mixture and freeze in a freezer-proof container, uncovered, for 1–2 hours, or until it begins to set around the edges. Turn the mixture into a bowl and stir with a fork until smooth. Spread half the mixture into another freezer-proof container. Pour over half the raspberry puree, then repeat the layers. Return to the container and freeze until completely frozen.

# CHILLED PEA SOUP

SERVES: 3–4    PREP TIME: 15 MIN. PLUS 2 HR. CHILLING TIME    COOK TIME: 10 MIN.

### INGREDIENTS

2 cups vegetable stock
or water

3 cups frozen peas

1 cup coarsely chopped scallions

1¼ cups plain yogurt

salt and pepper

### TO GARNISH

2 tablespoons chopped fresh mint

2 tablespoons chopped scallions
or chives

grated lemon rind

olive oil

**1.** Bring the stock to a boil in a large saucepan over medium heat. Reduce the heat, add the peas and scallions, and simmer for 5 minutes.

**2.** Let cool slightly, then strain twice, making sure that you remove any parts of skin. Pour into a large bowl, season with salt and pepper, and stir in the yogurt. Cover the bowl with plastic wrap and chill in the refrigerator for several hours, or until well chilled.

**3.** To serve, remove from the refrigerator, mix well, and ladle into serving bowls. Garnish with the chopped mint, scallions, grated lemon rind, and olive oil.

# PEACH MELBA MERINGUE

SERVES: 8    PREP TIME: 25 MIN. PLUS 15 MIN. COOLING TIME    COOK TIME: 50 MIN.

### INGREDIENTS

sunflower oil, for brushing

### RASPBERRY COULIS

2½ cups fresh raspberries

1 cup confectioners' sugar

### MERINGUE

2 teaspoons cornstarch

1½ cups superfine sugar

5 extra-large egg whites

1 teaspoon cider vinegar

### FILLING

3 peaches, peeled, pitted and chopped

2 cups fresh raspberries

1 cup crème fraîche or whipped cream

⅔ cup heavy cream

1. Preheat the oven to 300°F. Brush a 14 x 10-inch jellyroll pan with oil and line with parchment paper.

2. To make the raspberry coulis, process the raspberries and confectioners' sugar to a puree. Push through a strainer into a bowl and reserve.

3. To make the meringue, sift the cornstarch into a bowl and stir in the sugar. In a separate, grease-free bowl, beat the egg whites into stiff peaks, then beat in the vinegar. Gradually beat in the cornstarch-and-sugar mixture until stiff and glossy.

4. Spread the mixture evenly in the prepared pan, leaving a ½-inch border. Bake in the center of the preheated oven for 20 minutes, then reduce the heat to 225°F and cook for an additional 25–30 minutes, or until puffed up. Remove from the oven. Let cool for 15 minutes. Invert onto another piece of parchment paper and carefully remove the paper from the bottom.

5. To make the filling, place the peaches in a bowl with the raspberries. Add 2 tablespoons of the coulis and mix. In a separate bowl, beat together the crème fraîche and cream until thick. Spread over the meringue. Sprinkle the fruit over the cream, leaving a 1¼-inch border at one short edge. Using the parchment paper, lift and roll the meringue, starting at the short edge without the border, ending up seam side down. Lift onto a plate and serve with the coulis.

# CHOCOLATE BANANA SPLITS

SERVES: 4    PREP TIME: 15 MIN. PLUS COOLING AND CHILLING TIME, PLUS 2 HR. FREEZING TIME    COOK TIME: 5 MIN.

### INGREDIENTS

4 bananas

⅓ cup chopped, mixed nuts and chocolate rum sauce, to serve

### VANILLA ICE CREAM

1¼ cups milk

1 teaspoon vanilla extract

3 egg yolks

½ cup superfine sugar or granulated sugar

1¼ cups heavy cream, whipped

1. To make the vanilla ice cream, heat the milk and vanilla extract in a saucepan over medium heat until almost boiling. Beat together the egg yolks and sugar in a bowl. Remove the milk from the heat and stir a little into the egg mixture. Transfer the mixture to the pan and stir over low heat until thickened. Do not let boil. Remove from the heat.

2. Let cool for about 30 minutes, fold in the cream, cover with plastic wrap, and chill in the refrigerator for 1 hour. If using an ice cream machine, transfer the mixture and churn in the machine following the manufacturer's directions. Alternatively, freeze in a freezer-proof container, uncovered, for 1–2 hours, or until it begins to set around the edges. Turn the mixture into a bowl and stir with a fork until smooth. Return to the container and freeze for 30 minutes. Repeat twice again or until completely frozen.

3. Peel the bananas, slice lengthwise, and arrange on four serving dishes. Top with ice cream and nuts and serve with chocolate rum sauce.

PEACH MELBA
MERINGUE

# AUGUST

# TURBOT STICKS WITH CAPER MAYONNAISE

SERVES: 4    PREP TIME: 20 MIN.    COOK TIME: 5 MIN.

## INGREDIENTS

¾ cup dried white bread crumbs

finely grated rind of 1 lemon

2 tablespoons finely chopped fresh parsley

1 pound skinless turbot fillet

3 tablespoons all-purpose flour

1 egg, beaten

sunflower oil, for frying

salt and pepper

## CAPER MAYONNAISE

¼ cup mayonnaise

1 tablespoon capers, chopped

1 tablespoon lemon juice

1. Put the bread crumbs, lemon rind, and parsley into a food processor and process to fine crumbs. Place in a wide dish.

2. Cut the turbot into ¾ x 3-inch strips. Season the flour with salt and pepper and place in a wide dish. Put the egg into a separate wide dish.

3. Toss the fish in the seasoned flour to coat the strips evenly, then dip in the beaten egg and, finally, in the bread crumb mixture, turning to coat completely.

4. To make the caper mayonnaise, mix together the mayonnaise, capers, and lemon juice.

5. Heat enough oil for deep-frying in a large saucepan or deep-fryer to 375°F, checking the temperature with a thermometer. Add the fish strips in batches and cook, turning once, for 2–3 minutes, until golden. Drain on absorbent paper towels.

6. Serve the fish sticks hot, with the caper mayonnaise on the side.

# EGGS BAKED IN BEEFSTEAK TOMATOES

SERVES: 4     PREP TIME: 10 MIN.     COOK TIME: 25 MIN.

## INGREDIENTS

4 large beefsteak tomatoes

4 eggs

2 tablespoons chopped fresh oregano

¼ cup freshly grated Parmesan cheese

1 garlic clove, halved

4 slices sourdough bread or white bread

2 tablespoons olive oil

salt and pepper

**1.** Preheat the oven to 425°F. Cut a slice from the top of each tomato and scoop out the seeds and pulp. Place the tomatoes in a baking dish or pan.

**2.** Break an egg into each tomato, then sprinkle with oregano and salt and pepper. Sprinkle with the cheese and bake in the preheated oven for about 20 minutes, or until the eggs are just set, with runny yolks.

**3.** Meanwhile, rub the garlic over the bread, place on a baking sheet, and drizzle with oil. Bake in the oven for 5–6 minutes, or until golden.

**4.** Put each egg on a slice of toast and serve immediately.

# COLESLAW

**SERVES: 10–12** | **PREP TIME: 15 MIN.** | **COOK TIME: NO COOKING**

### INGREDIENTS

⅔ cup mayonnaise

⅓ cup plain yogurt

dash of Tabasco sauce

1 head of green cabbage

4 carrots

1 green bell pepper, seeded

salt and pepper

**1.** Mix together the mayonnaise, yogurt, and Tabasco sauce in a small bowl and season with salt and pepper. Chill the dressing in the refrigerator until required.

**2.** Cut the cabbage in half and then into quarters. Remove and discard the tough core in the center. Finely shred the cabbage leaves. Wash the leaves under cold running water and dry thoroughly on paper towels. Coarsely grate the carrots and bell pepper or shred in a food processor or on a mandoline.

**3.** Mix together the vegetables in a large serving bowl and toss to mix. Pour the dressing over the vegetables and toss until the vegetables are well coated. Cover and chill in the refrigerator until required.

# BEEF WITH TOMATOES & PEAS

**SERVES: 4**     **PREP TIME: 15 MIN.**     **COOK TIME: 1 HR. 15 MIN.**

## INGREDIENTS

4 tablespoons butter

1 onion, finely chopped

2 carrots, finely chopped

4 tomatoes, peeled and chopped

2 tablespoons all-purpose flour

1 teaspoon dry mustard

2½ cups beef stock

1 pound ground sirloin beef

1 cup frozen peas

salt and pepper

chopped fresh parsley, to garnish

**1.** Melt the butter in a saucepan. Add the onion and carrots and cook over low heat, stirring occasionally, for 5 minutes, until softened. Add the tomatoes and cook, stirring occasionally, for an additional 3 minutes.

**2.** Remove the pan from the heat and stir in the flour and dry mustard, then return to the heat and cook, stirring continuously, for 2 minutes. Gradually stir in the stock, a little at a time, then bring to a boil, stirring continuously. Cook, stirring continuously, for an additional few minutes, until thickened.

**3.** Add the beef and stir to break it up. Season with salt and pepper, then cover and simmer, stirring occasionally, for 45 minutes.

**4.** Gently stir in the peas, replace the lid, and simmer, stirring occasionally, for an additional 15 minutes. Taste and adjust the seasoning, adding salt and pepper, if needed. Garnish with parsley and serve.

# TUNA MELT ON BAGELS

SERVES: 8    PREP TIME: 35 MIN. PLUS 1 HR. 20 MIN. RISING TIME    COOK TIME: 30 MIN.

## INGREDIENTS

3⅔ cups white bread flour, plus extra for dusting

2¼ teaspoons active dry yeast

1 tablespoon granulated sugar

1½ teaspoons salt

1⅓ cups lukewarm water

olive oil, for greasing

⅓ cup poppy seeds

1 (12-ounce) can chunk light tuna in oil, drained and flaked

3 tablespoons mayonnaise

2 tablespoons snipped chives, plus extra to garnish

2 cups shredded cheddar cheese

1. Mix the flour, yeast, sugar, and salt in a large bowl. Make a well in the center and stir in just enough of the water to mix to a soft dough.

2. Invert the dough onto a lightly floured work surface and knead for about 10 minutes, until smooth. Cover and let stand in a warm place for about 1 hour, until doubled in size.

3. Invert the dough onto a lightly floured work surface and lightly knead until smooth. Divide into eight pieces and roll each piece into a smooth log shape. Form into a circle and firmly pinch together the ends. Cover and let stand for 20 minutes.

4. Preheat the oven to 425°F and grease a baking sheet. Bring a large saucepan of water to a boil, then lower the bagels into the water in batches and cook, turning once, for about 2 minutes, until they puff up.

5. Put the poppy seeds into a shallow bowl. Lift out the bagels with a slotted spoon and press them into the poppy seeds. Place the bagels on the prepared baking sheet and bake in the preheated oven for 20–25 minutes, until golden brown and firm. Transfer to a wire rack and let cool.

6. Preheat the broiler to high. Mix the tuna with the mayonnaise and chives. Slice the bagels in half and top with the tuna mixture. Sprinkle with the cheese, place on the broiler rack, and cook under the preheated broiler until the cheese is melted. Replace the bagel lids and serve sprinkled with chives.

# BARBECUED CHICKEN

SERVES: 4–6       PREP TIME: 15 MIN. PLUS 2 HR. MARINATING TIME       COOK TIME: 25 MIN.

## INGREDIENTS

4 chicken drumsticks (about 4 ounces each), skinned

chopped fresh parsley, to garnish

salad, to serve

### SAUCE

1 shallot, finely chopped

1 garlic clove, crushed

1 tablespoon tomato paste blended with ⅔ cup water

2 tablespoons red wine vinegar

1 tablespoon mustard

1 tablespoon Worcestershire sauce

1. To make the sauce, place all the sauce ingredients into a screw-top jar and shake vigorously until well blended.

2. Rinse the chicken drumsticks and pat dry with paper towels. Place the drumsticks in a large ovenproof dish, pour the sauce over the drumsticks, and let marinate for at least 2 hours, occasionally spooning the sauce over the chicken. When ready to cook, preheat the oven to 375°F.

3. Cook the chicken drumsticks in the preheated oven for 20–25 minutes, or until a fork can be inserted into the thickest part of the meat with ease and the juices run clear. A meat thermometer inserted into the thickest part of the meat, without touching the bone, should read 170°F. Spoon the sauce over the chicken or turn the chicken over during cooking.

4. Transfer to a serving plate, sprinkle with chopped parsley, and serve with salad.

# SPARERIBS IN BARBECUE SAUCE

SERVES: 4–6       PREP TIME: 15 MIN.       COOK TIME: 1 HR. 40 MIN.

## INGREDIENTS

2 tablespoons butter

2 tablespoons olive oil

1 onion, finely chopped

2 garlic cloves, finely chopped

1 celery stalk, finely chopped

1 (14½-ounce) can diced tomatoes

2 tablespoons tomato paste

2–3 tablespoons packed brown sugar

2 tablespoons orange juice

1 tablespoon honey

1 teaspoon whole-grain mustard

2 tablespoons red wine vinegar

1 tablespoon Worcestershire sauce

3¼ pounds pork spareribs

salt and pepper

1. Preheat the oven to 400°F. Melt the butter with the oil in a saucepan. Add the onion, garlic, and celery and cook over low heat, stirring occasionally, for 5 minutes, until softened. Stir in the tomatoes, tomato paste, sugar, orange juice, honey, mustard, vinegar, and Worcestershire sauce and season with salt and pepper. Increase the heat to medium and bring to a boil, then reduce the heat and simmer, stirring occasionally, for 15–20 minutes, until thickened. Remove the pan from the heat.

2. Spread out the spareribs in a shallow roasting pan and bake in the preheated oven for 25 minutes. Remove from the oven and spoon half the sauce over them. Reduce the oven temperature to 350°F, return the pan to the oven and cook for an additional 20 minutes.

3. Remove the pan from the oven and turn over the ribs. Spoon the remaining sauce over them and return the pan to the oven. Cook for an additional 25–30 minutes, until the meat is tender. Serve.

# PEPPERONI & ONION PIZZA

**MAKES: 1**  **PREP TIME: 20 MIN.**  **COOK TIME: 30 MIN.**

## INGREDIENTS

olive oil, for brushing and drizzling

1 (10-inch) pizza pie crust

¼ cup tomato paste

4 tomatoes, skinned and thinly sliced

2 red onions, finely chopped

4 slices prosciutto or other cooked ham, coarsely shredded

12 slices pepperoni

12 ripe black olives

½ teaspoon dried oregano

2 ounces mozzarella cheese, coarsely torn

salt

1. Preheat the oven to 425°F. Brush a baking sheet with oil and place the pizza pie crust on it.

2. Spread the tomato paste evenly over the crust. Arrange the tomato slices on the crust and season with salt. Sprinkle over the chopped onion and prosciutto and arrange the pepperoni on top. Add the olives and sprinkle with oregano. Add the cheese and drizzle with oil.

3. Bake in the preheated oven for 20–30 minutes, until golden and sizzling. Cut into slices and serve.

# SPICY SALMON FISH CAKES

SERVES: 4    PREP TIME: 25 MIN.    COOK TIME: 35 MIN.

## INGREDIENTS

4 potatoes, cut into medium chunks

1 pound skinless salmon fillet

2 tablespoons mayonnaise

1 egg, beaten

dash of milk, if needed

2 fresh jalapeño chiles, seeded and finely chopped

1 small bunch fresh cilantro leaves

all-purpose flour, for dusting

1 tablespoon olive oil

salt and pepper

1. Cook the potatoes in a large saucepan of lightly salted boiling water for 15 minutes, or until tender.

2. Meanwhile, lightly poach the salmon fillet in a saucepan of gently simmering water for 5–6 minutes (if in one piece), or until just cooked but still moist. Alternatively, cut into four equal pieces and cook in a microwave oven on medium for 3 minutes, then turn the pieces around so that the cooked parts are in the center, and cook for an additional 1–2 minutes—check after 1 minute; the fish should be barely cooked. Using a fork, flake the flesh into a bowl.

3. Drain the potatoes, return to the saucepan, and, while still warm, coarsely mash with a fork, adding the mayonnaise, egg, and milk, if needed—the mixture must remain firm, so only add the milk if necessary. Stir in the chiles and cilantro leaves and season with salt and pepper, then lightly mix in the salmon flakes.

4. With floured hands, form the mixture into eight small cakes. Heat the oil in a large nonstick skillet over medium–high heat, add the cakes, and cook for 5 minutes on each side, or until golden brown. Carefully remove with a spatula and serve.

# PAN-FRIED HALIBUT STEAKS WITH TOMATO SALSA

SERVES: 4    PREP TIME: 20 MIN.    COOK TIME: ABOUT 10 MIN.

## INGREDIENTS

1 tablespoon vegetable oil

3½ tablespoons butter

4 halibut steaks, about 1 inch thick

all-purpose flour, for dusting

juice of ½ lemon

salt and pepper

## TOMATO SALSA

3 firm tomatoes, halved, seeded, and finely diced

1 small red onion, finely diced

1 fresh green chile, seeded and finely chopped

3 tablespoons chopped fresh cilantro

juice of 1 lime

½ teaspoon sea salt

1. Combine all the tomato salsa ingredients in a serving bowl and let stand at room temperature.

2. Heat the oil and 3 tablespoons of the butter in a large skillet over medium–high heat. Dust the halibut steaks with flour and season with salt and pepper. Place in the skillet and cook for 5 minutes on one side and 3–4 minutes on the other, until golden and cooked through. Transfer to a warm serving dish.

3. Add the lemon juice to the skillet and simmer over medium heat for a few seconds, scraping up any sediment from the bottom of the skillet. Stir in the remaining butter and cook for a few seconds. Pour the sauce over the fish and serve with the tomato salsa.

**SPICY SALMON
FISH CAKES**

# BEEF WRAPS WITH LIME & HONEY

**SERVES: 4** | **PREP TIME: 10 MIN. PLUS 20 MIN. MARINATING TIME** | **COOK TIME: ABOUT 5 MIN.**

## INGREDIENTS

finely grated rind and juice of 1 lime

1 tablespoon honey

1 garlic clove, crushed

1 pound tenderloin steak

oil, for brushing

¼ cup mayonnaise

4 large wheat tortillas

1 red onion, thinly sliced

3-inch piece cucumber, sliced into ribbons

salt and pepper

**1.** Mix together the lime juice, honey, and garlic in a bowl and add the steak. Cover and let marinate in the refrigerator for 20 minutes.

**2.** Remove the steak from the marinade and season with salt and pepper. Heat a heavy skillet or ridged grill pan and brush with oil. Add the steak to the skillet and cook, turning once, for 5–6 minutes, until golden brown.

**3.** Remove the steak from the heat, let stand for 2 minutes, then cut into thin strips.

**4.** Mix together the mayonnaise and grated lime rind and spread over the tortillas. Sprinkle the onion over the mayonnaise mixture and add the steak strips and cucumber. Wrap the sides over and turn over one end. Serve.

# DINNERTIME BISCUITS

**MAKES: 10–12**     **PREP TIME: 20 MIN.**     **COOK TIME: ABOUT 10 MIN.**

## INGREDIENTS

3⅔ cups all-purpose flour, plus extra for dusting

½ teaspoon salt

2 teaspoons baking powder

4 tablespoons butter

1 cup milk, plus extra for glazing

butter, to serve

1. Preheat the oven to 425°F. Lightly dust a baking sheet with flour.

2. Sift the flour, salt, and baking powder into a bowl. Rub in the butter until the mixture resembles bread crumbs.

3. Make a well in the center and pour in the milk. Stir in, using a spatula, and form a soft dough.

4. Turn the dough onto a floured work surface and lightly flatten it until an even thickness of about ½ inch. Don't be too heavy-handed—biscuits need a light touch.

5. Use a 2½-inch pastry cutter to cut out the biscuits, then place them on the prepared baking sheet.

6. Glaze with a little milk and bake in the preheated oven for 10–12 minutes, until golden and well risen.

7. Serve while still warm with butter.

# CHOCOLATE-ORANGE ICE BOX COOKIES

**SERVES: 8**     **PREP TIME: 15 MIN. PLUS 4 HR. CHILLING TIME**     **COOK TIME: 5 MIN.**

## INGREDIENTS

butter, for greasing

1 pound semisweet dark chocolate, broken into pieces

3 small, loose-skinned oranges, such as tangerines, mandarins, or satsumas

4 egg yolks

1 cup crème fraîche or Greek-style plain yogurt

2 tablespoons raisins

whipped cream, to serve

1. Lightly grease a 9-inch loaf pan and line it with plastic wrap. Put the chocolate in a heatproof bowl set over a saucepan of gently simmering water. Stir over low heat until melted. Remove from the heat and let cool slightly.

2. Meanwhile, peel the oranges, removing all traces of pith. Cut the zest into thin strips. Beat the egg yolks into the chocolate, one at a time, then add most of the orange zest (reserving the rest for decoration), and all the crème fraîche and raisins, and beat until thoroughly combined. Spoon the mixture into the prepared pan, cover with plastic wrap, and chill for 3–4 hours, until set.

3. To serve, remove the pan from the refrigerator and invert the chocolate mold. Remove the plastic wrap and cut the mold into slices. Place the slices on serving plates and add whipped cream to serve. Decorate with the remaining orange zest.

# TOMATO & HERB RICOTTA TART

SERVES: 6    PREP TIME: **20 MIN.**    COOK TIME: **35 MIN.**

## INGREDIENTS

1 sheet ready-to-bake puff pastry

all-purpose flour, for dusting

1 tablespoon olive oil

4 scallions, finely chopped

1 cup ricotta cheese

2 eggs, beaten

3 tablespoons chopped fresh parsley

2 tablespoons chopped fresh mint

6 plum tomatoes or other small tomatoes, sliced

salt and pepper

chopped fresh herbs, to garnish

**1.** Preheat the oven to 400°C. Roll out the pastry on a lightly floured work surface to a rectangle about 1 inch larger than a 9 x 13-inch jellyroll pan. Carefully lift the pastry into the pan, tucking the edges evenly up the sides.

**2.** Heat the oil in a skillet, add the scallions, and sauté for 1 minute. Put the ricotta cheese and the eggs into a bowl, add the scallions, and stir to combine. Add the parsley and mint, then season well with salt and pepper.

**3.** Spread the filling over the puff pastry and arrange the tomato slices over the filling in an overlapping pattern.

**4.** Bake the tart in the preheated oven for 30–35 minutes, until the pastry is golden brown. Sprinkle with fresh herbs and serve warm.

# HALIBUT WITH BLUE CHEESE & BASIL BUTTER

**SERVES: 4     PREP TIME: 10 MIN.     COOK TIME: 10 MIN.**

### INGREDIENTS

1¼ sticks unsalted butter, at room temperature

1 cup crumbled blue cheese

2 tablespoons chopped fresh basil

4 halibut steaks (about 6–8 ounces each)

olive oil, for brushing

salt and pepper

1. Put the butter into a bowl and beat until soft, then stir in the cheese and basil, mixing evenly. Season with salt and pepper.

2. Spoon the mixture onto a sheet of plastic wrap, shape into a long log, and roll up in the plastic wrap. Let chill in the refrigerator until firm.

3. Preheat the broiler to high. Brush the halibut steaks with a little oil and season with salt and pepper. Broil the steaks for 8–10 minutes, turning once, until it flakes easily.

4. Serve the fish with a slice of chilled butter on each piece.

# ZUCCHINI WITH BUTTER & LEMON

**SERVES: 4     PREP TIME: 5 MIN. PLUS 30 MIN. MARINATING TIME     COOK TIME: 5 MIN.**

### INGREDIENTS

4 zucchini, sliced lengthwise into ¼-inch slices

1 tablespoon olive oil

2 tablespoons butter, melted

1 garlic clove, crushed

finely grated rind of 1 lemon

1 tablespoon lemon juice

salt and pepper

1. Place the zucchini slices in a bowl and add the oil, butter, garlic, lemon rind, and lemon juice. Turn to coat evenly, then cover, and let stand for 30 minutes.

2. Preheat a large skillet. Season the zucchini with salt and pepper.

3. Place the zucchini in the skillet and cook, turning occasionally and basting with any extra lemon butter, for 4–5 minutes, until golden and tender. Serve.

# SUMMER COUSCOUS SALAD

**SERVES: 4–6**     **PREP TIME: 20 MIN. PLUS 10 MIN. TO ABSORB THE WATER**     **COOK TIME: 15 MIN.**

### INGREDIENTS

2 cups couscous

½ teaspoon salt

2 cups warm water

1–2 tablespoons olive oil

4 scallions, finely chopped or sliced

1 bunch fresh mint, finely chopped

1 bunch fresh flat-leaf parsley, finely chopped

1 bunch fresh cilantro, finely chopped

1 tablespoon butter

½ preserved lemon, finely chopped

1. Preheat the oven to 350°F. Put the couscous into an ovenproof dish. Stir the salt into the water and then pour over the couscous. Cover and let the couscous absorb the water according to the package directions.

2. Drizzle the oil over the couscous. Using your fingers, rub the oil into the grains to break up the lumps and aerate them. Toss in the scallions and half the herbs. Dot the surface with the butter and cover with a piece of aluminum foil or wet wax paper. Bake in the preheated oven for about 15 minutes to heat through.

3. Fluff up the grains with a fork and transfer the couscous to a serving dish. Toss the remaining herbs into the couscous and sprinkle the preserved lemon over the top. Serve.

# BACON & CHICKEN BURGERS

**SERVES: 4     PREP TIME: 15 MIN. PLUS 1 HR. CHILLING TIME     COOK TIME: 10 MIN.**

### INGREDIENTS

1 pound ground chicken

1 onion, grated

2 garlic cloves, crushed

⅓ cup pine nuts, toasted

½ cup shredded Swiss cheese

2 tablespoons fresh, snipped chives

2 tablespoons whole-wheat flour

8 bacon strips

oil, for brushing and oiling

salt and pepper

crusty rolls and toppings of your choice, to serve

1. Place the ground chicken, onion, garlic, pine nuts, Swiss cheese, and chives in a food processor and season with salt and pepper. Using the pulse button, process the mixture together using short, sharp bursts. Scrape out onto a board and shape into four even patties. Coat in the flour, then cover and chill for 1 hour. Meanwhile, preheat the barbecue and soak eight wooden toothpicks in water for 30 minutes to prevent them from charring.

2. Wrap each burger with two bacon slices, securing in place with a presoaked wooden toothpick.

3. Oil the grill rack. Lightly brush each patty with a little oil and cook the burgers for 5 minutes on each side, or until cooked through. Transfer to serving plates and serve in crusty rolls with toppings of your choice.

# TARRAGON TURKEY

**SERVES: 4     PREP TIME: 10 MIN.     COOK TIME: ABOUT 15 MIN.**

### INGREDIENTS

4 turkey cutlets

4 teaspoons whole-grain mustard

8 fresh tarragon sprigs, plus extra to garnish

4 smoked bacon strips

oil, for oiling

salt and pepper

salad greens, to serve

1. Preheat the barbecue and soak four wooden toothpicks in water for 30 minutes to prevent them from charring. Season the turkey with salt and pepper, and using a blunt knife, spread the mustard evenly over the turkey.

2. Place two tarragon sprigs on top of each turkey cutlet and wrap a bacon strip around it to hold the herbs in place. Secure with a presoaked wooden toothpick.

3. Oil the grill rack. Cook the turkey over medium–hot coals for 5–8 minutes on each side. Transfer to serving plates and garnish with tarragon sprigs. Serve with salad greens.

BACON &
CHICKEN BURGERS

# CORN ON THE COB WITH BLUE CHEESE DRESSING

SERVES: 6     PREP TIME: 15 MIN. PLUS CHILLING TIME     COOK TIME: 20 MIN.

## INGREDIENTS

5 ounces blue cheese

⅔ cup cottage cheese

½ cup Greek-style yogurt

6 fresh ears of corn

salt and pepper

**1.** Crumble the blue cheese, then place in a bowl. Beat with a wooden spoon until creamy. Beat in the cottage cheese until thoroughly blended. Gradually beat in the yogurt and season with salt and pepper. Cover with plastic wrap and let chill in the refrigerator until required. Meanwhile, preheat the barbecue.

**2.** Fold back the husks on each corn cob and remove the silks. Smooth the husks back into place. Cut out six rectangles of aluminum foil, each large enough to enclose an ear of corn. Wrap the ears of corn in the foil.

**3.** Cook the ears of corn on the grill for 15–20 minutes, turning frequently. Unwrap the corn and discard the foil. Peel back the husk on one side of each and trim off with a sharp knife. Serve with the blue cheese dressing.

# PROSECCO & LEMON SORBET

**SERVES: 4**  **PREP TIME: 10 MIN. PLUS FREEZING TIME**  **COOK TIME: 5 MIN.**

## INGREDIENTS

¾ cup granulated sugar

½ cup water

finely grated rind and juice of 1 lemon

1½ cups prosecco or other dry sparkling white wine

fresh mint sprigs, to decorate

**1.** Put the sugar and water into a saucepan with the grated lemon rind and stir over low heat until the sugar dissolves.

**2.** Bring to a boil, then boil for 1 minute, until slightly reduced. Let cool, then strain through a strainer.

**3.** Add the lemon juice and prosecco to the lemon syrup and stir to combine, then pour into an ice cream machine and churn in the machine following the manufacturer's directions. Alternatively, pour into a container to freeze and beat once an hour until completely frozen.

**4.** Remove the sorbet from the freezer about 15 minutes before serving, then scoop into serving dishes. Decorate with mint sprigs and serve.

# PEANUT BUTTER S'MORES

SERVES: 4     PREP TIME: 5 MIN.     COOK TIME: 5 MIN.

## INGREDIENTS

½ cup smooth peanut butter

8 graham crackers or plain cookies

4 ounces semisweet dark chocolate, broken into squares

1. Preheat the barbecue. Spread the peanut butter on one side of each cracker.

2. Place the chocolate pieces on four of the crackers and invert the remaining crackers on top.

3. Toast the s'mores on the grill rack for about 1 minute, until the filling starts to melt. Turn carefully using tongs. Serve.

# CARROT CAKE

SERVES: 8     PREP TIME: 25 MIN.     COOK TIME: 40 MIN.

## INGREDIENTS

butter, for greasing

1 cup all-purpose flour

1½ teaspoons baking powder

pinch of salt

1 teaspoon allspice

½ teaspoon ground nutmeg

½ cup frimly packed light brown sugar

2 eggs, beaten

⅓ cup sunflower oil

2 carrots, peeled and shredded

1 banana, peeled and chopped

¼ cup chopped walnuts

store-bought frosting, to decorate

1. Preheat the oven to 350°F. Grease a 7-inch square cake pan and line the bottom and two sides with parchment paper.

2. Sift the flour, baking powder, salt, allspice, and nutmeg into a large bowl. Stir in the brown sugar, then add the eggs and sunflower oil and beat well. Stir in the carrots, banana, and chopped nuts.

3. Spoon the batter into the prepared pan and level the surface. Bake in the preheated oven for 35–40 minutes, or until risen, golden, and just firm to the touch. Cool in the pan for 5 minutes, then transfer to a wire rack to cool completely.

4. Spread the frosting over the top of the cake and serve.

PEANUT BUTTER
S'MORES

# STICKY LIME CHICKEN

SERVES: 4     PREP TIME: 25 MIN.     COOK TIME: 40 MIN.

## INGREDIENTS

4 skinless chicken breasts (about 5 ounces each)

juice and grated rind of 1 lime

1 tablespoon honey

1 tablespoon olive oil

1 garlic clove, chopped (optional)

1 tablespoon chopped fresh thyme

pepper

grated lemon rind, to garnish

roasted cherry tomatoes and chargrilled zucchini, to serve

1. Preheat the oven to 375°F. Arrange the chicken breasts in a shallow roasting pan.

2. Put the lime juice, lime rind, honey, oil, garlic (if using), and thyme in a small bowl and combine thoroughly. Spoon the mixture evenly over the chicken breasts and season with pepper.

3. Roast the chicken in the preheated oven, basting occasionally, for 35–40 minutes, or until a fork can be easily inserted into the thickest part of the meat with ease and the juices run clear. A meat thermometer inserted into the thickest part of the meat, without touching the bone, should read 170°F. As the chicken cooks, the liquid in the pan will thicken to create a sticky coating.

4. Remove from the oven and transfer to plates. Garnish with lemon rind and serve with roasted cherry tomatoes and chargrilled zucchini.

# ROASTED VEGETABLE & FETA CHEESE WRAPS

**MAKES: 4** **PREP TIME: 20 MIN.** **COOK TIME: 20 MIN.**

## INGREDIENTS

1 red onion, cut into eighths

1 red bell pepper, cored and cut into eighths

1 small eggplant, cut into eighths

1 zucchini, cut into eighths

¼ cup extra virgin olive oil

1 garlic clove, crushed

⅔ cup crumbled feta cheese

small bunch fresh mint, shredded

4 (10-inch) sandwich wraps

salt and pepper

**1.** Preheat the oven to 425°F. Mix together all of the vegetables, olive oil, and garlic, season with salt and pepper, and place in the oven in a nonstick roasting pan. Roast for 15–20 minutes, or until golden and cooked through.

**2.** Remove from the oven and let cool. Once cool, mix in the feta and mint.

**3.** Preheat a nonstick saucepan or griddle pan until almost smoking, then cook the wraps one at a time on both sides for 10 seconds.

**4.** Divide the vegetable-and-feta mixture among the wraps, placing it along the middle of each wrap. Roll up the wrap, cut them in half, and serve.

# SHRIMP & SCALLOP KABOBS

SERVES: 4–6 | PREP TIME: 25 MIN. PLUS 15 MIN. MARINATING TIME | COOK TIME: 5 MIN.

### INGREDIENTS

24 jumbo shrimp, heads removed

12 large scallops, corals attached

¼ – ⅓ cup olive oil, plus extra for oiling

juice of 1 lime

1 tablespoon chopped fresh cilantro

salt and pepper

lime wedges, to serve

**1.** Preheat the barbecue and soak eight wooden skewers, if using, in water for 30 minutes to prevent them from charring. Peel the shrimp but leave the tails attached. Slit down the back and remove the dark intestinal vein. Remove the tough muscle from the side of the scallops. Slice in half lengthwise through the coral.

**2.** Combine the olive oil and lime juice in a shallow dish. Add a pinch of salt and season with pepper. Add the scallops and shrimp and let marinate for 15 minutes.

**3.** Oil the grill rack. Reserving the marinade, thread the scallops and shrimp alternately onto the eight presoaked wooden skewers or metal skewers. Cook over hot coals for 4–6 minutes, turning and brushing with the marinade, until the shrimp are pink and cooked through. Transfer to serving plates and sprinkle with cilantro. Serve with lime wedges.

# VEGETABLE KABOBS WITH BLUE CHEESE

SERVES: 4–6 | PREP TIME: 15 MIN. | COOK TIME: 10 MIN.

### INGREDIENTS

5 thin leeks

18 small vine-ripened tomatoes, halved lengthwise

8 ounces cremini mushrooms, stems removed

1 stick butter, melted

oil, for oiling

1 cup crumbled blue cheese,

salt and pepper

**1.** Preheat the barbecue and soak 12 wooden skewers, if using, in water for 30 minutes to prevent them from charring. Trim the leeks to about 6 inches long. Slice in half lengthwise, and then widthwise into 1-inch pieces. Thread the leeks, tomatoes, and mushrooms alternately onto the 12 presoaked wooden skewers or metal skewers. Brush with melted butter and season with salt and pepper.

**2.** Oil the grill rack. Cook the kabobs over medium–hot coals, turning frequently, for 6–10 minutes, or until thoroughly cooked. Transfer to serving plates, sprinkle with the cheese, and serve.

# JERK CHICKEN

**SERVES: 4**   **PREP TIME: 30 MIN. PLUS 8 HR. MARINATING TIME**   **COOK TIME: 35 MIN.**

## INGREDIENTS

2 fresh red chiles, seeded and chopped

2 tablespoons vegetable oil, plus extra for brushing

2 garlic cloves, finely chopped

1 tablespoon finely chopped onion

1 tablespoon finely chopped scallion

1 tablespoon white wine vinegar

1 tablespoon lime juice

2 teaspoons raw brown sugar

1 teaspoon dried thyme

1 teaspoon ground cinnamon

1 teaspoon ground allspice

½ teaspoon freshly grated nutmeg

4 chicken parts

salt and pepper

fresh cilantro sprigs, to garnish

lime wedges, to serve

1. Place the chiles in a small bowl with the oil, garlic, onion, scallion, vinegar, lime juice, sugar, thyme, cinnamon, allspice, and nutmeg. Season with salt and pepper and mash thoroughly with a fork.

2. Using a sharp knife, make a series of diagonal slashes in the chicken parts and place them in a large nonmetallic dish. Spoon the jerk seasoning over the chicken, rubbing it well into the slashes. Cover and let marinate in the refrigerator for up to 8 hours.

3. Preheat the broiler. Remove the chicken from the marinade, discarding the marinade. Brush with oil and cook under the preheated broiler, turning frequently, for 30–35 minutes, or until a fork can be easily inserted into the thickest part of the meat with ease and the juices run clear. A meat thermometer inserted into the thickest part of the meat, without touching the bone, should read 170°F. Transfer to plates, garnish with cilantro sprigs, and serve with lime wedges.

# RASPBERRY & WHITE CHOCOLATE S'MORES

SERVES: 4     PREP TIME: 5 MIN.     COOK TIME: 5 MIN.

## INGREDIENTS

12 marshmallows, halved

8 graham crackers or plain cookies

¼ cup white chocolate chips

12 raspberries

**1.** Preheat the barbecue. Place the three marshmallow halves on each cracker.

**2.** Toast the s'mores on the grill rack until the marshmallows start to melt.

**3.** Top four of the crackers with white chocolate chips and raspberries, then invert the remaining cookies on top, pressing lightly. Serve.

# ARUGULA & PARMESAN SALAD

SERVES: 4–6   PREP TIME: 10 MIN.   COOK TIME: 5 MIN.

## INGREDIENTS

2 handfuls arugula

1 small fennel bulb

⅓ cup olive oil

2 tablespoons balsamic vinegar

⅓ cup pine nuts

4 ounces Parmesan cheese shavings

salt and pepper

1. Divide the arugula among serving plates.

2. Halve the fennel bulb and slice it finely. Arrange the sliced fennel over the arugula.

3. Put the oil and vinegar into a small bowl, season with salt and pepper, and beat together. Drizzle a little of the dressing over each serving.

4. Toast the pine nuts in a dry skillet until golden brown.

5. Top the salad with the Parmesan shavings and toasted pine nuts. Serve.

# TURKEY WITH MOLE SAUCE

SERVES: 4–6   PREP TIME: 25 MIN.   COOK TIME: 1½ HR.

## INGREDIENTS

4 turkey parts, each cut into 4 pieces

about 2¼ cups chicken stock, plus extra for thinning

about 1 cup water

1 onion, chopped

1 whole garlic bulb, divided into cloves and peeled

1 celery stalk, chopped

1 bay leaf

1 bunch of fresh cilantro, finely chopped

2¼ cups mole poblano or store-bought mole paste, thinned according to the package directions

¼–½ cup sesame seeds, to garnish

1. Preheat the oven to 375°F. Arrange the turkey in a large casserole dish. Pour the stock and water around the turkey, then add the onion, garlic, celery, bay leaf, and half the cilantro.

2. Bake in the preheated oven for 1–1½ hours, or until the turkey is very tender. Add extra liquid, if needed.

3. Warm the mole sauce in a saucepan with enough stock to make it the consistency of thin cream.

4. To toast the sesame seeds for the garnish, place the seeds in a dry skillet and dry-fry, shaking the skillet, until lightly golden.

5. Arrange the turkey pieces on a serving plate and spoon the warm mole sauce over the top. Sprinkle with the toasted sesame seeds and the remaining chopped cilantro and serve.

ARUGULA &
PARMESAN SALAD

# SEPTEMBER

# CHILLED BEET SOUP

SERVES: 6    PREP TIME: 25 MIN. PLUS 3 HR. CHILLING TIME    COOK TIME: 20 MIN.

### INGREDIENTS

4 cups chopped, peeled, cooked beets

2 lemons, peeled, seeded and chopped

5½ cups vegetable stock

3 extra-large eggs

1½ tablespoons honey, plus extra for drizzling

salt and pepper

sour cream and snipped fresh chives, to garnish

1. Put the beets and lemons into a large saucepan, pour in the stock, and bring to a boil. Reduce the heat and simmer for 20 minutes.

2. Remove the pan from the heat and let cool slightly. Ladle the soup into a food processor, in batches if necessary, and process to a puree. Push the soup through a strainer into a bowl to remove any membrane or fibers. Let cool completely.

3. Meanwhile, put the eggs, honey, and a pinch of salt into a food processor and process until thoroughly combined. Gradually add the mixture to the soup, stirring continuously.

4. Cover with plastic wrap and chill in the refrigerator for at least 3 hours. To serve, stir the soup and taste and adjust the seasoning, if necessary. Ladle into bowls, drizzle with honey, garnish with the sour cream and snipped chives, and serve.

# SCALLOPED POTATOES

SERVES: 8    PREP TIME: 20 MIN. PLUS 15 MIN. RESTING TIME    COOK TIME: 1 HR. 10 MIN.

### INGREDIENTS

1 tablespoon butter, plus extra for greasing

1 tablespoon all-purpose flour

1 cup heavy cream

2 cups milk

1 teaspoon salt

pinch of freshly grated nutmeg

pinch of freshly ground white pepper

4 fresh thyme sprigs

2 garlic cloves, finely chopped

12 Yukon gold potatoes (about 4 pounds), thinly sliced

1 cup shredded cheddar cheese or Monterey Jack cheese

salt and pepper

1. Preheat the oven to 375°F. Grease a 15 x 10-inch ovenproof dish.

2. Melt the butter in a saucepan over medium heat. Stir in the flour and cook, stirring continuously, for 2 minutes. Gradually beat in the cream and milk and bring to simmering point. Add the salt, nutmeg, white pepper, thyme, and garlic, reduce the heat to low, and simmer for 5 minutes. Remove the thyme sprigs.

3. Make a layer of half the potatoes in the prepared dish and season generously with salt and pepper. Top with half the sauce and cover with half the cheese. Repeat the layers with the remaining potatoes, sauce, and cheese.

4. Bake in the preheated oven for about 1 hour, or until the top is browned and the potatoes are tender. Remove from the oven and let rest for 15 minutes before serving.

CHILLED
BEET SOUP

# ROCKY ROAD CHOCOLATE MUFFINS

MAKES: 12     PREP TIME: 15 MIN.     COOK TIME: 20 MIN.

## INGREDIENTS

oil or melted butter, for greasing (if using)

1¾ cups all-purpose flour

⅔ cup unsweetened cocoa powder

1 tablespoon baking powder

pinch of salt

½ cup granulated sugar

½ cup white chocolate chips

1 cup white miniature marshmallows, cut in half

2 eggs

1 cup milk

6 tablespoons butter, melted and cooled

1. Preheat the oven to 400°F. Grease a 12-cup muffin pan or line with 12 muffin cups. Sift together the flour, cocoa powder, baking powder, and salt into a large bowl. Stir in the sugar, chocolate chips, and marshmallows.

2. Lightly beat the eggs in a large bowl, then beat in the milk and butter. Make a well in the center of the dry ingredients and pour in the beaten liquid ingredients. Gently stir until just combined; do not overmix.

3. Spoon the mixture into the prepared muffin pan. Bake in the preheated oven for about 20 minutes, until risen and firm to the touch.

4. Let the muffins cool in the pan for 5 minutes, then serve warm or transfer to a wire rack and let cool.

# DRIED FRUIT & SUNFLOWER SEED COOKIES

MAKES: 18    PREP TIME: 15 MIN.    COOK TIME: 15 MIN.

## INGREDIENTS

6 tablespoons unsalted butter, softened, plus extra for greasing

⅓ cup firmly packed light brown sugar

1 egg, beaten

1¾ cups all-purpose flour

½ teaspoon freshly grated nutmeg

⅓ cup golden raisins

¼ cup sunflower seeds

raw brown sugar or granulated sugar, for sprinkling

1. Preheat the oven to 400°F. Lightly grease a large baking sheet.

2. Put the butter and brown sugar into a mixing bowl or food processor and beat together until soft and fluffy. Add the egg and beat thoroughly, then stir in the flour, nutmeg, golden raisins, and sunflower seeds, mixing evenly to a fairly soft dough.

3. Break off small pieces of the dough and use your hands to roll them into walnut-size balls. Arrange the balls on the prepared baking sheet and press to flatten slightly.

4. Sprinkle the cookies with a little raw brown sugar and bake in the preheated oven for 12–15 minutes, or until golden brown. Transfer to a wire rack to cool.

# APPLE & BLACKBERRY WAFFLES

SERVES: 4 — PREP TIME: 10 MIN. — COOK TIME: ABOUT 10 MIN.

## INGREDIENTS

1¼ cups all-purpose flour

1½ teaspoons baking powder

pinch of salt

1 cup milk

1 extra-large egg

2 tablespoons sunflower oil, plus extra for brushing

2 crisp Pippin apples, peeled, cored, and grated

1½ cups blackberries

maple syrup, for drizzling

**1.** Preheat a waffle maker to high. Sift together the flour, baking powder, and salt into a mixing bowl and make a well in the center.

**2.** Add the milk and egg, then beat to a smooth, bubbly batter. Add the oil and apple and beat well to mix.

**3.** Brush the waffle maker with a little oil, add a ladleful of batter, and cook until puffed and golden. You will need to do this in batches, keeping the cooked waffles warm while you cook the remaining batter.

**4.** Serve the waffles hot in stacks of two, topped with blackberries and a drizzle of maple syrup.

# FRIED CHICKEN WINGS

SERVES: 4 | PREP TIME: 20 MIN. | COOK TIME: 25 MIN.

## INGREDIENTS

12 chicken wings

1 egg

¼ cup milk

½ cup all-purpose flour

1 teaspoon paprika

2 cups bread crumbs

4 tablespoons butter

salt and pepper

1. Preheat the oven to 425°F. Separate the chicken wings into three pieces each. Discard the bony tip. Beat the egg with the milk in a shallow dish. Add the flour and paprika to a separate shallow dish, season with salt and pepper, and combine. Place the bread crumbs in another shallow dish.

2. Dip the chicken pieces into the egg to coat well, then drain and roll in the seasoned flour. Remove, shaking off any excess, then roll the chicken in the bread crumbs, gently pressing them onto the surface and shaking off any excess.

3. Put the butter in a shallow roasting pan large enough to hold all the chicken pieces in a single layer. Place the pan in the preheated oven and melt the butter. Remove from the oven and arrange the chicken, skin side down, in the pan. Return to the oven and bake for 10 minutes. Turn and bake for an additional 10 minutes, or until a fork can be inserted into the thickest part of the meat with ease and the juices run clear. A meat thermometer inserted into the thickest part of the meat, without touching the bone, should read 170°F.

4. Remove the chicken from the pan. Serve hot or at room temperature.

# HUSH PUPPIES

MAKES: 30–35 | PREP TIME: 20 MIN. | COOK TIME: ABOUT 15 MIN.

## INGREDIENTS

2 cups cornmeal

½ cup all-purpose flour, sifted

1 small onion, finely chopped

1 tablespoon granulated sugar

2 teaspoons baking powder

½ teaspoon salt

¾ cup milk

1 egg, beaten

vegetable oil, for deep-frying

1. Stir together the cornmeal, flour, onion, sugar, baking powder, and salt in a bowl and make a well in the center.

2. Beat together the milk and egg in a small bowl, then pour into the dry ingredients and stir until a thick batter forms.

3. Heat enough oil for deep-frying in a large saucepan or deep-fryer to 350°F, checking the temperature with a thermometer.

4. Drop in as many spoonfuls of the batter as will fit without overcrowding the skillet and cook, stirring continuously, until the hush puppies puff up and turn golden.

5. Remove from the oil with a slotted spoon and drain on paper towels. Reheat the oil, if necessary, and cook the remaining batter. Serve hot.

# ITALIAN-STYLE SAUSAGES & MASHED POTATOES

SERVES: 4 · PREP TIME: 20 MIN. · COOK TIME: 1 HR. 20 MIN.

## INGREDIENTS

1 tablespoon olive oil

8 Italian-style sausages

### ONION GRAVY

3 onions, halved and thinly sliced

4 tablespoons butter

½ cup Marsala or port

½ cup vegetable stock

salt and pepper

### MASHED POTATOES

8 Yukon gold or russet potatoes (about 2 pounds), peeled and cut into chunks

4 tablespoons butter

3 tablespoons hot milk

2 tablespoons chopped fresh parsley

**1.** Place a skillet over low heat with the oil and add the sausages. (Alternatively, you may want to broil the sausages.) Cover the skillet and cook for 25–30 minutes, turning the sausages from time to time, until browned all over.

**2.** Meanwhile, prepare the onion gravy by placing the onions in a skillet with the butter and sautéing over low heat until soft, stirring continuously. Continue to cook for about 30 minutes, or until the onions are brown and have started to caramelize.

**3.** Pour in the Marsala and stock and continue to let simmer until the onion gravy is thick. Season with salt and pepper.

**4.** To make the mashed potatoes, bring a large saucepan of lightly salted water to a boil. Add the potatoes, bring back to a boil, and cook for 15–20 minutes. Drain well and mash with a potato masher until smooth. Season with salt and pepper. Add the butter, milk, and parsley and stir well.

**5.** Serve the sausages with the mashed potatoes, and the onion gravy spooned over the top.

# POTATO GNOCCHI

SERVES: 4    PREP TIME: 35 MIN.    COOK TIME: 40 MIN.

## INGREDIENTS

4 russet potatoes

⅔ cup freshly grated Parmesan cheese

1 egg, beaten

1⅔ cups all-purpose flour, plus extra for dusting

## WALNUT PESTO

40 g/1½ oz fresh flat-leaf parsley

2 tablespoons capers, rinsed

2 garlic cloves

¾ cup extra virgin olive oil

½ cup walnut halves

½ cup freshly grated Parmesan cheese

salt and pepper

1. Boil the potatoes in their skins in a large saucepan of lightly salted water for 30–35 minutes, until tender. Drain well and let cool slightly.

2. Meanwhile, to make the walnut pesto, chop the parsley, capers, and garlic, then put in a mortar with the oil and walnuts and season with salt and pepper. Pound with a pestle to a coarse paste. Add the cheese.

3. Peel the skins off the potatoes and push the flesh through a strainer into a bowl. While still hot, season well with salt and pepper and add the Parmesan cheese. Beat in the egg and sift in the flour. Lightly mix together, then turn out onto a lightly floured work surface. Knead lightly until the mixture becomes a smooth dough.

4. Roll the dough out with your hands into a long log. Cut into 1-inch pieces and gently press with a fork to create the traditional ridged effect. Transfer to a floured baking sheet and cover with a clean dish towel.

5. Bring a large saucepan of lightly salted water to a boil. Carefully add the gnocchi, in small batches, return to a boil, and cook for 2–3 minutes, or until they rise to the surface. Remove with a slotted spoon and transfer to a warm serving dish while you cook the remaining gnocchi.

6. Serve the gnocchi in serving bowls with a good spoonful of the walnut pesto on top.

# CHEESE & ZUCCHINI GRATIN

SERVES: 4    PREP TIME: 20 MIN.    COOK TIME: ABOUT 10 MIN.

## INGREDIENTS

3 zucchini

4 tablespoons butter, plus extra for greasing

⅓ cup all-purpose flour

2½ cups milk

1 teaspoon Dijon mustard

1 cup shredded cheddar cheese

8 slices cooked ham

1 cup fresh white or whole-wheat bread crumbs

salt and pepper

snipped fresh chives or parsley, to garnish

1. Lightly grease a shallow ovenproof dish and set aside. Cook the zucchini in a saucepan of boiling water for 4–5 minutes, or until tender. Drain well, set aside, and keep warm.

2. Meanwhile, melt 3 tablespoons of the butter in a separate saucepan, then stir in the flour and cook gently for 1 minute, stirring. Remove the pan from the heat and gradually beat in the milk. Return to the heat and bring gently to a boil, stirring continuously, until the sauce thickens. Simmer for 2–3 minutes, stirring. Remove the pan from the heat and stir in the mustard and ¾ cup of the cheese. Season with salt and pepper.

3. Preheat the broiler to medium–high. Cut each slice of ham in half widthwise, then wrap a half slice of ham around each zucchini. Place the ham-wrapped zucchini in a single layer in the prepared dish and pour the cheese sauce evenly over the top to cover.

4. Mix together the remaining cheese and the bread crumbs and sprinkle evenly over the cheese sauce. Add pats of the remaining butter, then place under the broiler for a few minutes, until lightly browned and bubbling. Garnish with snipped fresh chives and serve.

POTATO
GNOCCHI

# CHICKEN FAJITAS

SERVES: 4     PREP TIME: 20 MIN. PLUS 2–3 HR. CHILLING TIME     COOK TIME: ABOUT 10 MIN.

## INGREDIENTS

3 tablespoons olive oil, plus extra for drizzling

3 tablespoons maple syrup or honey

1 tablespoon red wine vinegar

2 garlic cloves, crushed

2 teaspoon dried oregano

1–2 teaspoon crushed red pepper

4 skinless, boneless chicken breasts

2 red bell peppers, seeded and cut into 1-inch strips

8 tortillas, warmed

salt and pepper

1. Place the oil, maple syrup, vinegar, garlic, oregano, and crushed red pepper in a large, shallow dish or bowl, season with salt and pepper, and mix together.

2. Slice the chicken across the grain into 1-inch thick slices. Toss in the marinade until well coated. Cover and chill in the refrigerator for 2–3 hours, turning occasionally.

3. Heat a griddle pan or skillet until hot. Lift the chicken slices from the marinade with a slotted spoon, lay on the griddle pan, and cook over medium–high heat for 3–4 minutes on each side, or until cooked through. Remove the chicken to a warm serving plate and keep warm. Add the bell peppers, skin side down, to the pan and cook for 2 minutes on each side. Transfer to the serving plate. Serve with the warm tortillas to be used as wraps.

# PAD THAI

SERVES: 4–6     PREP TIME: 15 MIN.     COOK TIME: 10 MIN.

## INGREDIENTS

8 ounces thick rice noodles

2 tablespoons peanut oil or vegetable oil

2 garlic cloves, chopped

2 fresh red chiles, seeded and chopped

6 ounces pork tenderloin, thinly sliced

4 ounces shrimp, peeled, deveined and chopped

8 fresh Chinese chives, snipped

2 tablespoons Thai fish sauce

juice of 1 lime

2 teaspoons jaggery or light brown sugar

2 eggs, beaten

1 cup fresh bean sprouts

¼ cup chopped fresh cilantro

¾ cup chopped unsalted peanuts

1. Prepare the noodles according to the package directions, until soft. Drain well and set aside.

2. Heat a wok over medium–high heat, then add the oil. Stir-fry the garlic, chiles, and pork for 2–3 minutes. Add the shrimp and stir-fry for an additional 2–3 minutes.

3. Add the chives and noodles, then cover and cook for 1–2 minutes. Add the fish sauce, lime juice, sugar, and eggs. Cook, stirring and tossing continuously to mix in the eggs.

4. Stir in the bean sprouts, cilantro, and peanuts and mix well, then transfer to serving dishes. Serve.

CHICKEN
FAJITAS

# SPICY FRIED EGGS

SERVES: 2    PREP TIME: 10 MIN.    COOK TIME: 20 MIN.

### INGREDIENTS

2 tablespoons olive oil

1 large onion, finely chopped

2 green or red bell peppers, seeded and coarsely chopped

1 garlic clove, finely chopped

½ teaspoon crushed red pepper

4 plum tomatoes, peeled and coarsely chopped

2 eggs

salt and pepper

**1.** Heat the oil in a large nonstick skillet. Add the onion and cook until golden. Add the bell peppers, garlic, and crushed red pepper and cook until the peppers are soft.

**2.** Stir in the tomatoes and season with salt and pepper. Place over low heat and simmer for 10 minutes.

**3.** Using the back of a spoon, make two depressions in the mixture in the skillet. Break the eggs into the depressions, season with salt and pepper, cover, and cook for 3–4 minutes, until the eggs are set. Serve.

# PEANUT BUTTER & JELLY WAFFLE SANDWICH

SERVES: 4 | PREP TIME: 10 MIN. | COOK TIME: 10 MIN.

## INGREDIENTS

1¼ cups all-purpose flour

1½ teaspoons baking powder

1 tablespoon granulated sugar

pinch of salt

1 cup milk

1 extra-large egg

2 tablespoons melted butter

confectioners' sugar, for dusting

## FILLING

¼ cup chunky peanut butter

¼ cup strawberry jelly or raspberry preserves

**1.** Sift the flour, baking powder, sugar, and salt into a bowl. Add the milk, egg, and butter and beat to a smooth batter. Let stand for 5 minutes.

**2.** Preheat a waffle maker to high. Pour the batter into the waffle maker and cook until golden brown. Repeat this process using the remaining batter, while keeping the cooked waffles warm.

**3.** Spread half the waffles with peanut butter and the remainder with jelly. Sandwich the two together with the peanut butter and jelly inside.

**4.** Dust with confectioners' sugar and serve.

# 15 SEPTEMBER

# FIGS WITH HONEY & ALMONDS

SERVES: 4    PREP TIME: 5 MIN.    COOK TIME: NO COOKING

### INGREDIENTS

8 large ripe figs

¼ cup Greek-style yogurt or crème fraîche

¼ cup honey

½ cup toasted slivered almonds

ground cinnamon, for sprinkling

1. Cut the figs widthwise almost to the bottom, then push the sides to open out. Divide among four serving plates.

2. Spoon the yogurt into the figs and drizzle the honey over them.

3. Sprinkle the almonds on top and sprinkle lightly with cinnamon to serve.

# 16 SEPTEMBER

# HAZELNUT SHORTBREAD

MAKES: 12    PREP TIME: 15 MIN.    COOK TIME: 15 MIN.

### INGREDIENTS

1 stick unsalted butter, softened, plus extra for greasing

½ cup granulated sugar, plus extra for sprinkling

1 egg, beaten

1⅔ cups all-purpose flour

½ cup toasted hazelnuts, finely chopped

1. Preheat the oven to 350°F. Lightly grease a shallow 8½-inch square cake pan.

2. Put the butter and sugar into a mixing bowl and cream together with a handheld mixer until smooth. Gradually add the egg, beating to mix evenly. Add the flour and hazelnuts and mix well, kneading lightly with your hands to a soft dough.

3. Press the dough into the prepared pan, pressing with your knuckles to spread evenly.

4. Bake in the preheated oven for about 15 minutes, or until firm and pale golden brown.

5. Cut the shortbread into 12 slices with a sharp knife and sprinkle with sugar. Let cool in the pan until firm before removing.

# SALAMI PASTA SALAD

**SERVES: 4–6** | **PREP TIME: 25 MIN.** | **COOK TIME: 10 MIN.**

## INGREDIENTS

12 ounces dried penne

2 tablespoons pesto sauce

3 tablespoons olive oil

1 orange bell pepper, seeded and diced

1 yellow bell pepper, seeded and diced

1 red onion, finely diced

1 cup pitted ripe black olives

12 cherry tomatoes, halved

6-ounce piece Milano salami, cut into small chunks

4 ounces mozzarella cheese, torn into small pieces

salt and pepper

fresh basil sprigs, to garnish

**1.** Bring a large, heavy saucepan of lightly salted water to a boil. Add the penne, bring back to a boil, and cook according to the package directions, or until just tender but still firm to the bite.

**2.** Drain the pasta well and transfer to a bowl. Mix together the pesto sauce and olive oil and stir into the hot pasta. Let cool, stirring occasionally.

**3.** Add the bell peppers, onion, olives, tomatoes, salami, and mozzarella cheese to the pasta and toss well to mix. Season with salt and pepper. Garnish with basil sprigs and serve.

# SAUSAGE & BEER CASSEROLE

SERVES: 4     PREP TIME: 10 MIN.     COOK TIME: 40–45 MIN.

## INGREDIENTS

1 tablespoon sunflower oil

8 Italian-style sausages

1 onion, sliced

1 large green bell pepper, seeded and sliced

⅔ cup beer

1 (14½-ounce) can Italian tomatoes

1½ cups fresh or frozen corn kernels

2 tablespoons Worcestershire sauce

1 teaspoon dried thyme

salt and pepper

crusty bread, to serve

**1.** Heat the oil in a large saucepan or flameproof casserole dish, add the sausages, and cook, turning occasionally, for 6–8 minutes, until golden. Remove from the pan and keep warm.

**2.** Add the onion and green bell pepper to the pan and cook over medium heat for 3–4 minutes, until soft.

**3.** Return the sausages to the pan and stir in the beer. Bring to a boil, then add the tomatoes, corn, Worcestershire sauce, and thyme. Season well with salt and pepper.

**4.** Bring to a boil, then reduce the heat, cover, and simmer gently for 30–35 minutes. Serve hot with crusty bread.

# EASY APPLE CAKE

SERVES: 8    PREP TIME: 15 MIN.    COOK TIME: 50 MIN.

## INGREDIENTS

4 Pippin apples, peeled, cored, and diced

2 tablespoons apple juice

⅓ cup light brown sugar

1 stick unsalted butter, at room temperature, plus extra for greasing

2 extra-large eggs, beaten

1¾ cups all-purpose flour

2½ teaspoons baking powder

1½ teaspoons allspice

⅓ cup finely chopped hazelnuts

1. Preheat the oven to 375°F. Grease a deep, 8-inch loose-bottom round cake pan and line the bottom with parchment paper. Sprinkle the apples with the apple juice.

2. Reserve 1 tablespoon of the sugar, then put the sugar and butter into a mixing bowl and beat until pale and fluffy. Gradually add the eggs, beating thoroughly after each addition. Sift together the flour, baking powder, and spice into the mixture and evenly fold in with a metal spoon.

3. Stir the apples and juice into the batter, then spoon into the prepared pan and level the surface with a spatula.

4. Mix the hazelnuts with the reserved sugar and sprinkle the mixture over the surface of the cake.

5. Bake in the preheated oven for 45–50 minutes, until firm and golden brown. Let cool for 10 minutes in the pan, then invert onto a wire rack to cool completely.

# PEAR & PECAN SPONGE CAKE

**SERVES: 8**     **PREP TIME: 20 MIN.**     **COOK TIME: 45 MIN.**

### INGREDIENTS

1 extra-large egg

½ cup firmly packed
light brown sugar

3 tablespoons light corn syrup

3 tablespoons milk

3 tablespoons sunflower oil

1 cup all-purpose flour

1½ teaspoons baking powder

1 teaspoon ground ginger

1 teaspoon ground cinnamon

Greek-style yogurt
or whipped cream, to serve

### TOPPING

1 tablespoon butter

1 tablespoon light corn syrup

4 ripe pears

4 pecans, halved

**1.** Preheat the oven to 350°F. To make the topping, put the butter and corn syrup into a saucepan and heat gently, stirring, until melted. Pour into a deep 8½-inch round cake pan, spreading to cover the bottom.

**2.** Thinly peel the pears, cut in half lengthwise, and use a teaspoon to scoop out the cores.

**3.** Place a pecan half in the cavity of each pear half and arrange cut side down in the pan.

**4.** To make the cake, put the egg, sugar, corn syrup, milk, and oil into a mixing bowl and beat together. Sift together the flour, baking powder, ginger, and cinnamon and stir into the egg mixture. Beat well to make a smooth batter.

**5.** Pour the batter over the pears. Bake in the preheated oven for 35–40 minutes, or until risen and springy to the touch.

**6.** Let cool in the pan for 5 minutes, then invert onto a serving plate and serve with yogurt.

# 21 SEPTEMBER
# APPLE PANCAKES WITH MAPLE SYRUP

MAKES: 18  PREP TIME: 15 MIN.  COOK TIME: 10 MIN.

### INGREDIENTS

1⅔ cups all-purpose flour

2½ teaspoons baking powder

½ cup granulated sugar

1 teaspoon ground cinnamon

1 egg

1 cup milk

2 apples, peeled and grated

1 teaspoon butter

3 tablespoons maple syrup

**1.** Mix together the flour, baking powder, sugar, and cinnamon in a bowl and make a well in the center. Beat together the egg and the milk and pour into the well. Using a wooden spoon, gently incorporate the dry ingredients into the liquid until well combined, then stir in the grated apple.

**2.** Gently heat the butter in a large nonstick skillet. Add tablespoons of the pancake batter to form small circles. Cook each pancake for about 1 minute, until it starts to bubble lightly on the top and looks set, then flip it over and cook the other side for 30 seconds, or until cooked through. The pancakes should be golden brown. Remove from the skillet and repeat the process until all of the pancake batter has been used. Serve with the maple syrup drizzled over the pancakes.

# 22 SEPTEMBER
# BRAZIL NUT BRITTLE

MAKES: 20 PIECES  PREP TIME: 10 MIN. PLUS COOLING TIME  COOK TIME: 10 MIN.

### INGREDIENTS

sunflower oil, for brushing

12 ounces semisweet dark chocolate, broken into pieces

¾ cup chopped Brazil nuts

6 ounces white chocolate, coarsely chopped

6 ounces fudge, coarsely chopped

**1.** Brush the bottom and sides of a baking pan with oil.

**2.** Melt half the dark chocolate in a medium saucepan over low heat and spread in the prepared pan.

**3.** Sprinkle with the chopped Brazil nuts, white chocolate, and fudge. Melt the remaining dark chocolate pieces and pour over the top.

**4.** Let stand in a cool place to set, then break up into jagged pieces, using the tip of a strong knife.

# MINI MACARONS

**MAKES: 30    PREP TIME: 25 MIN. PLUS 30 MIN. STANDING TIME    COOK TIME: 15 MIN.**

## INGREDIENTS

¾ cup almond meal (ground almonds)

1 cup confectioners' sugar

2 extra-large egg whites

¼ cup superfine sugar or granulated sugar

½ teaspoon vanilla extract

selection of sugar sprinkles, to decorate

## BUTTERCREAM

6 tablespoons unsalted butter, softened

1 teaspoon vanilla extract

1⅓ cups confectioners' sugar, sifted

edible pink, yellow, and green food coloring pastes or liquids

**1.** Place the almond meal and confectioners' sugar in a food processor and process for 15 seconds. Sift the mixture into a bowl. Line two baking sheets with parchment paper.

**2.** Place the egg whites in a large bowl and beat until soft peaks form. Gradually beat in the superfine sugar to make a firm, glossy meringue. Beat in the vanilla extract.

**3.** Using a spatula, fold the almond mixture into the meringue one-third at a time. When all the dry ingredients are thoroughly incorporated, continue to cut and fold the mixture until it forms a shiny batter with a thick, ribbonlike consistency.

**4.** Pour the mixture into a pastry bag fitted with a ½-inch plain tip. Pipe 60 tiny circles onto the prepared baking sheets. Tap the baking sheets firmly on a work surface to remove air bubbles. Top with the sprinkles. Let stand at room temperature for 30 minutes. Meanwhile, preheat the oven to 325°F.

**5.** Bake in the preheated oven for 10–15 minutes. Let cool for 10 minutes, then carefully peel the macarons off the parchment paper. Let cool completely.

**6.** To make the buttercream, beat the butter and vanilla extract in a bowl until pale and fluffy. Gradually beat in the confectioners' sugar until smooth and creamy. Divide the buttercream into three bowls and color each with pink, yellow, or green food coloring. Use to sandwich together pairs of macarons.

# BAKED BEANS WITH CORN

**SERVES: 4–6**    **PREP TIME: 20 MIN.**    **COOK TIME: 1 HR. 35 MIN.**

## INGREDIENTS

⅓ cup olive oil or ¾ stick butter

6 onions, finely sliced

3–4 garlic cloves, finely chopped

1 teaspoon cumin seeds

1 teaspoon dried oregano leaves

1 (28-ounce) can diced tomatoes

4 cups peeled, seeded, and diced butternut squash or pumpkin

1 (29-ounce) can pinto beans, rinsed and drained

2 tablespoons chopped, pitted green olives

2 tablespoons raisins

1 tablespoon confectioners' sugar

1 teaspoon crushed red pepper

## TOPPING

6 cups fresh corn kernels

1½ cups milk

1 egg, beaten

1. Heat ¼ cup of the oil in a heavy saucepan, add the onions and garlic, and cook over low heat, stirring occasionally, for 20–30 minutes, or until the onions are soft and golden but not browned.

2. Add the cumin seeds, oregano, and tomatoes and heat until simmering, mashing the tomatoes down with a vegetable masher, for 10 minutes, or until you have a thick, sticky sauce.

3. Add the squash and heat until simmering. Reduce the heat to low, cover, and cook for an additional 10–15 minutes, or until the squash is softened but not collapsed. Stir in the beans, olives, and raisins. Reheat gently and simmer for 5 minutes to marry the flavors.

4. Preheat the oven to 350°F. To make the topping, put the corn in a food processor with the milk and blend to a puree. Transfer to a saucepan and cook, stirring continuously, for 5 minutes, or until the mixture has thickened slightly. Remove from the heat and let cool to room temperature. Stir in the egg.

5. Spread the bean mixture in an ovenproof dish and top with a thick layer of the corn mixture—the bean bottom and the topping should be of roughly equal thickness. Drizzle with the remaining oil or dab with pats of butter over the surface and sprinkle with the sugar and crushed pepper.

6. Bake in the preheated oven for 30 minutes, or until browned and bubbling. Serve hot.

# LASAGNA

**SERVES: 6**    **PREP TIME: 30 MIN.**    **COOK TIME: 1 HR. 15 MIN.**

## INGREDIENTS

2 tablespoons olive oil

2 ounces pancetta or bacon, chopped

1 onion, chopped

1 garlic clove, finely chopped

1 pound ground sirloin beef

2 celery stalks, chopped

2 carrots, chopped

2 cups tomato-based pasta sauce from a jar

2 pounds ricotta cheese

½ cup grated Parmesan cheese

1 egg

2 tablespoons dried basil

8 ounces oven-ready lasagna noodles

8 ounces mozzarella cheese, shredded

1. Preheat the oven to 375°F. Heat the oil in a large, heavy saucepan. Add the pancetta and cook over medium heat, stirring occasionally, for 3 minutes, or until the fat begins to run. Add the onion and garlic and cook, stirring occasionally, for 5 minutes, or until softened.

2. Add the beef and cook, breaking it up with a wooden spoon, until browned all over. Stir in the celery and carrots and cook for 5 minutes. Drain and set aside.

3. Meanwhile, heat the pasta sauce in a separate small saucepan.

4. Mix together the ricotta, Parmesan, egg, and dried basil in a bowl.

5. In a 9 x 13-inch ovenproof dish, spread a thin layer of pasta sauce along the bottom. Make alternate layers starting with three to four lasagna noodles, overlapping the edges, one-half of the ricotta mixture, one-half of the beef mixture, and one-fourth of the mozzarella. Repeat the layers of sauce, noodles, ricotta, meat, and mozzarella. Finally, make a layer of sauce and noodles before pouring the remaining sauce over the noodles and topping with the remaining mozzarella. Cover and bake in the oven for 45 minutes, until the noodles are tender, then remove the cover and bake for 10 minutes, or until golden brown. Serve immediately.

BAKED BEANS
WITH CORN

# ROASTED BUTTERNUT SQUASH

**SERVES: 4** · **PREP TIME: 40 MIN.** · **COOK TIME: 1 HR. 10 MIN.**

## INGREDIENTS

1 butternut squash

1 onion, chopped

2–3 garlic cloves, crushed

4 small tomatoes, chopped

1⅓ cups chopped cremini mushrooms,

½ cup drained, rinsed, and coarsely chopped canned lima beans

1 zucchini, trimmed and shredded

1 tablespoon chopped fresh oregano, plus extra to garnish

2 tablespoons tomato paste

1¼ cups water

4 scallions, trimmed and chopped

1 tablespoon Worcestershire sauce, or to taste

pepper

**1.** Preheat the oven to 375°F. Prick the squash all over with the tip of a sharp knife, then roast for 40 minutes, or until tender. Remove from the oven and let rest until cool enough to handle.

**2.** Cut the squash in half, scoop out and discard the seeds, then scoop out some of the flesh, making hollows in both halves. Chop the scooped-out flesh and put in a bowl. Place the two squash halves side by side in a large roasting pan.

**3.** Add the onion, garlic, tomatoes, and mushrooms to the squash flesh in the bowl. Add the lima beans, zucchini, and oregano, season with pepper, and mix well. Spoon the filling into the two halves of the squash, packing it down as firmly as possible.

**4.** Mix the tomato paste with the water, scallions, and Worcestershire sauce in a small bowl and pour around the squash.

**5.** Cover loosely with a large sheet of aluminum foil and bake for 30 minutes, or until piping hot. Serve in bowls, garnished with some chopped oregano.

# CHICKEN & WILD MUSHROOM CANNELLONI

SERVES: 4    PREP TIME: 20 MIN.    COOK TIME: 1 HR. 50 MIN.

### INGREDIENTS

butter, for greasing

2 tablespoons olive oil

2 garlic cloves, crushed

1 large onion, finely chopped

8 ounces wild mushrooms, sliced

12 ounces ground chicken

4 ounces prosciutto, diced

⅔ cup Marsala wine

1 cup canned diced tomatoes

1 tablespoon shredded fresh
basil leaves

2 tablespoons tomato paste

10–12 dried cannelloni tubes

1 quantity White Sauce
(see page 287)

1 cup freshly grated Parmesan cheese

salt and pepper

**1.** Preheat the oven to 375°F. Lightly grease a large ovenproof dish. Heat the olive oil in a heavy skillet. Add the garlic, onion, and mushrooms and cook over low heat, stirring frequently, for 8–10 minutes. Add the ground chicken and prosciutto and cook, stirring frequently, for 12 minutes, or until browned all over. Stir in the Marsala wine, tomatoes and their can juices, basil, and tomato paste and cook for 4 minutes. Season with salt and pepper, then cover and simmer for 30 minutes. Uncover, stir, and simmer for 15 minutes.

**2.** Bring a large, heavy saucepan of lightly salted water to a boil. Add the cannelloni, bring back to a boil, and cook according to the package directions, until just tender but still firm to the bite. Using a slotted spoon, transfer to a plate and pat dry.

**3.** Using a teaspoon, fill the cannelloni tubes with the chicken-and-mushroom mixture and transfer to the dish. Pour the White Sauce over them to cover completely and sprinkle with the grated Parmesan cheese.

**4.** Bake in the preheated oven for 30 minutes, or until golden brown and bubbling. Serve immediately.

# MEATBALL SANDWICH

**SERVES: 4** | **PREP TIME: 20 MIN.** | **COOK TIME: 15–20 MIN.**

## INGREDIENTS

1 pound ground sirloin beef

1 small onion, grated

2 garlic cloves, crushed

¼ cup dried white bread crumbs

1 teaspoon hot chili sauce

whole-wheat flour, for dusting

peanut oil, for pan-frying

salt and pepper

4 sub rolls or small baguettes, to serve

## FILLING

1 tablespoon olive oil

1 small onion, sliced

¼ cup mayonnaise

½ cup sliced jalapeños (from a jar)

2 tablespoons yellow mustard

1. Place the ground beef, onion, garlic, bread crumbs, and chili sauce into a bowl. Season with salt and pepper and mix thoroughly. Shape the mixture into 20 small, equal balls, using floured hands. Cover and chill for 10 minutes, or until required.

2. Heat a shallow depth of oil in a wok or heavy skillet until hot, then cook the meatballs, in batches, for 6–8 minutes, turning often, until golden brown and firm. Drain on paper towels and keep hot.

3. To make the filling, heat the olive oil in a clean saucepan and sauté the onion over a moderate heat, stirring occasionally, until soft and golden brown.

4. Slice the rolls in half lengthwise and spread with mayonnaise. Arrange the onion, meatballs, and jalapeños over the bottom half, spread the mustard over them, and top with the other half. Serve.

# THE REUBEN SANDWICH

**SERVES: 2** | **PREP TIME: 25 MIN.** | **COOK TIME: 5 MIN.**

## INGREDIENTS

2 tablespoons margarine, softened

4 slices rye bread

4–6 ounces cooked salt beef

1 cup drained store-bought sauerkraut

1 cup shredded Swiss cheese

vegetable oil, for frying

chopped pickles, to serve

## DRESSING

2 tablespoons mayonnaise

2 tablespoons ketchup or chili sauce

1 green bell pepper, seeded and finely chopped

2 tablespoons pimiento, finely chopped

1. To make the dressing, mix together all the dressing ingredients in a bowl until well blended.

2. Spread the margarine on one side of each slice of bread and lay margarine side down. Spread the other sides with 1 tablespoon of the dressing.

3. Divide the salt beef between two slices, tucking in the sides to fit. Divide the sauerkraut and make an even layer on top of the salt beef, before covering with the cheese. Top with the remaining slices of bread, margarine side facing up, and press firmly to compress the layers.

4. Heat the oil in a nonstick griddle pan or skillet over medium–high heat and carefully slide the sandwiches into the pan. Using a spatula, press down on the tops of the sandwiches. Cook for 3 minutes, or until the undersides are crisp and golden. Carefully turn the sandwiches, press down again, and cook for an additional 2 minutes, or until golden, the cheese is melted, and the salt beef is hot.

5. Remove from the heat and transfer the sandwiches to a cutting board. Cut in half and serve with pickles.

# STEAK & FRIES

SERVES: 4     PREP TIME: 20 MIN.     COOK TIME: 1 HR.

## INGREDIENTS

4 tenderloin steaks
(about 8 ounces each)

4 teaspoons Tabasco sauce

salt and pepper

## FRIES

4 russet potatoes, peeled

2 tablespoons sunflower oil

## HERB BUTTER

1 bunch of basil or flat-leaf parsley

6 tablespoons unsalted butter,
softened

**1.** To make the fries, preheat the oven to 400°F. Cut the potatoes into thick, even sticks. Rinse them under cold running water and then dry well on a clean dish towel. Place in a bowl, add the oil, and toss together until coated.

**2.** Spread the fries on a baking sheet and cook in the preheated oven for 40–45 minutes, turning once, until golden.

**3.** To make the herb butter, finely chop enough basil to fill ¼ cup. Place the butter in a small bowl and beat in the chopped basil with a fork until completely incorporated. Cover with plastic wrap and let chill in the refrigerator until required.

**4.** Preheat a ridged grill pan or skillet to high. Sprinkle each steak with 1 teaspoon of the Tabasco sauce, rubbing it in well. Season with salt and pepper.

**5.** Cook the steaks in the preheated pan for 2½ minutes each side for rare, 4 minutes each side for medium, and 6 minutes each side for well done. Transfer to serving plates and serve topped with the herb butter and accompanied by the fries.

# OCTOBER

# SOUFFLÉ BAKED POTATOES

SERVES: 4     PREP TIME: **10 MIN.**     COOK TIME: **1 HR. 35 MIN.**

## INGREDIENTS

4 large russet potatoes

oil, for brushing

2 tablespoons milk or light cream

2 eggs, separated

1 cup shredded Monterey Jack cheese, Meunster cheese, or cheddar cheese

1 tablespoon butter

4 scallions, finely chopped

salt and pepper

**1.** Preheat the oven to 400°F. Place the potatoes on a baking sheet, brush with oil, and rub with salt. Bake in the preheated oven for 1–1¼ hours, until tender. (Do not turn off the oven.)

**2.** Cut a slice from the top of the potatoes and scoop out the flesh, leaving about a ¼-inch thick shell. Put the flesh into a bowl. Add the milk, egg yolks, and half the cheese and mash together.

**3.** Melt the butter in a small saucepan, add the scallions, and sauté for 1–2 minutes, until soft. Stir into the potato mixture and season with salt and pepper.

**4.** Beat the egg whites in a grease-free bowl until they hold soft peaks. Fold them lightly into the potato mixture, then spoon the mixture back into the shells.

**5.** Place the filled potatoes on the baking sheet and sprinkle the remaining cheese on top. Bake for 15–20 minutes, until golden. Serve.

# PORK CHOPS WITH APPLESAUCE

SERVES: 4     PREP TIME: 20 MIN.     COOK TIME: 40 MIN.

## INGREDIENTS

4 pork rib chops on the bone, each about 1¼ inches thick, at room temperature

1½ tablespoons sunflower oil or canola oil

salt and pepper

## APPLESAUCE

3 Granny Smith apples, peeled, cored, and diced

¾ cup granulated sugar, plus extra, if needed

finely grated zest of ½ lemon

½ tablespoon lemon juice, plus extra, if needed

¼ cup water

¼ teaspoon ground cinnamon

pat of butter

1. Preheat the oven to 400°F.

2. To make the applesauce, put the apples, sugar, lemon zest, lemon juice, and water into a heavy saucepan over high heat and bring to a boil, stirring to dissolve the sugar. Reduce the heat to low, cover, and simmer for 15–20 minutes, until the apples are tender and fall apart when you mash them against the side of the pan. Stir in the cinnamon and butter and beat the apples until they are as smooth or chunky as you like. Stir in extra sugar or lemon juice, if needed. Remove the pan from the heat, cover, and keep the applesauce warm.

3. Meanwhile, pat the chops dry and season with salt and pepper. Heat the oil in a large ovenproof skillet over medium–high heat. Add the chops and cook for 3 minutes on each side to brown.

4. Transfer the pan to the oven and roast the chops for 7–9 minutes, until cooked through and the juices run clear when you cut the chops. To check with a meat thermometer, insert it into the thickest part of the meat, away from any bone, fat, or gristle; it should read at least 160°F. Remove the pan from the oven, cover with aluminum foil, and let stand for 3 minutes. Gently reheat the applesauce, if necessary.

5. Transfer the chops to plates and spoon the pan juices over them. Serve accompanied by the applesauce.

# MINI SALMON & BROCCOLI PIES

**MAKES: 8  PREP TIME: 35 MIN. PLUS 30 MIN. CHILLING TIME  COOK TIME: 45–50 MIN.**

## INGREDIENTS

2 cups broccoli florets

4 ounces salmon fillet

salt and pepper

salad, to serve

## WHITE SAUCE

2 tablespoons butter

¼ cup all-purpose flour

1¼ cups warm milk

## PIE DOUGH

1¾ cups all-purpose flour, plus extra for dusting

pinch of salt

1 stick butter

about 3 tablespoons iced water

1 egg, lightly beaten with 1 tablespoon water

1. Cook the broccoli in lightly salted boiling water for 5–10 minutes, until tender. Drain and let cool. Meanwhile, bring a saucepan of lightly salted water to a boil, then reduce the heat to low. Add the fish and poach, turning once, for 5 minutes, until the flesh flakes easily. Remove from the pan and let cool.

2. To make the white sauce, melt the butter in a saucepan, add the flour, and cook over low heat, stirring continuously, for 2 minutes. Gradually stir in the warm milk. Bring to a boil, stirring continuously, then simmer, stirring, until thickened and smooth. Season, remove from the heat, and let cool, stirring occasionally.

3. Meanwhile, make the pie dough. Sift the flour and salt into a bowl. Add the butter and cut into the flour. Rub in with your fingertips until the mixture resembles bread crumbs. Stir in the water and mix to a smooth dough, adding more water, if necessary. Shape into a ball, cover, and chill for 30 minutes.

4. Remove the skin and flake the flesh of the fish into a bowl. Break up the broccoli florets and add to the bowl. Stir in the white sauce and season with salt and pepper. Mix well.

5. Preheat the oven to 400°F. Roll out the dough on a lightly floured surface and stamp out 16 circles with a 4-inch cutter. Put 8 circles into a muffin pan. Add spoonfuls of the salmon mixture without filling the pastry shells completely. Brush the edges of the remaining circles with water and use to cover the pies, pressing with the tines of a fork to seal.

6. Brush the tops with the beaten egg mixture and bake for 20–25 minutes, until golden brown. Serve with salad.

# BAKED SEA BASS

SERVES: 4    PREP TIME: 20 MIN.    COOK TIME: 50 MIN.

### INGREDIENTS

3-pound fresh sea bass or
2 (1½-pound) sea bass, gutted

2–4 sprigs fresh rosemary

½ lemon, thinly sliced

2 tablespoons olive oil,
plus extra for brushing

fresh bay leaves, to garnish

lemon wedges, to serve

### GARLIC SAUCE

2 teaspoons coarse sea salt

2 teaspoons capers

2 garlic cloves, crushed

¼ cup water

2 fresh bay leaves

1 teaspoon lemon juice
or wine vinegar

2 tablespoons olive oil

pepper

1. Preheat the oven to 375°F. Scrape off the scales from the fish and cut off the sharp fins. Make diagonal cuts along both sides. Wash and dry thoroughly. Place a sprig of rosemary in the cavity of each of the smaller fish with half the lemon slices, or put two sprigs and all the lemon slices in the large fish.

2. Brush a roasting pan with oil, then brush the fish with the rest of the oil. Cook in the preheated oven for 30 minutes for the small fish or 45–50 minutes for the large fish, until the thickest part of the fish is opaque.

3. To make the garlic sauce, crush the salt and capers with the garlic in a mortar with a pestle and then work in the water. Alternatively, work in a food processor until smooth.

4. Bruise the bay leaves and remaining sprigs of rosemary and put into a bowl. Add the garlic mixture, lemon juice, and oil and pound together until the flavors are released. Season with pepper.

5. Place the fish on a serving dish and, if desired, remove the skin. Spoon some of the sauce over the fish and serve the rest separately. Remove the bruised bay leaves, garnish with fresh bay leaves, and serve with lemon wedges. Do not eat the bay leaves.

# SOUTHERN-STYLE CHICKEN DRUMSTICKS

**SERVES: 4**     **PREP TIME: 15 MIN. PLUS 1 HR. CHILLING TIME**     **COOK TIME: 30 MIN.**

## INGREDIENTS

8 chicken drumsticks

2 cups milk

1¾ cups all-purpose flour

1 teaspoon garlic salt

½ teaspoon cayenne pepper

1 tablespoon dried parsley

1 teaspoon dried thyme

1 extra-large egg, beaten

sunflower oil, for deep-frying

1. Place the drumsticks in a large bowl and pour the milk over them. Cover and chill in the refrigerator for 1 hour.

2. Put the chicken and milk into a large saucepan and heat over medium heat until boiling. Reduce the heat, cover, and simmer gently for 20 minutes, until the chicken is cooked. Drain well and let cool slightly.

3. Mix together the flour, garlic salt, cayenne pepper, parsley, and thyme in a shallow bowl. Put the egg into a separate shallow bowl. Dip the chicken drumsticks in the seasoned flour to coat evenly. Dip into the beaten egg, then dip again into the seasoned flour.

4. Heat enough oil for deep-frying in a large saucepan or deep-fryer to 340°F, checking the temperature with a thermometer. Lower the chicken drumsticks into the oil and cook, in batches, for 6–8 minutes, or until a fork can be easily inserted into the thickest part of the meat with ease and the juices run clear. A meat thermometer inserted into the thickest part of the meat, without touching the bone, should read 170°F. Keep the cooked chicken warm while you cook the remaining drumsticks.

5. Remove the chicken with a slotted spoon, drain on absorbent paper towels, and serve.

## 06 OCTOBER

# LAMB CHOPS IN TOMATO SAUCE

**SERVES: 4**   **PREP TIME: 25 MIN.**   **COOK TIME: 30 MIN.**

### INGREDIENTS

8 lamb chops

2 tablespoons butter

2 tablespoons olive oil

1 onion, finely chopped

2 garlic cloves, finely chopped

1 celery stalk, finely chopped

2 ounces pancetta or bacon, diced

1 (14½-ounce) can diced tomatoes

2 tablespoons tomato paste

brown sugar, to taste

2 tablespoons chopped fresh basil

1 tablespoon red wine vinegar

2 cups shelled fresh or frozen fava beans, gray skins removed

salt and pepper

1. Season the chops with salt and pepper. Melt the butter with the oil in a large skillet. Add the chops and cook over medium heat for 1–1½ minutes on each side, until evenly browned. Remove the chops from the skillet and set aside.

2. Add the onion, garlic, celery, and pancetta to the skillet and cook over low heat, stirring occasionally, for 5 minutes, until the onion has softened. Stir in the tomatoes, tomato paste, sugar, basil, vinegar, and ½ cup of water and season with salt and pepper. Increase the heat to medium and bring to a boil, then reduce the heat and simmer, stirring occasionally, for 10 minutes.

3. Return the chops to the skillet and add the fava beans. Partly cover and simmer for 10 minutes, until the lamb is tender and cooked through. Transfer to a serving dish and serve.

## 07 OCTOBER

# ROASTED VEGETABLES

**SERVES: 4–6**   **PREP TIME: 25 MIN.**   **COOK TIME: 1 HR.**

### INGREDIENTS

3 parsnips, cut into 2-inch chunks

4 baby turnips, cut into quarters

3 carrots, cut into 2-inch chunks

1 butternut squash, peeled and cut into 2-inch chunks

3 sweet potatoes, peeled and cut into 2-inch chunks

2 garlic cloves, finely chopped

2 tablespoons chopped fresh rosemary

2 tablespoons chopped fresh thyme

2 teaspoons chopped fresh sage

3 tablespoons olive oil

salt and pepper

chopped fresh mixed herbs, such as parsley, thyme, and mint, to garnish

1. Preheat the oven to 425°F.

2. Arrange all the vegetables in a single layer in a large roasting pan. Sprinkle the garlic and herbs over the vegetables. Pour the oil over the top and season well with salt and pepper.

3. Toss all the ingredients together until they are well mixed and coated with the oil (you can let them marinate at this stage to let the flavors be absorbed).

4. Roast the vegetables at the top of the preheated oven for 50–60 minutes, until they are cooked and nicely browned. Turn the vegetables over halfway through the cooking time.

5. Serve with a good handful of fresh herbs sprinkled on top and a final sprinkling of salt and pepper.

LAMB CHOPS IN
TOMATO SAUCE

# MUSHROOM & WALNUT OPEN TART

**SERVES: 4**  **PREP TIME: 20 MIN.**  **COOK TIME: 30–40 MIN.**

## INGREDIENTS

1 tablespoon olive oil

1 tablespoon butter

1 red onion, sliced

1 garlic clove, crushed

1 pound cremini mushrooms, sliced

¾ cup chopped walnuts

2 tablespoons chopped fresh flat-leaf parsley, plus extra to garnish

1 rolled dough pie crust, thawed if frozen

all-purpose flour, for dusting

beaten egg, for glazing

salt and pepper

1. Preheat the oven to 400°F. Heat the oil and butter in a large skillet, add the onion, and sauté for 2–3 minutes, until soft, but not brown.

2. Add the garlic and mushrooms and cook, stirring, for 3–4 minutes, until soft. Cook until any liquid has evaporated, then remove from the heat and stir in the walnuts and parsley and season with salt and pepper.

3. Roll out the rolled dough pie crust on a lightly floured work surface to a 14-inch circle and place on a large baking sheet. Pile the mushroom mixture onto the dough, leaving a 3½-inch border around the edge.

4. Lift the edges of the dough and tuck up around the filling, leaving an open center. Brush the dough with beaten egg to glaze.

5. Bake in the preheated oven for 25–30 minutes, until the pastry is golden brown. Serve warm, sprinkled with parsley.

# BLUE CHEESE, FIG & WALNUT BREAD

**MAKES: 1 LOAF**  **PREP TIME: 30 MIN. PLUS 30 MIN. SOAKING TIME**  **COOK TIME: 55 MIN.**

## INGREDIENTS

butter, for greasing

½ cup coarsely chopped dried figs

¼ cup Marsala wine

1¼ cups all-purpose flour

1 tablespoon baking powder

3 eggs

1 cup crème fraîche or sour cream

6 ounces blue cheese, such as Roquefort or Gorgonzola

¼ cup coarsely chopped walnuts

salt and pepper

1. Lightly grease and line the bottom and sides of a 9-inch loaf pan with parchment paper. Put the figs in a small bowl, pour the wine over them, and let soak for about 30 minutes.

2. Preheat the oven to 350°F.

3. Sift the flour and baking powder into a large bowl. In a separate bowl, beat together the eggs and crème fraîche until smooth. Stir the egg mixture into the flour until everything is well combined. Season with salt and pepper.

4. Crumble the blue cheese and add 1 cup to the batter. Add the figs and wine, then stir in half the walnuts. Turn the dough into the prepared pan, sprinkle with the remaining cheese and walnuts, and bake in the preheated oven for 40 minutes, or until the loaf is golden brown.

5. Cover the pan loosely with aluminum foil and return to the oven for an additional 15 minutes, or until a toothpick inserted into the center of the loaf comes out clean.

6. Let the loaf cool slightly in the pan, then invert onto a wire rack to cool completely.

MUSHROOM &
WALNUT OPEN TART

# MASHED POTATOES

**SERVES: 4**  **PREP TIME: 10 MIN.**  **COOK TIME: 25 MIN.**

## INGREDIENTS

8 Yukon gold or russet potatoes (about 2 pounds)

4 tablespoons butter

3 tablespoons hot milk

salt and pepper

1. Peel the potatoes, placing them in cold water as you prepare the others to prevent them from turning brown.

2. Cut the potatoes into even chunks. Cook in a large saucepan of lightly salted boiling water over medium heat, covered, for 20–25 minutes, until they are tender. Test with the point of a knife, but make sure you test right to the middle to avoid lumps.

3. Remove the pan from the heat and drain the potatoes. Return the potatoes to the hot pan and mash with a potato masher until smooth.

4. Add the butter and continue to mash until it is all mixed in, then add the milk (it is better hot because the potatoes absorb it more quickly to produce a creamier texture).

5. Taste the mashed potatoes and season with salt and pepper, if necessary. Serve.

# CHORIZO & CHEESE QUESADILLAS

**SERVES: 4**  **PREP TIME: 20 MIN.**  **COOK TIME: 20 MIN.**

## INGREDIENTS

1 cup shredded mozzarella cheese

1 cup shredded cheddar cheese

8 ounces cooked chorizo sausage, outer casing removed, or ham, diced

4 scallions, finely chopped

2 fresh green chiles, such as poblano, seeded and finely chopped

8 tortillas

vegetable oil, for brushing

salt and pepper

1. Place the cheeses, chorizo, scallions, and chiles in a bowl, season with salt and pepper, and mix together. Divide the mixture among four tortillas, then top with the remaining tortillas.

2. Brush a large, nonstick or heavy skillet with oil and heat over medium heat. Add one quesadilla and cook, pressing it down with a spatula, for 4–5 minutes, or until the underside is crisp and lightly browned. Turn over and cook the other side until the cheese is melting. Remove from the skillet and keep warm. Cook the remaining quesadillas individually.

3. Cut each quesadilla into quarters, arrange on serving plates, and serve.

# CHICKEN & VEGETABLE CASSEROLE

SERVES: 4     PREP TIME: 20 MIN.     COOK TIME: 45 MIN.

## INGREDIENTS

3 tablespoons olive oil

2 leeks, sliced

2 garlic cloves, sliced

2 large skinless, boneless chicken breasts (about 6 ounces each), cut into bite-size pieces

2 sweet potatoes, peeled and cut into chunks

2 parsnips, scrubbed and sliced

1 red bell pepper, seeded and cut into strips

1 yellow bell pepper, seeded and cut into strips

9 ounces mixed wild mushrooms, cleaned

4 tomatoes, coarsely chopped

2 cups cold cooked long-grain white rice

1 small bunch fresh parsley, chopped

1 cup shredded Muenster cheese, Monterey Jack cheese, or sharp cheddar cheese

salt and pepper

**1.** Preheat the oven to 350°F.

**2.** Heat the oil in a large skillet over medium heat, add the leeks and garlic, and cook, stirring frequently, for 3–4 minutes, until softened. Add the chicken and cook, stirring frequently, for 5 minutes. Add the sweet potatoes and parsnips and cook, stirring frequently, for 5 minutes, or until golden and beginning to soften. Add the bell peppers and mushrooms and cook, stirring frequently, for 5 minutes. Stir in the tomatoes, rice, and parsley and season with salt and pepper.

**3.** Spoon the mixture into an ovenproof dish, sprinkle with the cheese, and bake in the preheated oven for 20–25 minutes. Cut into the chicken to check the chicken is tender and cooked through, with no sign of pink. Serve.

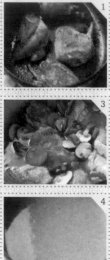

# CHICKEN STEW

SERVES: 4–6      PREP TIME: 35 MIN.      COOK TIME: 40 MIN.

## INGREDIENTS

3½-pound chicken, cut into 8 pieces

2 tablespoons all-purpose flour, seasoned with salt and pepper

4 tablespoons butter, plus extra for the pasta

1 tablespoon sunflower oil, plus extra if needed

4 shallots, finely chopped

1 pound cremini mushrooms, sliced

2 tablespoons brandy

1¼ cups white wine

2 carrots, thinly sliced

8 ounces dried ribbon pasta, such as pappardelle or tagliatelle

½ cup crème fraîche or heavy cream

salt and pepper

**1.** Coat the chicken pieces with the seasoned flour, shaking off any excess, and set aside. Melt 2 tablespoons of the butter with the oil in a flameproof casserole dish over medium heat. Add the chicken pieces to the dish and cook for 3–5 minutes, until golden brown, removing each piece when it is browned and adding extra oil, if necessary. Wipe out the casserole dish.

**2.** Melt the remaining butter in the casserole dish. Add the shallots and sauté, stirring, for 2–3 minutes, or until soft. Add the mushrooms and a pinch of salt and continue sautéing until they absorb the liquid they release. Return the chicken to the casserole dish. Light the brandy in a ladle and pour it over the chicken.

**3.** When the flames die down, add the wine and carrots and enough water to cover all the ingredients. Bring to a boil, then reduce the heat to low and simmer for 20–25 minutes, or until a fork can be inserted into the thickest part of the meat with ease and the juices run clear. A meat thermometer inserted into the thickest part of the meat, without touching the bone, should read 170°F. Meanwhile, preheat the oven to 225°F.

**4.** Bring a large, heavy saucepan of lightly salted water to a boil. Add the pasta, bring back to a boil, and cook according to the package directions, until just tender but still firm to the bite. Drain well, toss with butter, and keep warm in the preheated oven. Using tongs and a slotted spoon transfer the chicken and the vegetables to a serving platter and keep warm in the oven. Skim any fat off the cooking juices, stir in the crème fraîche, and bring to a boil, stirring, for 2–3 minutes to reduce. Taste and adjust the seasoning, if necessary, then pour the sauce over the chicken. Serve with the pasta.

# BLACKBERRY CRUMB CUPCAKES

MAKES: 6          PREP TIME: 20 MIN.          COOK TIME: 30 MIN.

## INGREDIENTS

1 cup all-purpose flour

2 teaspoons baking powder

1 stick butter, softened, plus extra for greasing

½ cup granulated sugar

2 eggs

1¼ cups blackberries

whipped cream, to serve

## CRUMB TOPPING

¾ cup all-purpose flour

1 teaspoon baking powder

¼ cup raw brown sugar or granulated sugar

4 tablespoons butter, chilled and diced

**1.** Preheat the oven to 375°F. Grease six 1-cup ovenproof teacups or ramekins (individual ceramic dishes) with butter.

**2.** To make the crumb topping, mix the flour, baking powder, and sugar in a bowl. Add the butter and rub in until the mixture resembles coarse bread crumbs.

**3.** To make the cake, sift the flour and baking powder into a bowl. Add the butter, granulated sugar, and eggs and, using an electric handheld mixer, beat together until smooth. Spoon the batter into the cups or dishes and level the surface. Top with the blackberries. Spoon the crumb topping over the blackberries.

**4.** Put the cups or dishes on a baking sheet and bake in the preheated oven for 25–30 minutes, until the crumb topping is golden brown. Serve warm with whipped cream.

# 15 OCTOBER

# NUTTY OAT BARS

MAKES: 16    PREP TIME: 10 MIN.    COOK TIME: 25 MIN.

## INGREDIENTS

2 cups rolled oats

1 cup chopped hazelnuts

½ cup all-purpose flour

1 stick butter, plus extra for greasing

2 tablespoons light corn syrup

⅓ cup firmly packed light brown sugar

1. Preheat the oven to 350°F. Grease a 9-inch square cake pan.

2. Place the rolled oats, hazelnuts, and flour in a large mixing bowl and stir together.

3. Place the butter, corn syrup, and sugar in a saucepan over low heat and stir until melted. Pour onto the dry ingredients and mix well. Spoon the batter into the prepared cake pan and smooth the surface with the back of a spoon.

4. Bake in the preheated oven for 20–25 minutes, or until golden and firm to the touch. Mark into 16 pieces and let cool in the pan. When completely cold, cut with a sharp knife and remove from the pan.

# 16 OCTOBER

# CHOCOLATE PEANUT BUTTER SQUARES

MAKES : 20    PREP TIME: 20 MIN.    COOK TIME: 35 MIN.

## INGREDIENTS

10 ounces milk chocolate

2¾ cups all-purpose flour

1 teaspoon baking powder

2 sticks butter

1½ cups firmly packed light brown sugar

2 cups rolled oats

⅔ cup chopped mixed nuts

1 egg, beaten

1 (14-ounce) can condensed milk

¼ cup chunky peanut butter

1. Preheat the oven to 350°F.

2. Finely chop the chocolate. Sift the flour and baking powder into a large bowl. Add the butter to the flour mixture and rub in using your fingertips until the mixture resembles bread crumbs. Stir in the sugar, rolled oats, and nuts.

3. Put one-quarter of the mixture into a bowl and stir in the chopped chocolate. Set aside.

4. Stir the egg into the remaining mixture, then press into the bottom of a 12 x 8-inch baking pan. Bake in the preheated oven for 15 minutes.

5. Meanwhile, mix together the condensed milk and peanut butter. Pour the mixture over the baked bottom layer and spread evenly, then sprinkle the reserved chocolate mixture on top and press down lightly.

6. Return to the oven and bake for an additional 20 minutes, until golden brown. Let cool in the pan, then cut into squares.

# FRESH TOMATO SOUP WITH PASTA

**SERVES: 4** | **PREP TIME: 15 MIN.** | **COOK TIME: 55 MIN.**

### INGREDIENTS

1 tablespoon olive oil

4 large plum tomatoes

1 onion, cut into quarters

1 garlic clove, thinly sliced

1 celery stalk, coarsely chopped

2 cups chicken stock

2 ounces small dried pasta shapes

salt and pepper

chopped fresh flat-leaf parsley, to garnish

1. Pour the oil into a large, heavy saucepan and add the tomatoes, onion, garlic, and celery. Cover and cook over low heat, occasionally shaking gently, for 45 minutes, until pulpy.

2. Transfer the mixture to a food processor and process to a smooth puree.

3. Push the puree through a strainer into a clean saucepan.

4. Add the stock and bring to a boil. Add the pasta, return to a boil, and cook according to the package directions, until just tender but still firm to the bite. Season with salt and pepper. Garnish with parsley and serve.

# MEATLOAF

SERVES: 4–6    PREP TIME: 20 MIN.    COOK TIME: 45 MIN.

### INGREDIENTS

vegetable oil, for greasing

1 thick slice white bread, crusts removed

1½ pounds ground beef, pork, or lamb

1 medium egg

1 tablespoon finely chopped scallions

1 beef bouillon cube, crumbled

1 teaspoon dried mixed herbs

salt and pepper

### TO SERVE

gravy

mashed potatoes

cooked runner beans

1. Preheat the oven to 350°F and lightly grease a 9-inch loaf pan. Put the bread into a small bowl and add enough water to soak. Let stand for 5 minutes, then drain and squeeze well to remove the water. Crumble the bread into small pieces.

2. Combine the bread with the beef, egg, scallions, bouillon cube, and herbs in a bowl and season with salt and pepper. Transfer the mixture to the prepared loaf pan.

3. Bake the meatloaf in the preheated oven for 30–45 minutes, until the juices run clear when it is pierced with a skewer. Cut into slices and serve with gravy, mashed potatoes, and runner beans.

# POT ROAST WITH POTATOES & DILL

SERVES: 6    PREP TIME: 30 MIN.    COOK TIME: ABOUT 3 HR.

### INGREDIENTS

2½ tablespoons all-purpose flour, seasoned with salt and pepper

3½-pound rolled brisket

2 tablespoons vegetable oil

2 tablespoons butter

1 onion, finely chopped

2 celery stalks, diced

2 carrots, peeled and diced

1 teaspoon dill seeds

1 teaspoon dried thyme or oregano

1½ cups red wine

⅔–1 cup beef stock

5 boiled potatoes, cut into chunks

1. Preheat the oven to 275°F. Put 2 tablespoons of the flour in a shallow dish. Dip the meat to coat. Heat the oil in a flameproof casserole dish and brown the meat all over. Transfer to a plate. Add half the butter to the casserole dish and cook the onion, celery, carrots, dill seeds, and thyme for 5 minutes. Return the meat and juices to the dish.

2. Pour in the wine and enough stock to reach one-third of the way up the meat. Bring to a boil, cover, and cook in the oven for 3 hours, turning the meat every 30 minutes. After it has been cooking for 2 hours, add the potatoes and more stock, if necessary.

3. When ready, transfer the meat and vegetables to a warm serving dish. Strain the cooking liquid to remove any solids, then return the liquid to the casserole dish.

4. Mix the remaining butter and flour to a paste. Bring the cooking liquid to a boil. Beat in small pieces of the flour-and-butter paste, beating continuously until the sauce is smooth. Pour the sauce over the meat and vegetables. Serve.

MEATLOAF

# FISH & POTATO STEW

SERVES: 4   PREP TIME: **25 MIN.**   COOK TIME: **50 MIN.**

## INGREDIENTS

1½ tablespoons olive oil, plus extra for brushing

1 onion, finely chopped

3 large garlic cloves, 2 chopped and 1 halved

1 tablespoon fennel seeds

½ teaspoon crushed red pepper, or to taste

pinch of saffron threads

1 (14½-ounce) can diced tomatoes

½ cup fish stock or water

2 bay leaves

4 Yukon gold or russet potatoes, thinly sliced

2 pounds mixed fish, such as monkfish, red snapper, and Alaskan pollock, boned, skinned, and trimmed as necessary

2 red bell peppers, seeded and sliced

2 tablespoons chopped fresh parsley

salt and pepper

1. Preheat the oven to 350°F.

2. Heat the oil in a saucepan over medium heat. Add the onion and sauté, stirring, for 2 minutes. Add the chopped garlic, fennel seeds, crushed red pepper, and saffron and continue sautéing for an additional 1 minute, or until the onion is soft. Add the tomatoes, stock, and bay leaves and season with salt and pepper. Cover and bring to a boil, then reduce the heat to low and simmer for 10 minutes. Taste and adjust the seasoning with salt and pepper, if necessary. Remove and discard the bay leaves.

3. Meanwhile, rub the garlic halves all over a 1½-quart ovenproof dish, pressing down firmly, then set aside the dish, discarding the garlic. Bring a large saucepan of lightly salted water to a boil, add the potatoes, bring back to a boil, and cook for 8–10 minutes, or until they are starting to soften but still hold their shape. Drain well, pat dry, and set aside.

4. Place the prepared dish on a baking sheet and arrange half the potatoes in a layer at the bottom of the dish. Place the fish and red bell peppers on top. Spoon the tomato sauce over the layers, sprinkle with the parsley, and shake the dish slightly. Arrange the remaining potatoes on top to cover all the other ingredients and lightly brush with oil. Bake in the preheated oven for 20–25 minutes, or until the fish and potatoes are tender when pierced with the tines of a fork. Serve.

# FETA & SPINACH POCKETS

MAKES: 6     PREP TIME: 25 MIN.     COOK TIME: 20 MIN.

## INGREDIENTS

2 tablespoons olive oil, plus extra for greasing

1 bunch scallions, chopped

1 pound spinach leaves, coarsely chopped, thawed if frozen

1 egg, beaten

1 cup crumbled feta cheese

½ teaspoon freshly grated nutmeg

6 sheets phyllo pastry

4 tablespoons butter, melted

1 tablespoon sesame seeds

salt and pepper

1. Preheat the oven to 400°F. Grease a baking sheet with oil.

2. Heat the oil in a wok or large skillet, add the scallions, and sauté for 1–2 minutes. Add the spinach and stir until the leaves are wilted. Cook, stirring occasionally, for 2–3 minutes. Drain off any free liquid and let cool slightly.

3. Stir the egg, cheese, and nutmeg into the spinach and season well with salt and pepper.

4. Brush three sheets of pastry with butter. Place another three sheets on top and brush with butter. Cut each sheet down the middle to make six long strips in total. Place a spoonful of the spinach filling on the end of each strip.

5. Lift one corner of pastry over the filling to the opposite side, then turn over the opposite way to enclose. Continue to fold over down the strip to make a triangular pocket, finishing with the seam underneath.

6. Place the pockets on the baking sheet, brush with butter, and sprinkle with the sesame seeds. Bake in the preheated oven for 12–15 minutes, or until golden brown and crisp. Serve.

# PAPRIKA PORK

SERVES: 4    PREP TIME: 15 MIN.    COOK TIME: 35 MIN.

### INGREDIENTS

1½ pounds pork tenderloin

2 tablespoons sunflower oil

2 tablespoons butter

1 onion, chopped

1 tablespoon paprika

¼ cup all-purpose flour

1¼ cups chicken stock

¼ cup dry sherry

2 cups sliced white button mushrooms

⅔ cup sour cream

salt and pepper

**1.** Cut the pork into 1½-inch cubes. Heat the oil and butter in a large saucepan. Add the pork and cook over medium heat, stirring, for 5 minutes, or until browned. Transfer to a plate with a slotted spoon.

**2.** Add the chopped onion to the saucepan and cook, stirring occasionally, for 5 minutes, or until softened. Stir in the paprika and flour and cook, stirring continuously, for 2 minutes. Gradually stir in the stock and bring to a boil, stirring continuously.

**3.** Return the pork to the saucepan, add the sherry and sliced mushrooms, and season with salt and pepper. Cover and simmer gently for 20 minutes, or until the pork is tender. Stir in the sour cream and serve.

# THAI CHICKEN

SERVES: 4    PREP TIME: 20 MIN. PLUS 2 HR. MARINATING TIME    COOK TIME: 25 MIN.

### INGREDIENTS

6 garlic cloves, coarsely chopped

1 teaspoon pepper

8 chicken legs

1 tablespoon Thai fish sauce

¼ cup dark soy sauce

fresh ginger, cut into matchsticks, to garnish

**1.** Put the garlic in a mortar, add the pepper, and pound to a paste with a pestle. Using a sharp knife, make three to four diagonal slashes on both sides of the chicken legs. Spread the garlic paste over the chicken legs and place them in a dish. Add the fish sauce and soy sauce and turn the chicken to coat well. Cover with plastic wrap and let marinate in the refrigerator for 2 hours.

**2.** Preheat the broiler to medium–high. Drain the chicken legs, reserving the marinade. Put them on the broiler rack and cook under the preheated broiler, turning and basting frequently with the reserved marinade, for 20–25 minutes, or until a fork can be inserted into the thickest part of the meat with ease and the juices run clear. A meat thermometer inserted into the thickest part of the meat, without touching the bone, should read 170°F. Garnish with ginger and serve.

# CRÈME BRÛLÉE

**SERVES: 4–6**　　　**PREP TIME: 15 MIN. PLUS 2 HR. CHILLING TIME**　　　**COOK TIME: 5 MIN.**

### INGREDIENTS

2–3 cups mixed berries, such as blueberries, and pitted fresh cherries

1½–2 tablespoons orange liqueur or orange flower water

1 cup mascarpone cheese

1 cup crème fraîche or Greek-style yogurt

2–3 tablespoons packed dark brown sugar

**1.** Prepare the fruit, if necessary, and lightly rinse, then place in the bottoms of four to six ⅔-cup ramekins (individual ceramic dishes). Sprinkle the fruit with the liqueur.

**2.** Cream the mascarpone cheese in a bowl until soft, then gradually beat in the crème fraîche.

**3.** Spoon the cheese mixture over the fruit, smoothing the surface and making sure that the tops are level. Chill in the refrigerator for at least 2 hours.

**4.** Sprinkle the tops with the sugar. Using a chef's blow torch, heat the tops until caramelized (about 2–3 minutes). Alternatively, cook under a preheated broiler, turning the dishes, for 3–4 minutes, or until the tops are lightly caramelized all over.

**5.** Serve warm or chill in the refrigerator for 15–20 minutes before serving.

# COCONUT FUDGE BALLS

MAKES: 16     PREP TIME: 15 MIN. PLUS CHILLING TIME     COOK TIME: 5 MIN.

### INGREDIENTS

1 (14-ounce) can condensed milk

2 cups dried coconut

½ teaspoon ground cinnamon

few drops edible yellow food coloring (optional)

1. Place the condensed milk in a saucepan and heat gently, stirring, for 1 minute.

2. Stir in 1 cup of the coconut with the cinnamon and food coloring, if using. Cook over moderate heat, stirring, for 3–4 minutes, until the mixture thickens and begins to clump together in one piece.

3. Remove from the heat and let stand until the mixture is cool enough to handle. Break off bite-size balls of the mixture and roll into small balls with your hands.

4. Put the remaining coconut into a bowl and roll the balls in it to coat evenly, then place on a chilled plate and let set.

# 26 OCTOBER

## SLICED BEEF IN BLACK BEAN SAUCE

SERVES: 4–6    PREP TIME: 15 MIN.    COOK TIME: 5 MIN.

### INGREDIENTS

3 tablespoons peanut oil

1 pound beef tenderloin, thinly sliced

1 red bell pepper, seeded and thinly sliced

1 green bell pepper, seeded and thinly sliced

1 bunch scallions, sliced

2 garlic cloves, crushed

1 tablespoon grated fresh ginger

2 tablespoons black bean sauce

1 tablespoon sherry

1 tablespoon soy sauce

1. Heat 2 tablespoons of the oil in a wok over high heat and stir-fry the beef for 1–2 minutes. Remove and set aside.

2. Add the remaining oil and bell peppers and stir-fry for 2 minutes.

3. Add the scallions, garlic, and ginger and stir-fry for 30 seconds.

4. Add the black bean sauce, sherry, and soy sauce, then stir in the beef and heat until bubbling. Serve.

# 27 OCTOBER

## FRENCH ONION SOUP

SERVES: 6    PREP TIME: 15 MIN.    COOK TIME: 1½ HR.

### INGREDIENTS

3 tablespoons olive oil

6 onions (about 1½ pounds), thinly sliced

4 garlic cloves, 3 chopped and 1 halved

1 teaspoon sugar

2 teaspoons chopped fresh thyme, plus extra sprigs to garnish

2 tablespoons all-purpose flour

½ cup dry white wine

5 cups vegetable stock

6 slices French bread

2½ cups shredded Swiss cheese

1. Heat the oil in a large, heavy saucepan over medium–low heat, add the onions, and cook, stirring occasionally, for 10 minutes, or until they are just beginning to brown. Stir in the chopped garlic, sugar, and chopped thyme, then reduce the heat and cook, stirring occasionally, for 30 minutes, or until the onions are golden brown.

2. Sprinkle in the flour and cook, stirring continuously, for 1–2 minutes. Stir in the wine. Gradually stir in the stock and bring to a boil, skimming off any scum that rises to the surface, then reduce the heat and simmer for 45 minutes. Meanwhile, preheat the broiler to medium.

3. Toast the bread on both sides under the broiler, then rub the toast with the cut edges of the halved garlic clove.

4. Ladle the soup into six heatproof bowls set on a baking sheet. Place a piece of toast floating in each bowl and divide the shredded cheese among them. Place under the broiler for 2–3 minutes, or until the cheese has just melted. Garnish with thyme sprigs and serve.

# BEAN CASSEROLE WITH POTATOES, CORN & SQUASH

**SERVES: 4–6**     **PREP TIME: 35 MIN. PLUS SOAKING TIME**     **COOK TIME: 2 HR. 45 MIN.**

## INGREDIENTS

1 cup dried lima beans

4 Yukon gold potatoes, peeled and cubed

1 butternut squash, seeded and cubed

2 cups fresh or frozen corn kernels

salt and pepper

chopped fresh basil leaves and crumbled feta cheese, to serve

## SALSA

2–3 fresh yellow or red chiles, seeded and chopped

1 small onion, finely chopped

6 scallions, green parts included, finely chopped

2–3 garlic cloves, finely chopped

2 tablespoons olive oil

**1.** Soak the beans in cold water overnight. Drain, rinse, and transfer to a large saucepan with enough water to cover by two fingers' width. Do not add salt. Bring to a boil, then reduce the heat and simmer gently for 1½–2 hours, or until the beans are tender.

**2.** Meanwhile, put all the salsa ingredients in a small saucepan and cook over medium heat, stirring frequently, for 5 minutes to marry the flavors. Set aside.

**3.** When the beans are tender, add the potatoes and squash and add enough boiling water to submerge all the ingredients. Return to a boil, then reduce the heat, cover, and cook gently for 20–30 minutes, or until the vegetables are tender. Season with salt and pepper.

**4.** Stir in the corn kernels and reheat until simmering. Stir in the salsa and cook for an additional 10 minutes to marry the flavors and reduce the cooking juices. The dish should be juicy but not soupy. Sprinkle with the chopped basil and crumbled cheese and serve.

# PUMPKIN WHOOPIE PIES

MAKES: 12    PREP TIME: 30 MIN.    COOK TIME: 10 MIN.

## INGREDIENTS

2¼ cups all-purpose flour

½ teaspoon baking powder

½ teaspoon baking soda

1½ teaspoons ground cinnamon

¼ teaspoon salt

1 cup firmly packed light brown sugar

½ cup sunflower oil

1 extra-large egg, beaten

1 teaspoon vanilla extract

½ cup canned pumpkin puree

## CINNAMON & MAPLE FILLING

1 cup cream cheese

6 tablespoons unsalted butter, softened

2 tablespoons maple syrup

1 teaspoon ground cinnamon

¾ cup confectioners' sugar, sifted

1. Preheat the oven to 350°F. Line two to three large baking sheets with parchment paper. Sift together the all-purpose flour, baking powder, baking soda, cinnamon, and salt.

2. Place the sugar and oil in a large bowl and beat with an electric mixer for 1 minute. Beat in the egg and vanilla extract, then the pumpkin puree. Stir in the sifted flour mixture and beat until thoroughly incorporated.

3. Pipe or spoon 24 mounds of the batter onto the prepared baking sheets, spaced well apart to allow for spreading. Bake, one sheet at a time, in the preheated oven for 8–10 minutes, until risen and just firm to the touch. Cool for 5 minutes, then using a spatula transfer to a cooling rack and let cool completely.

4. For the cinnamon-and-maple filling, place the cream cheese and butter in a bowl and beat together until well blended. Beat in the maple syrup, cinnamon, and confectioners' sugar until smooth.

5. To assemble, spread or pipe the filling over the flat side of half the cakes. Top with the rest of the cakes.

# BAKED PUMPKIN WITH GRUYÈRE CHEESE

SERVES: 4–6     PREP TIME: 25 MIN.     COOK TIME: 1 HR. 15 MIN.

## INGREDIENTS

1 large pumpkin

1¼ cups heavy cream

3 garlic cloves, thinly sliced

1 tablespoon fresh thyme leaves

1 cup shredded Gruyère cheese
Swiss cheese, or Muenster cheese

salt and pepper

crusty bread, to serve

**1.** Preheat the oven to 350°F.

**2.** Cut horizontally straight through the top quarter of the pumpkin to form a lid. Scoop out the seeds. Put the pumpkin in a large, deep ovenproof dish. Heat together the cream and garlic in a saucepan until just below boiling point. Remove from the heat, season with salt and pepper, and stir in the thyme. Pour into the pumpkin and set the lid on top.

**3.** Bake in the preheated oven for 1 hour, or until the flesh is tender—the exact cooking time will depend on the size of the pumpkin. Be careful to avoid overcooking the pumpkin, or it may collapse. Remove from the oven, lift off the lid, and sprinkle with the Gruyère cheese. Return to the oven and bake for an additional 10 minutes.

**4.** Serve the soft pumpkin flesh with a generous portion of the cheesy cream and crusty bread.

# HALLOWEEN MUD PIE

**SERVES: 6–8** | **PREP TIME: 30 MIN.** | **COOK TIME: 35–40 MIN.**

## INGREDIENTS

3 ounces semisweet dark chocolate

6 tablespoons unsalted butter

⅓ cup firmly packed light brown sugar

2 eggs, beaten

½ cup light cream

1 teaspoon vanilla extract

## PIE DOUGH

1⅓ cups all-purpose flour, plus extra for dusting

¼ cup unsweetened cocoa powder

¼ cup firmly packed light brown sugar

6 tablespoons unsalted butter

2–3 tablespoons cold water

## TOPPING

1 cup heavy whipping cream

3 ounces plain chocolate

**1.** Preheat the oven to 400°F. To make the pie dough, sift the flour and cocoa powder into a bowl and stir in the sugar. Rub in the butter with your fingertips until the mixture resembles fine bread crumbs. Add just enough water to bind to a dough.

**2.** Roll out the dough on a lightly floured work surface to a circle large enough to line an 8-inch, 1¼-inch deep tart pan. Use the dough to line the pan. Prick the bottom with a fork, cover with a piece of parchment paper and fill with pie weights or dried beans, then bake the pastry shell in the preheated oven for 10 minutes. Remove from the oven and remove the paper and weights. Reduce the oven temperature to 350°F.

**3.** For the filling, put the chocolate and butter into a saucepan and heat over low heat, stirring, until melted. Put the sugar and eggs into a bowl and beat together until smooth, then stir in the chocolate mixture, cream, and vanilla extract.

**4.** Pour the chocolate mixture into the pastry shell and bake in the oven for 20–25 minutes, or until just set. Let cool.

**5.** To make the topping, whip the cream until it just holds its shape, then spread over the pie. Melt the chocolate in a bowl set over a saucepan of simmering water, making sure the bowl doesn't come in contact with the water, then spoon into a pastry bag and pipe decorations over the cream. Serve cold.

# NOVEMBER

# BEEF WITH HERB DUMPLINGS

**SERVES: 6**    **PREP TIME: 35 MIN.**    **COOK TIME: 2 HR. 20 MIN.**

### INGREDIENTS

2 tablespoons sunflower oil

2 large onions, thinly sliced

8 carrots, sliced

¼ cup all-purpose flour

2 pounds boneless beef chuck, cut into cubes

2 cups stout

2 teaspoons light brown sugar

2 bay leaves

1 tablespoon chopped fresh thyme

### HERB DUMPLINGS

1 cup all-purpose flour

1½ teaspoons baking powder

¼ cup lard or vegetable shortening

2 tablespoons chopped fresh parsley

about ¼ cup water

**1.** Preheat the oven to 325°F. Heat the oil in a flameproof casserole dish. Add the onions and carrots and cook over low heat, stirring occasionally, for 5 minutes, or until the onions are softened. Meanwhile, place the flour in a plastic food bag. Add the beef to the bag, tie the top, and shake well to coat. Do this in batches, if necessary.

**2.** Remove the vegetables from the casserole dish with a slotted spoon and reserve. Add the beef to the casserole dish, in batches, and cook, stirring frequently, until browned all over. Return all the meat and the onions and carrots to the casserole dish and sprinkle in any remaining flour. Pour in the stout and add the sugar, bay leaves, and thyme. Bring to a boil, cover, and transfer to the preheated oven to bake for 1¾ hours.

**3.** To make the herb dumplings, sift the flour and baking powder into a bowl. Stir in the lard and parsley and add enough of the water to make a soft dough. Shape into small balls between the palms of your hands. Add to the casserole dish and return to the oven for 30 minutes. Remove and discard the bay leaves. Serve.

# CHICKEN-FRIED STEAK

**SERVES: 4**    **PREP TIME: 20 MIN.**    **COOK TIME: 45 MIN.**

### INGREDIENTS

4 minute steaks (6 ounces each)

2 eggs, beaten

¼ cup milk

1 cup all-purpose flour

1 tablespoon paprika

½ teaspoon white pepper

vegetable oil, for frying

salt and pepper

### GRAVY

4 ounces bulk sausage or sausage meat removed from the casings

3 scallions, chopped

3 tablespoons butter

¼ cup all-purpose flour

2½ cups milk

**1.** Generously season both sides of the steaks with salt and pepper. Put the eggs and milk into a pie plate, beat together, and set aside. Put the flour, paprika, and white pepper into a second pie plate and mix well to combine. One at a time, dip the steaks into the egg mixture, turning to coat completely, and then dredge in the flour, coating on both sides. Place the egged-and-floured steaks on a plate and let stand for 10 minutes.

**2.** Add about ¼ inch of the oil to a large skillet and place over medium–high heat. When the oil begins to shimmer, add the steaks and cook for about 3–4 minutes on each side, until golden brown and cooked through. Remove from the skillet and drain for about 2 minutes on a wire rack set over some paper towels. If working in batches, keep the cooked steaks warm in a low oven until the remainder have been cooked.

**3.** To make the gravy, cook the sausages until browned, breaking up the meat into small pieces. Add the white parts of the scallion and the butter and sauté for a few minutes until the onions are translucent.

**4.** Stir in the flour and cook for 3 minutes. Gradually beat in the milk until combined. When it reaches simmering point, reduce the heat to low and cook, stirring occasionally, for 15 minutes. If the gravy thickens too much, add some more milk. Serve the gravy over the steaks.

BEEF WITH HERB
DUMPLINGS

# MINI POPOVERS

MAKES: 6    PREP TIME: 15 MIN.    COOK TIME: 35 MIN.

## INGREDIENTS

2 tablespoons beef dripping or sunflower oil

1¼ cups all-purpose flour

½ teaspoon salt

2 eggs

1 cup milk

**1.** Grease six individual metal molds with the dripping, then divide the remaining dripping among the molds. Preheat the oven to 425°F, placing the molds in the oven so the dripping can melt while the oven heats.

**2.** Sift together the flour and salt into a large mixing bowl and make a well in the center. Break the eggs into the well, add the milk, and beat, gradually drawing in the flour from the side to make a smooth batter. Remove the molds from the oven and spoon in the batter until they are about halfway full.

**3.** Bake in the preheated oven for 30–35 minutes, without opening the door, until the popovers are well risen, puffed, and golden brown. Serve.

# CHILI-SPICED MAPLE-GLAZED TURKEY CUTLETS

**SERVES: 4**   **PREP TIME: 10 MIN.**   **COOK TIME: 15 MIN.**

### INGREDIENTS

4 turkey cutlets

2 tablespoons olive oil

1 garlic clove, crushed

⅓ cup maple syrup

2 tablespoons tomato paste

2 tablespoons Worcestershire sauce

3 tablespoons lime juice

1½ teaspoons hot chili sauce

salt and pepper

chopped fresh flat-leaf parsley, to garnish

**1.** Place the turkey cutlets between two pieces of plastic wrap and beat with a rolling pin until thin. Season with salt and pepper.

**2.** Heat the oil in a large skillet, add the turkey, and cook over high heat, turning once, for 3–4 minutes, until golden brown.

**3.** Mix together the garlic, maple syrup, tomato paste, Worcestershire sauce, lime juice, and chili sauce, then spoon the glaze over the turkey.

**4.** Turn the turkey in the glaze to coat, then reduce the heat to low, cover the skillet, and cook gently for 8–10 minutes, until the turkey is tender and thoroughly cooked, with no traces of pink when cut into with a knife.

**5.** Season with salt and pepper, sprinkle with parsley, and serve.

# CHICKEN MOLE POBLANO

SERVES: 4 · PREP TIME: 30 MIN. · COOK TIME: 1 HR. 20 MIN.

### INGREDIENTS

3 tablespoons olive oil

4 chicken parts (about 6 ounces each), halved

1 onion, chopped

2 garlic cloves, finely chopped

1 hot dried red chile, rehydrated and finely chopped

1 tablespoon sesame seeds, toasted, plus extra to garnish

1 tablespoon chopped almonds

½ teaspoon each of ground cinnamon, cumin, and cloves

3 tomatoes, peeled and chopped

2 tablespoons raisins

1½ cups chicken stock

1 tablespoon peanut butter

1 ounce semisweet dark chocolate, grated, plus extra to garnish

salt and pepper

1. Heat the oil in a large skillet. Add the chicken and cook until browned on all sides. Remove the chicken with a slotted spoon and set aside.

2. Add the onion, garlic, and chile and cook for 5 minutes, or until softened. Add the sesame seeds, almonds, and spices and cook, stirring, for 2 minutes. Add the tomatoes, raisins, stock, peanut butter, and chocolate and stir well.

3. Season with salt and pepper and simmer for 5 minutes. Transfer the mixture to a food processor and process until smooth (you may need to do this in batches). Return the mixture to the skillet, add the chicken, and bring to a boil. Reduce the heat, cover, and simmer for 1 hour, adding more liquid, if necessary, until a fork can be easily inserted into the thickest part of the meat with ease and the juices run clear. A meat thermometer inserted into the thickest part of the meat, without touching the bone, should read 170°F.

4. Serve garnished with sesame seeds and a little grated chocolate.

# CHICKEN & CORN SOUP

SERVES: 6 · PREP TIME: 35 MIN. · COOK TIME: 50 MIN.

### INGREDIENTS

3-pound roasted chicken

½ teaspoon saffron threads

3 tablespoons vegetable oil

2 onions, thinly sliced

3 celery stalks, sliced

7 cups vegetable stock

8 black peppercorns

1 mace blade

4 ounces egg noodles

2½ cups frozen corn kernels

pinch of dried sage

2 tablespoons chopped fresh parsley

salt and pepper

1. Remove the skin from the chicken, cut the meat off the bones, and cut into small pieces. Put the saffron into a bowl, pour in hot water to cover, and let soak.

2. Heat the oil in a saucepan. Add the onions and celery and cook over low heat, stirring occasionally, for 5 minutes, until softened. Increase the heat to medium, pour in the stock, add the peppercorns and mace, and bring to a boil. Reduce the heat and simmer for 25 minutes.

3. Increase the heat to medium, add the chicken, noodles, corn, sage, parsley, and saffron with its soaking water, season with salt and pepper, and bring back to a boil. Reduce the heat and simmer for an additional 20 minutes.

4. Remove the pan from the heat, taste, and adjust the seasoning, if necessary, and ladle into serving bowls.

CHICKEN MOLE
POBLANO

# SQUASH, SWEET POTATO & GARLIC SOUP

SERVES: 4–6    PREP TIME: 35 MIN.    COOK TIME: 1 HR. 20 MIN.

## INGREDIENTS

1 acorn or butternut squash

1 sweet potato
(about 12 ounces)

4 shallots

2 tablespoons olive oil

5–6 garlic cloves, unpeeled

3½ cups chicken stock

½ cup crème fraîche or sour cream

pepper

snipped fresh chives, to garnish

1. Preheat the oven to 375°F. Cut the squash, sweet potato, and shallots in half lengthwise, through to the stem end. Scoop the seeds out of the squash. Brush the cut sides with the oil.

2. Place the vegetables, cut side down, in a shallow roasting pan and add the garlic. Roast in the preheated oven for about 40 minutes, until tender and light brown. Cool.

3. When cool, scoop the flesh from the sweet potato and squash halves and place in a saucepan with the shallots. Peel the garlic and add the soft insides to the other vegetables.

4. Add the stock. Bring just to a boil, reduce the heat, and simmer, partly covered, for about 30 minutes, stirring occasionally, until the vegetables are tender.

5. Let the soup cool slightly, then transfer to a food processor and process until smooth, working in batches, if necessary. (If using a food processor, strain off the cooking liquid and set aside. Process the soup solids with enough cooking liquid to moisten them, then combine with the remaining liquid.)

6. Return the soup to the rinsed-out saucepan. Season with pepper, then simmer for 5–10 minutes, until completely heated through. Ladle into serving bowls and swirl the crème fraîche over the top. Garnish with extra pepper and snipped chives and serve.

# BUTTERNUT SQUASH & MUSHROOM RISOTTO

SERVES: 4     PREP TIME: 35 MIN.     COOK TIME: 1 HR.

## INGREDIENTS

2 tablespoons olive oil

1 large onion,
finely chopped

6 sage leaves,
finely chopped

2 teaspoons chopped fresh
thyme leaves

1 large butternut squash, peeled,
seeded, and cut into ¾ inch chunks

8 ounces cremini mushrooms, sliced

1¼ cups vegetable stock

1 cup dry white wine

2 cups risotto rice

¾ cup freshly grated Parmesan cheese

salt and pepper

crispy fried sage leaves,
to garnish

**1.** Preheat the oven to 400°F. Heat the oil in a large saucepan. Add the onion, sage, and thyme. Cover and cook over low heat for 5 minutes, until the onion turns translucent.

**2.** Stir in the butternut squash, mushrooms, stock, and wine. Bring to a boil, then remove from the heat and ladle everything in the pan into a large ovenproof casserole dish. Stir in the rice.

**3.** Cover the casserole dish with a tight fitting lid and bake for 40–45 minutes, until the rice and vegetables are tender. Stir in half the cheese, then season with salt and pepper. Serve sprinkled with the remaining cheese and fried sage leaves to garnish.

# HAM & MUSHROOM QUICHE

**SERVES: 4–6**    **PREP TIME: 30 MIN. PLUS 30 MIN. CHILLING TIME**    **COOK TIME: 45–50 MIN.**

### INGREDIENTS

1 tablespoon butter

1 small onion, finely chopped

2 cups sliced white button mushrooms

5 ounces cooked ham, diced

2 eggs, beaten

1 cup light cream

½ cup shredded Swiss cheese,

salt and pepper

### PASTRY DOUGH

1⅔ cups all-purpose flour, plus extra for dusting

1 stick butter

2–3 tablespoons cold water

**1.** To make the pastry dough, sift the flour into a bowl and rub in the butter with your fingertips until the mixture resembles fine bread crumbs. Stir in just enough water to bind to a soft dough.

**2.** Roll out the dough on a lightly floured work surface and use to line a 9-inch tart pan. Press into the edges, trim the excess, and prick the bottom with a fork. Chill in the refrigerator for 15 minutes. Preheat the oven to 400°F.

**3.** Prick the bottom of the pastry shell with a fork, line it with parchment paper, and fill with pie weights or dried beans. Bake the pastry shell in the preheated oven for 10 minutes, until lightly browned. Remove from the oven and remove the paper and weights, then bake for an additional 10 minutes.

**4.** Melt the butter in a skillet, add the onion, and sauté for 2 minutes, then add the mushrooms and sauté, stirring, for an additional 2–3 minutes. Add the ham, then spread the mixture evenly in the pastry shell.

**5.** Put the eggs into a bowl with the cream and beat together, then season with salt and pepper. Pour into the pastry shell and sprinkle with the cheese. Bake for 20–25 minutes, until golden brown and just set.

# CHUNKY POTATO & SPINACH CURRY

SERVES: 4    PREP TIME: 30 MIN.    COOK TIME: 25 MIN.

## INGREDIENTS

4 tomatoes

2 tablespoons peanut oil or vegetable oil

2 onions, cut into thick wedges

1-inch piece fresh ginger, peeled and finely chopped

1 garlic clove, chopped

2 tablespoons ground coriander

4 Yukon gold potatoes, peeled and cut into chunks

2½ cups vegetable stock

1 tablespoon red curry paste

8 ounces spinach

cooked rice or noodles, to serve

1. Put the tomatoes in a heatproof bowl and cover with boiling water. Let stand for 2–3 minutes, then plunge into cold water and peel off the skins. Cut each tomato into quarters and remove and discard the seeds and the core in the center. Set aside.

2. Heat the oil in a preheated wok, add the onions, ginger, and garlic, and stir-fry over medium–high heat for 2–3 minutes, until starting to soften. Add the coriander and potatoes and stir-fry for 2–3 minutes. Add the stock and curry paste and bring to a boil, stirring occasionally. Reduce the heat and simmer gently for 10–15 minutes, until the potatoes are tender.

3. Add the spinach and the tomato quarters and cook, stirring, for 1 minute, or until the spinach has wilted. Serve with rice.

# PAN-FRIED HOT & SPICY SALMON

SERVES: 4    PREP TIME: 5 MIN.    COOK TIME: 5 MIN.

## INGREDIENTS

½ teaspoon crushed red pepper

¾-inch piece fresh ginger, grated

1 tablespoon sesame oil

finely grated rind and juice of 1 lemon

4 salmon fillet pieces

1 tablespoon sunflower oil

salt and pepper

sautéed potatoes and seasonal vegetables, to serve

1. Put the red pepper, ginger, sesame oil, lemon rind, and half the lemon juice into a nonmetallic bowl and mix together.

2. Add the salmon to the mixture and turn to coat evenly. Cover and let stand for 5 minutes. Season with salt and pepper.

3. Preheat a heavy skillet or ridged grill pan. Add the sunflower oil, then place the salmon in the skillet skin side down. Cook for about 2 minutes, until the skin is golden and crisp, then turn and cook the other side for about 2 minutes, until golden and just firm.

4. Squeeze the remaining lemon juice over the salmon and serve with sautéed potatoes and vegetables.

# VEGETABLE CHILI

**SERVES: 4** | **PREP TIME: 35 MIN.** | **COOK TIME: 1 HR. 10 MIN.**

### INGREDIENTS

1 eggplant, cut into 1-inch slices

1 tablespoon olive oil, plus extra for brushing

1 large red onion, finely chopped

2 red or yellow bell peppers, seeded and finely chopped

3–4 garlic cloves, finely chopped or crushed

1 (28-ounce) can diced tomatoes

1 tablespoon mild chili powder

½ teaspoon ground cumin

½ teaspoon dried oregano

2 small zucchini, quartered lengthwise and sliced

1 (15-ounce) can kidney beans, drained and rinsed

2 cups water

1 tablespoon tomato paste

6 scallions, finely chopped

1 cup shredded cheddar cheese

salt and pepper

1. Brush the eggplant slices on one side with olive oil. Heat half the oil in a large, heavy skillet over medium–high heat. Add the eggplant slices, oiled side up, and cook for 5–6 minutes, or until browned on one side. Turn the slices over, cook on the other side until browned, and transfer to a plate. Cut into bite-size pieces.

2. Heat the remaining oil in a large saucepan over medium heat. Add the onion and bell peppers and cook, stirring occasionally, for 3–4 minutes, or until the onion is just softened, but not browned.

3. Add the garlic and cook for an additional 2–3 minutes, or until the onion begins to brown.

4. Add the tomatoes, chili powder, cumin, and oregano. Season with salt and pepper. Bring just to a boil, reduce the heat, cover, and simmer gently for 15 minutes.

5. Add the zucchini, eggplant pieces, and kidney beans. Stir in the water and the tomato paste. Return to a boil, then cover and continue simmering for 45 minutes, or until the vegetables are tender. Taste and adjust the seasoning if necessary. Ladle into serving bowls and top with scallions and cheese.

# 13 NOVEMBER

# CINNAMON SWIRLS

MAKES: 12    PREP TIME: 30 MIN. PLUS 1 HR. 10 MIN. STANDING TIME    COOK TIME: 30 MIN.

## INGREDIENTS

1⅔ cups white bread flour

½ teaspoon salt

2¼ teaspoons active dry yeast

2 tablespoons butter, cut into small pieces, plus extra for greasing

1 egg, lightly beaten

½ cup lukewarm milk

2 tablespoons maple syrup, for glazing

## FILLING

4 tablespoons butter, softened

2 teaspoons ground cinnamon

¼ cup firmly packed light brown sugar

⅓ cup dried currants

1. Grease a baking sheet with a little butter.

2. Sift the flour and salt into a mixing bowl. Stir in the yeast. Rub in the butter with your fingertips until the mixture resembles bread crumbs. Add the egg and milk and mix to form a dough.

3. Form the dough into a ball, place in a greased bowl, cover, and let stand in a warm place for about 40 minutes, or until doubled in size.

4. Knead the dough for 1 minute, then roll out to a rectangle measuring 12 x 9 inches.

5. To make the filling, cream together the butter, cinnamon, and sugar until light and fluffy. Spread the filling evenly over the dough rectangle, leaving a 1-inch border all around. Sprinkle the dried currants evenly over the top.

6. Roll up the dough from one long edge, and press down to seal. Cut the roll into 12 slices. Place them, cut side down, on the baking sheet, cover, and let stand for 30 minutes. Meanwhile, preheat the oven to 375°F.

7. Bake the swirls in the preheated oven for 20–30 minutes, or until well risen. Brush with the maple syrup and let cool slightly before serving.

# 14 NOVEMBER

# CHOCOLATE FUDGE BROWNIES

MAKES: 16    PREP TIME: 25 MIN.    COOK TIME: 45 MIN.

## INGREDIENTS

1 cup cream cheese

½ teaspoon vanilla extract

1 cup granulated sugar

2 eggs

¾ stick butter, plus extra for greasing

¼ cup unsweetened cocoa powder

¾ cup all-purpose flour

1¼ teaspoons baking powder

½ cup chopped pecans

## FUDGE FROSTING

4 tablespoons butter

1 tablespoon milk

⅔ cup confectioners' sugar

2 tablespoons unsweetened cocoa powder

1. Preheat the oven to 350°F. Lightly grease and line a shallow 8-inch square cake pan.

2. Place the cheese, vanilla extract, and 5 teaspoons of the sugar in a large bowl and beat together until smooth.

3. Place the eggs and remaining sugar in a separate bowl and beat together until light and fluffy. Place the butter and cocoa powder in a small saucepan and heat gently, stirring until the butter melts and the mixture combines, then stir it into the egg mixture.

4. Fold in the flour, baking powder, and nuts, pour half of the batter into the pan, and smooth the top. Carefully spread the cheese mixture over the batter, then cover it with the remaining batter. Bake in the preheated oven for 40–45 minutes. Let cool in the pan.

5. To make the fudge frosting, melt the butter with the milk in a saucepan. Stir in the confectioners' sugar and cocoa powder. Spread the frosting over the brownies, let set, then cut into squares or rectangles.

~328~

CINNAMON
SWIRLS

# RATATOUILLE

SERVES: 4    PREP TIME: 30 MINS    COOK TIME: ABOUT 1 HR.

## INGREDIENTS

⅔ cup olive oil

2 onions, sliced

2 garlic cloves

2 eggplants, coarsely chopped

4 zucchini, coarsely chopped

2 yellow bell peppers, seeded and chopped

2 red bell peppers, seeded and chopped

1 bouquet garni of sprigs of parsley, bay leaf, and thyme tied together

1 (14¼-ounce) can diced tomatoes

salt and pepper

**1.** Heat the oil in a large saucepan. Add the onions and cook over low heat, stirring occasionally, for 5 minutes, or until softened. Add the garlic and cook, stirring frequently, for an additional 2 minutes.

**2.** Add the eggplants, zucchini, and bell peppers. Increase the heat to medium and cook, stirring occasionally, until the peppers begin to brown. Add the bouquet garni, reduce the heat, cover, and simmer gently for 40 minutes.

**3.** Stir in the diced tomatoes and season with salt and pepper. Replace the lid and simmer gently for an additional 10 minutes. Remove and discard the bouquet garni. Serve warm or cold.

# SHRIMP EGG FOO YUNG

SERVES: 4–6    PREP TIME: 10 MIN.    COOK TIME: 10 MIN.

## INGREDIENTS

1 tablespoon peanut oil or vegetable oil

4 ounces large shrimp, peeled and deveined

4 eggs, lightly beaten

1 teaspoon salt

pinch of white pepper

2 tablespoons finely chopped Chinese chives or regular chives

**1.** Heat a wok or large skillet over high heat and add the oil. Add the shrimp and stir-fry for about 4 minutes, or until just pink.

**2.** Season the eggs with the salt and pepper and pour the mixture over the shrimp. Stir-fry for 1 minute, then add the chives.

**3.** Cook for an additional 4 minutes, stirring all the time, until the eggs are cooked through but still soft in texture. Serve.

# CHICKEN GUMBO

SERVES: 4–6    PREP TIME: **30 MIN.**    COOK TIME: **2½ HR.**

### INGREDIENTS

3½-pound chicken, cut into 6 parts

2 celery stalks, 1 broken in half and 1 finely chopped

1 carrot, chopped

2 onions, 1 sliced and 1 chopped

2 bay leaves

¼ teaspoon salt

¼ cup peanut oil or vegetable oil

⅓ cup all-purpose flour

2 large garlic cloves, crushed

1 green bell pepper, cored, seeded, and diced

1 pound fresh okra, trimmed, then cut widthwise into ½-inch slices

8 ounces andouille sausage or Polish kielbasa, sliced

2 tablespoons tomato paste

1 teaspoon dried thyme

½ teaspoon salt

½ teaspoon cayenne pepper

¼ teaspoon pepper

1 (14½-ounce) can Italian tomatoes

cooked long-grain rice and hot pepper sauce, to serve

**1.** Put the chicken into a large saucepan with water to cover over medium–high heat and bring to a boil, skimming the surface to remove the foam. When the foam stops rising, reduce the heat to medium, add the celery stalk halves, carrot, sliced onion, 1 bay leaf, and salt, and simmer for 20 minutes, or until a fork can be inserted into the thickest part of the meat with ease and the juices run clear. A meat thermometer inserted into the thickest part of the meat, without touching the bone, should read 170°F. Strain the chicken, reserving 4 cups of the liquid. When the chicken is cool enough to handle, remove and discard the skin and bones, as well as the ingredients remaining in the pan. Cut the chicken meat into bite-size pieces and reserve.

**2.** Heat the oil in a large saucepan over medium–high heat for 2 minutes. Reduce the heat to low, sprinkle in the flour, and stir to make a paste. Stir continuously for 30 minutes, or until the paste turns hazelnut brown. If black specks appear, it is burned and you will have to start again.

**3.** Add the chopped celery, chopped onion, garlic, green bell pepper, and okra to the saucepan. Increase the heat to medium–high and cook, stirring frequently, for 5 minutes. Add the sausage and cook, stirring frequently, for 2 minutes.

**4.** Stir in the remaining ingredients, including the second bay leaf and the reserved cooking liquid. Bring to a boil, crushing the tomatoes with a wooden spoon. Reduce the heat to medium–low and simmer, uncovered, for 30 minutes, stirring occasionally.

**5.** Add the chicken to the pan and simmer for an additional 30 minutes. Taste and adjust the seasoning, if necessary. Remove and discard the bay leaves and spoon the gumbo over the rice. Serve with a bottle of hot pepper sauce on the side.

# BRAISED BEEF WITH RED WINE & CRANBERRIES

SERVES: 4     PREP TIME: 15 MIN.     COOK TIME: 1 HR. 40 MIN.

## INGREDIENTS

2 tablespoons olive oil

6 shallots, quartered

1¼ pounds chuck steak, cubed

1 tablespoon all-purpose flour

1¼ cups red wine

2 tablespoons tomato paste

1 tablespoon Worcestershire sauce

2 bay leaves

1 cup fresh or frozen cranberries

salt and pepper

mashed potatoes and seasonal vegetables, to serve

**1.** Heat the oil in a large, flameproof casserole dish, add the shallots, and sauté, stirring, for 2–3 minutes, until beginning to brown. Remove from the dish and keep warm.

**2.** Add the steak and cook, stirring, for 3–4 minutes, or until evenly browned. Stir in the flour and cook for 1 minute.

**3.** Add the wine and bring to a boil, then boil for 1 minute. Return the shallots to the dish with the tomato paste, Worcestershire sauce, and bay leaves and season with salt and pepper. Stir in the cranberries.

**4.** Reduce the heat to low, cover tightly with a lid, and let simmer gently for 1–1½ hours, until the beef is tender.

**5.** Remove and discard the bay leaves, adjust the seasoning, if desired, and serve with mashed potatoes and vegetables.

# BAKED SWEET POTATO WITH GARLIC SALSA

SERVES: 4–6    PREP TIME: 20 MIN.    COOK TIME: 1 HR. 5 MIN.

## INGREDIENTS

6 sweet potatoes (about 2¼ pounds)

chopped fresh cilantro, to garnish

### GARLIC SALSA

2 tablespoons olive oil

4 garlic cloves, crushed

juice of 3–4 oranges (about ⅔ cup)

juice and grated rind of 1 lemon

½ teaspoon sea salt

1. Preheat the oven to 350°F.

2. Wash the sweet potatoes and pat dry. Bake in the preheated oven for 40 minutes, then test for softness with a knife—they may need an additional 20 minutes to cook, depending on their size and shape.

3. Meanwhile, make the garlic salsa. Heat the oil and garlic in a small saucepan, add the citrus juices, lemon rind, and salt and let simmer for 3–4 minutes, or until blended.

4. When the sweet potatoes are perfectly tender, remove from the oven. When cool enough to handle, remove the skins and dice the flesh into bite-size pieces.

5. Fold the diced sweet potato into the dressing. Serve at room temperature with the chopped cilantro sprinkled over them.

# FARFALLE WITH BLUE CHEESE & HAM

SERVES: 4    PREP TIME: 15 MIN.    COOK TIME: 20 MIN.

## INGREDIENTS

1 cup crème fraîche or sour cream

8 ounces cremini mushrooms, quartered

1 pound dried farfalle (pasta bow ties)

½ cup crumbled blue cheese

1 tablespoon chopped fresh flat-leaf parsley, plus extra sprigs to garnish

6 ounces cooked ham, diced

salt and pepper

1. Pour the crème fraîche into a saucepan, add the mushrooms, and season with salt and pepper. Bring to just below a boil, then lower the heat and simmer gently, stirring occasionally, for 8–10 minutes, until the cream has thickened.

2. Meanwhile, bring a large, heavy saucepan of lightly salted water to a boil. Add the farfalle, bring back to a boil, and cook according to the package directions, until just tender but still firm to the bite.

3. Remove the pan of mushrooms from the heat and stir in the blue cheese until it has melted. Return the pan to low heat and stir in the chopped parsley and ham.

4. Drain the pasta and add it to the sauce. Toss lightly, then divide among serving plates, garnish with the sprigs of parsley, and serve.

# VEGETABLE & BLACK BEAN EGG ROLLS

SERVES: 4          PREP TIME: 30 MIN.          COOK TIME: 15 MIN.

### INGREDIENTS

2 tablespoons peanut oil or vegetable oil, plus extra for deep-frying

4 scallions, cut into 2-inch lengths and shredded lengthwise

1-inch piece fresh ginger, peeled and finely chopped

1 large carrot, peeled and cut into matchsticks

1 red bell pepper, seeded and cut into matchsticks

⅓ cup black bean sauce

½ cup fresh bean sprouts

1 (8-ounce) can water chestnuts, drained and coarsely chopped

2-inch piece cucumber, cut into matchsticks

8 egg roll wrappers

sweet chili dipping sauce, to serve (optional)

**1.** Heat the oil in a preheated wok, add the scallions, ginger, carrot, and red bell pepper, and stir-fry over medium–high heat for 2–3 minutes. Add the black bean sauce, bean sprouts, water chestnuts, and cucumber and stir-fry for 1–2 minutes. Let cool.

**2.** Remove the egg roll wrappers from the package, but keep them in a pile, covered with plastic wrap, to prevent them from drying out. Lay one wrapper on a work surface in front of you in a diamond shape and brush the edges with water. Put a spoonful of the filling near one corner and fold the corner over the filling. Roll over again and then fold the side corners over the filling. Roll up to seal the filling completely. Repeat with the remaining wrappers and filling.

**3.** Heat the oil for deep-frying in the wok to 375°F, or until a cube of bread browns in 30 seconds. Add the rolls, in 2–3 batches, and cook for 2–3 minutes, until crisp and golden all over. Remove with a slotted spoon, drain on paper towels, and keep warm while you cook the remaining rolls. Serve with the sweet chili dipping sauce, if using.

# GREEN BEAN CASSEROLE

SERVES: 4–6     PREP TIME: 10 MIN.     COOK TIME: 40–45 MIN.

### INGREDIENTS

5 cups 1½-inch green bean pieces (about 1 pound)

1 (10¾-ounce) can condensed mushroom soup

1 cup milk

1 teaspoon soy sauce

1 tablespoon vegetable oil

1 tablespoon butter

1 onion, sliced into rings

salt

1. Preheat the oven to 350°F. Bring a saucepan of lightly salted water to a boil and add the beans. Bring back to a boil and cook for 5 minutes. Drain well.

2. Put the soup, milk, and soy sauce into a bowl and mix together, then stir in the beans. Transfer to a 1½-quart casserole dish and distribute evenly. Bake in the preheated oven for 25–30 minutes, until bubbling and golden.

3. Meanwhile, heat the oil and butter in a skillet, add the onion rings, and sauté over high heat, stirring frequently, until golden brown and crisp. Remove and drain on absorbent paper towels.

4. Arrange the onion rings on top of the casserole and bake for an additional 5 minutes. Serve hot.

# MASHED YAMS WITH PARSLEY BUTTER

**SERVES: 4**  **PREP TIME: 10 MIN.**  **COOK TIME: 25 MIN.**

### INGREDIENTS

4 tablespoons butter, softened

2 tablespoons chopped fresh parsley

2 pounds yams, scrubbed

salt

1. Reserving 2 tablespoons, put the butter into a bowl with the parsley and beat together. Turn out onto a square of aluminum foil or plastic wrap, shape into a block, and chill in the refrigerator until required.

2. Cut the yams into even chunks. Bring a large saucepan of lightly salted water to a boil, add the yams, bring back to a boil, and cook, covered, for 15–20 minutes, until tender.

3. Drain the yams well, then cover the pan with a clean dish towel and let stand for 2 minutes. Remove the skins and mash with a potato masher until fluffy.

4. Add the reserved butter to the yams and stir in evenly. Spoon the mashed yams into a serving dish and serve hot, topped with chunks of parsley butter.

# THANKSGIVING ROASTED TURKEY

SERVES: 8–10   PREP TIME: 20 MIN.   COOK TIME: 2 HR. 45 MIN.

**INGREDIENTS**

6½-pound oven-ready turkey

1 onion, halved

fresh thyme sprigs

6 tablespoons butter, softened

½ cup maple syrup

1 tablespoon finely chopped fresh thyme

1 cup chicken stock

1 tablespoon lemon juice

salt and pepper

traditional trimmings, to serve

1. Preheat the oven to 350°F. Put the turkey into a roasting pan and put the onion and thyme sprigs into the cavity.

2. Put the butter, maple syrup, and chopped thyme into a bowl and mix together. Lift the turkey skin away from the breast and spread a little of the butter mixture on the meat. Replace the skin and brush more of the glaze over the skin.

3. Sprinkle the turkey with salt and pepper and roast in the preheated oven for 2½ hours, basting occasionally with the glaze and juices. If the skin begins to overbrown, cover it loosely with aluminum foil.

4. Cook until a meat thermometer inserted into the thickest part of the meat—in the inner thigh area near the breast—without touching the bone, has a reading of 180°F. Or cook until the turkey is tender and the juices run clear when the tip of a sharp knife is inserted into the thickest part of the meat. Gently pull the leg away from the body; the leg should give and no traces of pink or blood should remain. Remove from the oven, cover with foil, and let rest for about 20 minutes before carving.

5. Skim any fat from the pan juices and stir in the stock and lemon juice. Bring to a boil and boil until slightly reduced. Season with salt and pepper.

6. Serve the turkey with the gravy and trimmings.

# CREAMED SPINACH WITH NUTMEG

SERVES: 4   PREP TIME: 5 MIN.   COOK TIME: 5 MIN.

**INGREDIENTS**

1 tablespoon butter

2 pounds young spinach

¾ cup light cream

½ teaspoon freshly grated nutmeg

salt and pepper

1. Melt the butter in a large skillet or saucepan, add the spinach, and cook, stirring, until the leaves are wilted.

2. Continue to cook over medium heat, stirring occasionally, until most of the free liquid has evaporated.

3. Stir in the cream and nutmeg, and season with salt and pepper. Serve.

THANKSGIVING
ROASTED TURKEY

# APPLE PIE

SERVES: 6–8     PREP TIME: 40 MIN. PLUS 30 MIN. CHILLING TIME     COOK TIME: 50 MIN.

### INGREDIENTS

1⅓ cups all-purpose flour

pinch of salt

6 tablespoons butter, cut into pieces

⅓ cup lard, cut into small pieces

about 1–2 tablespoons water

beaten egg or milk, for glazing

### FILLING

6–8 Granny Smith apples (about 1½–2¼ pounds), peeled, cored, and sliced

½ cup firmly packed light brown sugar, plus extra for sprinkling

½–1 teaspoon ground cinnamon

1. Sift the flour and salt into a mixing bowl. Add the butter and lard, and rub in with your fingertips until the mixture resembles fine bread crumbs. Add enough cold water to mix to a firm dough. Wrap in plastic wrap and chill for 30 minutes.

2. Preheat the oven to 425°F. Thinly roll out almost two-thirds of the dough and use to line a deep 9-inch pie plate.

3. For the filling, mix the apples with the sugar and cinnamon, and pack into the pastry shell.

4. Roll out the remaining dough to form a lid. Dampen the edges of the pie rim with water and position the lid, firmly pressing together the edges. Trim and crimp the edges. Use the dough trimmings to cut out leaves or other shapes. Dampen and attach to the top of the pie. Glaze the pie with beaten egg, make one or two slits in the top, and place the pie on a baking sheet.

5. Bake in the preheated oven for 20 minutes, then reduce the temperature to 350°F and bake for an additional 30 minutes, or until the pastry is a light golden brown. Sprinkle with sugar and serve hot or cold.

# PUMPKIN PIE

SERVES: 4–6     PREP TIME: 40 MIN.     COOK TIME: 1 HR.

### INGREDIENTS

all-purpose flour, for dusting

1 sheet rolled dough pie crust

1 (15-ounce) can pumpkin puree

2 eggs, lightly beaten

¾ cup granulated sugar

1 teaspoon ground cinnamon

½ teaspoon ground ginger

¼ teaspoon ground cloves

½ teaspoon salt

1 (12-ounce) can evaporated milk

### EGGNOG WHIPPED CREAM

1½ cups heavy cream

½ cup confectioners' sugar

1 tablespoon brandy, or to taste

1 tablespoon light or dark rum, or to taste

freshly grated nutmeg, to decorate

1. Preheat the oven to 400°F. Lightly dust a rolling pin with flour and use to roll out the dough on a lightly floured work surface into a 12-inch circle. Line a deep 9-inch pie plate with the dough, trimming the excess. Prick the bottom of the pastry shell with a fork, line with parchment paper, and fill with pie weights or dried beans. Bake the pastry shell in the preheated oven for 10 minutes, until lightly browned. Remove from the oven and remove the paper and beans. Reduce the oven temperature to 350°F.

2. Meanwhile, put the pumpkin puree, eggs, sugar, cinnamon, ginger, cloves, and salt into a bowl and beat together, then beat in the evaporated milk. Pour the mixture into the pastry shell, return to the oven, and bake for 40–50 minutes, until the filling is set and a fork inserted in the center comes out clean. Transfer to a wire rack and set aside to cool completely.

3. Meanwhile, make the eggnog whipped cream. Put the cream in a bowl and beat until it has thickened and increased in volume. Just as it starts to stiffen, sift over the confectioners' sugar and continue beating until it holds stiff peaks. Add the brandy and rum and beat, being careful not to overbeat or the mixture will separate. Cover and chill until required. When ready to serve, grate some nutmeg over the whipped cream. Serve.

APPLE PIE

# PARKER HOUSE ROLLS

MAKES: 12     PREP TIME: 40 MIN. PLUS 1 HR. 10 MIN. RESTING TIME     COOK TIME: 15 MIN.

## INGREDIENTS

½ cup milk

¼ cup water

5 tablespoons butter, softened, plus extra for brushing

2¼ cups white bread flour, plus extra for dusting

2¼ teaspoons active dry yeast

1 tablespoon sugar

½ teaspoon salt

1 extra-large egg, beaten

sunflower oil, for greasing

1. Put the milk, water, and 2 tablespoons of the butter into a small saucepan and heat to 110–113°F. Put the flour, yeast, sugar, and salt into a large bowl, stir, and make a well in the center. Slowly pour in 6 tablespoons of the milk mixture, then add the egg and beat, drawing in the flour from the side. Add the remaining milk, tablespoon by tablespoon, until a soft dough forms.

2. Grease a bowl and set aside. Invert the dough onto a lightly floured work surface and knead for 8–10 minutes, until smooth and elastic. Shape the dough into a ball, roll it around in the greased bowl, cover with plastic wrap, and set aside for 1 hour, or until doubled in size.

3. Invert the dough onto a lightly floured work surface and punch down to release the air. Cover with the upturned bowl and let rest for 10 minutes. Meanwhile, preheat the oven to 400°F and dust a baking sheet with flour. Melt the remaining butter in a small saucepan over medium heat.

4. Lightly flour a rolling pin and use to roll out the dough to a thickness of ¼ inch. Using a floured 3¼-inch round cutter, cut out 12 circles, rerolling the trimmings, if necessary. Brush the middle of a dough circle with butter. Use a floured chopstick or wooden spoon handle to make an indentation just off-center, then fold along the indentation and pinch the edges together to seal. Place on the prepared sheet, cover with a dish towel, and let rise while you shape the remaining rolls.

5. Lightly brush the tops of the rolls with butter and bake in the preheated oven for 12–15 minutes, until the rolls are golden brown and the bottoms sound hollow when tapped. Transfer to a wire rack to cool. Serve warm or at room temperature.

# SPICED APPLE MACARONS

MAKES: 16    PREP TIME: 40 MIN. PLUS 30 MIN. STANDING TIME    COOK TIME: 25 MIN.

## INGREDIENTS

¾ cup almond meal (ground almonds)

1 cup confectioners' sugar

1 teaspoon ground cinnamon

2 extra-large egg whites

¼ cup superfine sugar or granulated sugar

½ teaspoon freshly grated nutmeg

## FILLING

3 Granny Smith apples, peeled, cored, and chopped

3 tablespoons superfine sugar or granulated sugar

1 tablespoon water

1. Place the almond meal, confectioners' sugar, and cinnamon in a food processor and process for 15 seconds. Sift the mixture into a bowl. Line two baking sheets with parchment paper.

2. Place the egg whites in a large bowl and beat until holding soft peaks. Gradually beat in the superfine sugar to make a firm, glossy meringue.

3. Using a spatula, fold the almond mixture into the meringue one-third at a time. When all the dry ingredients are thoroughly incorporated, continue to cut and fold the mixture until it forms a shiny batter with a thick, ribbonlike consistency.

4. Pour the mixture into a pastry bag fitted with a ½-inch plain tip. Pipe 32 small mounds onto the prepared baking sheets. Tap the baking sheets firmly onto a work surface to remove air bubbles. Sprinkle with the grated nutmeg. Let stand at room temperature for 30 minutes. Meanwhile, preheat the oven to 325°F.

5. Bake in the preheated oven for 10–15 minutes. Let cool for 10 minutes, then carefully peel the macarons off the parchment paper. Let cool completely.

6. To make the filling, place the apples, sugar, and water in a small saucepan. Cover and simmer for 10 minutes, until soft. Mash with a fork to make a puree, then let cool. Use to sandwich together pairs of macarons.

# WHISKEY FLUMMERY

SERVES: 4        PREP TIME: 10 MIN.        COOK TIME: 1–2 MIN.

## INGREDIENTS

3 tablespoons rolled oats

1 cup heavy cream

finely grated rind and juice of
1 small orange

3 tablespoons honey

2 tablespoons whiskey

1 cup raspberries

**1.** Sprinkle the oats into a dry skillet and stir over medium heat for 1–2 minutes, until lightly toasted. Remove and cool.

**2.** Put the cream into a bowl and beat until thick, then gradually add the orange rind, orange juice, honey, and whiskey, beating until it just holds its shape.

**3.** Reserving four raspberries for decoration, stir the remainder into the mixture with the oats. Spoon into serving dishes and serve chilled, topped with the reserved raspberries.

# DECEMBER

# YULE LOG

SERVES: 8     PREP TIME: 40 MIN. PLUS COOLING TIME     COOK TIME: 15 MIN.

## INGREDIENTS

butter, for greasing

¾ cup granulated sugar, plus extra for sprinkling

4 eggs, separated

1 teaspoon almond extract

1 cup all-purpose flour, plus extra for dusting

1½ teaspoons baking powder

10 ounces semisweet dark chocolate, broken into squares

1 cup heavy cream

2 tablespoons rum

holly and confectioners' sugar, to decorate

1. Preheat the oven to 375°F. Grease and line a 16 x 11-inch jellyroll pan, then dust with flour.

2. Reserve 2 tablespoons of the granulated sugar and beat the remainder with the egg yolks in a bowl until thick and pale. Stir in the almond extract. Beat the egg whites in a separate grease-free bowl until soft peaks form. Gradually beat in the reserved sugar until stiff and glossy. Sift together the flour and baking powder. Add half the flour mixture to the egg yolk mixture and fold in, then fold in one-quarter of the egg whites. Fold in the remaining flour mixture, followed by the remaining egg whites. Spoon the batter into the pan, spreading it out evenly with a spatula. Bake in the preheated oven for 15 minutes, until lightly golden.

3. Sprinkle granulated sugar over a sheet of parchment paper and invert the cake onto the paper. Roll up and let cool.

4. Place the chocolate in a heatproof bowl. Bring the cream to boiling point in a small saucepan, then pour it over the chocolate and stir until the chocolate has melted. Beat with an electric mixer until smooth and thick. Reserve about one-third of the chocolate mixture and stir the rum into the remainder. Unroll the cake and spread the chocolate-and-rum mixture over it. Reroll and place on a plate or cake board. Spread the reserved chocolate mixture evenly over the top and sides. Mark with a fork so that the surface resembles tree bark. Just before serving, decorate with holly and a sprinkling of confectioners' sugar to resemble snow.

# PECAN PIE

SERVES: 8     PREP TIME: 35 MIN. PLUS 30 MIN. CHILLING TIME     COOK TIME: ABOUT 1 HR.

## INGREDIENTS

### PIE DOUGH

1⅔ cups all-purpose flour, plus extra for dusting

1 stick unsalted butter

2 tablespoons granulated sugar

### FILLING

4 tablespoons unsalted butter

½ cup firmly packed light brown sugar

½ cup light corn syrup

2 extra-large eggs, beaten

1 teaspoon vanilla extract

1 cup coarsely chopped pecans

1. To make the pie dough, place the flour in a bowl and rub in the butter with your fingertips until it resembles fine bread crumbs. Stir in the sugar and add enough cold water to mix to a firm dough. Wrap in plastic wrap and chill for 15 minutes, until firm enough to roll out.

2. Preheat the oven to 400°F. Roll out the dough on a lightly floured surface and use to line a 9-inch loose-bottom round tart pan. Prick the bottom with a fork. Chill for 15 minutes.

3. Place the tart tin on a baking sheet, cover with a piece of parchment paper and fill with pie weights or dried beans. Bake the pastry shell in the preheated oven for 10 minutes, until lightly browned. Remove from the oven and remove paper and weights. Put back in the oven and bake for an additional five minutes. Reduce the oven temperature to 350°F.

4. To make the filling, place the butter, sugar, and corn syrup in a saucepan and heat gently until melted. Remove from the heat and quickly beat in the eggs and vanilla extract.

5. Stir the chopped pecans into the mixture. Pour into the pastry shell and bake for 35–40 minutes, until the filling is just set. Serve warm or cold.

YULE LOG

# TURKEY SOUP WITH RICE, MUSHROOMS & SAGE

**SERVES: 4–5**     **PREP TIME: 20 MIN.**     **COOK TIME: ABOUT 1 HR.**

## INGREDIENTS

3 tablespoons butter

1 onion, finely chopped

1 celery stalk, finely chopped

25 large fresh sage leaves, finely chopped

¼ cup all-purpose flour

5 cups turkey stock or chicken stock

½ cup brown rice

3¼ cups sliced white button mushrooms

1½ cups diced cooked turkey

1 cup heavy cream

salt and pepper

sprigs of fresh sage, to garnish

freshly grated Parmesan cheese, to serve

**1.** Melt half the butter in a large saucepan over medium–low heat. Add the onion, celery, and sage and cook for 3–4 minutes, until the onion is softened, stirring frequently. Stir in the flour and continue cooking for 2 minutes.

**2.** Slowly add about one-quarter of the stock and stir well, scraping the bottom of the pan to mix in the flour. Pour in the remaining stock, stirring to combine completely, and bring just to a boil.

**3.** Stir in the rice and season with salt and pepper. Reduce the heat and simmer gently, partly covered, for about 30 minutes, until the rice is just tender, stirring occasionally.

**4.** Meanwhile, melt the remaining butter in a large skillet over medium heat. Add the mushrooms and season with salt and pepper. Cook for about 8 minutes, until they are golden brown, stirring occasionally at first, then more often after they start to brown. Add the mushrooms to the soup.

**5.** Add the turkey to the soup and stir in the cream. Continue simmering for about 10 minutes, until heated through. Taste and adjust the seasoning, if necessary. Ladle into serving bowls, garnish with sage, and serve with Parmesan cheese.

# BACON-WRAPPED ITALIAN-STYLE SAUSAGES

MAKES: 8    PREP TIME: 15 MIN.    COOK TIME: 20 MIN.

### INGREDIENTS

8 Italian-style sausages

2 tablespoons yellow mustard

24 prunes

8 bacon strips

1. Preheat the broiler. Using a sharp knife, cut a slit along the length of each sausage about three-quarters of the way through. Spread the mustard inside the slits and press 3 prunes into each sausage.

2. Wrap a strip of bacon around each sausage.

3. Place the sausages on a broiler rack and cook under the the preheated broiler, turning occasionally, for 15–20 minutes, until cooked through and browned all over.

# LAYERED CASSEROLE

SERVES: 4–6     PREP TIME: 20 MIN.     COOK TIME: ABOUT 1 HR.

## INGREDIENTS

3 tablespoons olive oil

5 parsnips, peeled and thinly sliced

1 teaspoon fresh thyme leaves

1 teaspoon granulated sugar

1¼ cups heavy cream

5 tomatoes, thinly sliced

1 teaspoon dried oregano

1½ cups shredded cheddar cheese

salt and pepper

**1**. Preheat the oven to 350°F.

**2**. Heat the oil in a skillet over medium heat, add the parsnips, thyme, and sugar, season with salt and pepper, and cook, stirring frequently, for 6–8 minutes, until golden and softened.

**3**. Spread half the parsnips over the bottom of a casserole dish. Pour over half the cream, then arrange half the tomatoes in an even layer across the parsnips. Season with salt and pepper and sprinkle over half the oregano. Sprinkle over half the cheddar cheese. Top with the remaining parsnips and tomatoes. Sprinkle with the remaining oregano, season with salt and pepper, and pour over the remaining cream. Sprinkle the remaining cheese over the top.

**4**. Cover with aluminum foil and bake in the preheated oven for 40 minutes, or until the parsnips are tender. Remove the foil and return to the oven for an additional 5–10 minutes, until the top is golden and bubbling. Serve.

LAYERED
CASSEROLE

# BANANA WALNUT LOAF CAKE

MAKES: 1 LOAF　　　PREP TIME: 10 MIN.　　　COOK TIME: ABOUT 1 HR.

### INGREDIENTS

2 cups all-purpose flour

1½ teaspoons baking powder

1 cup firmly packed
light brown sugar

½ cup chopped walnuts

2 extra-large eggs

½ cup sunflower oil,
plus extra for greasing

2 ripe bananas, mashed

½ cup milk

1 teaspoon vanilla extract

8 walnut halves

**1.** Preheat the oven to 350°F. Grease an 8-inch loaf pan and line with parchment paper.

**2.** Sift together the flour and baking powder into a mixing bowl and stir in the sugar and chopped walnuts.

**3.** Put the eggs, oil, bananas, milk, and vanilla extract into a bowl and beat together, then stir into the dry ingredients and mix together.

**4.** Spoon the batter into the prepared pan, smoothing it level with a spatula. Arrange the walnut halves over the surface.

**5.** Bake in the preheated oven for about 1 hour, or until risen, firm, and golden brown. Let cool in the pan for 15 minutes, then invert onto a wire rack to cool completely.

# SMOKED SALMON RISOTTO

SERVES: 4    PREP TIME: 20 MIN.    COOK TIME: 15–20 MIN.

## INGREDIENTS

4 tablespoons unsalted butter

1 onion, finely chopped

½ small fennel bulb, finely chopped

2½ cups risotto rice

1¼ cups white wine or vermouth

5 cups hot fish stock

6 ounces hot smoked salmon, flaked

6 ounces smoked salmon slices

2 tablespoons fresh chervil leaves or chopped flat-leaf parsley

salt and pepper

**1.** Melt half the butter in a large saucepan over medium heat, add the onion and fennel, and cook, stirring frequently, for 5–8 minutes, until transparent and soft. Add the rice and stir well to coat the grains in the butter. Cook, stirring, for 3 minutes, then add the wine, stir, and let simmer until most of the liquid has been absorbed.

**2.** With the stock simmering in a separate saucepan, add a ladleful to the rice and stir well. Cook, stirring continuously, until nearly all the liquid has been absorbed before adding another ladleful of stock. Continue to add the remaining stock in the same way until the rice is cooked but still firm to the bite and most or all of the stock has been added.

**3.** Remove from the heat and stir in the two types of salmon and the remaining butter. Season with salt and pepper and serve sprinkled with the chervil.

# CRANBERRY & PINE NUT BISCOTTI

MAKES: 18–20     PREP TIME: 35 MIN. PLUS 3–4 MIN. COOLING TIME     COOK TIME: 35 MIN.

## INGREDIENTS

butter or oil, for greasing

⅓ cup firmly packed light brown sugar

1 extra-large egg

1¼ cups all-purpose flour, plus extra for dusting

½ teaspoon baking powder

1 teaspoon ground allspice

⅓ cup dried cranberries

⅓ cup pine nuts, toasted

1. Preheat the oven to 350°F. Grease a baking sheet.

2. Beat together the sugar and egg until pale and thick enough to form a trail when the beaters are lifted.

3. Sift the flour, baking powder, and allspice and fold into the mixture. Stir in the cranberries and pine nuts and mix lightly to a smooth dough.

4. With lightly floured hands, shape the mixture into a long roll, about 12 inches long. Press to flatten slightly.

5. Lift the dough onto the baking sheet and bake in the preheated oven for 20–25 minutes, until golden. Do not turn off the oven.

6. Cool for 3–4 minutes, then cut into ½-inch thick slices and arrange on the baking sheet.

7. Bake in the oven for 10 minutes, or until golden. Remove from the oven, transfer to a wire rack, and let cool.

# CHRISTMAS TREE COOKIES

MAKES: 12     PREP TIME: 35 MIN. PLUS 45 MIN. CHILLING TIME     COOK TIME: ABOUT 10 MIN.

## INGREDIENTS

1¼ cups all-purpose flour, plus extra for dusting

1 teaspoon ground cinnamon

½ teaspoon ground nutmeg

½ teaspoon ground ginger

5 tablespoons unsalted butter, diced, plus extra for greasing

3 tablespoons honey

White Icing (optional, see page 357) and narrow gold or silver ribbon, to decorate

1. Sift the flour and spices into a bowl and rub in the butter until the mixture resembles bread crumbs. Add the honey and mix together well to form a soft dough. Wrap the dough in plastic wrap and chill in the refrigerator for 30 minutes.

2. Meanwhile, preheat the oven to 350°F and lightly grease two baking sheets with butter. Divide the dough in half. Roll out a piece of dough on a floured work surface to about ¼ inch thick. Cut out tree shapes using a cutter or cardboard template. Repeat with the remaining piece of dough.

3. Put the cookies on the prepared baking sheets and, using a toothpick, make a hole through the top of each cookie large enough to thread the ribbon through. Chill in the refrigerator for 15 minutes.

4. Bake the cookies in the preheated oven for 10–12 minutes, until golden. Let cool on the baking sheets for 5 minutes, then transfer to a wire rack to cool completely. Decorate the trees with White Icing, or simply leave them plain, then thread a length of ribbon through each hole and knot.

# SNOWFLAKE CHRISTMAS WHOOPIE PIES

MAKES: 14     PREP TIME: 40 MIN.     COOK TIME: ABOUT 10 MIN.

### INGREDIENTS

2⅔ cups all-purpose flour

2 teaspoons baking powder

large pinch of salt

½ cup almond meal (ground almonds)

1 stick butter, softened

¾ cup granulated sugar, plus extra for sprinkling

1 extra-large egg, beaten

1 teaspoon almond extract

½ cup milk

1 tablespoon edible silver balls

### BUTTERCREAM

1¼ sticks unsalted butter, softened

½ cup heavy cream

2¼ cups confectioners' sugar, sifted

### WHITE ICING

1 cup confectioners' sugar

1–2 tablespoons warm water

**1.** Preheat the oven to 350°F. Line two to three large baking sheets with parchment paper. Sift together the all-purpose flour, baking powder, and salt. Stir in the almond meal.

**2.** Place the butter and sugar in a large bowl and beat with an electric mixer until pale and fluffy. Beat in the egg and almond extract, followed by half the flour mixture and then the milk. Stir in the rest of the flour mixture and beat until thoroughly incorporated.

**3.** Pipe or spoon 28 mounds of the mixture onto the prepared baking sheets, spaced well apart to allow for spreading. Bake in the preheated oven, one sheet at a time, for 10–12 minutes, until risen and just firm to the touch. Cool for 5 minutes, then, using a spatula, transfer to a wire rack and let cool completely.

**4.** For the buttercream, place the butter in a bowl and beat with an electric mixer for 2–3 minutes, until pale and creamy. Beat in the cream, then gradually beat in the confectioners' sugar and continue beating for 2–3 minutes, until the buttercream is light and fluffy.

**5.** For the white icing, sift the confectioners' sugar into a bowl and gradually stir in enough water to make a smooth, thick icing that is thick enough to coat the back of a wooden spoon.

**6.** To assemble, spread or pipe the buttercream on the flat side of half of the cakes. Top with the rest of the cakes. Spoon the icing into a small paper pastry bag, snip the end, and pipe snowflake patterns on the top of the whoopie pies. Decorate with silver balls and sprinkle with granulated sugar. Let set.

# 11 DECEMBER

# TUSCAN CHRISTMAS CAKE

**SERVES: 14     PREP TIME: 50 MIN.     COOK TIME: 1½ HR.**

### INGREDIENTS

1 cup hazelnuts

1 cup almonds

½ cup chopped candied peel

½ cup finely chopped dried apricots

⅓ cup finely chopped candied pineapple

grated rind of 1 orange

½ cup all-purpose flour

2 tablespoons unsweetened cocoa powder

1 teaspoon ground cinnamon

¼ teaspoon ground coriander

¼ teaspoon freshly grated nutmeg

¼ teaspoon ground cloves

½ cup granulated sugar

¾ cup honey

1. Preheat the oven to 350°F. Line an 8-inch round loose-bottom cake pan with parchment paper.

2. Spread out the hazelnuts on a baking sheet and toast in the preheated oven for 10 minutes, until golden brown. Transfer to a dish towel and rub off the skins.

3. Meanwhile, spread out the almonds on a baking sheet and toast in the oven for 10 minutes, until golden. Watch carefully because they burn easily.

4. Reduce the oven temperature to 300°F. Chop all the nuts and place in a large bowl. Add the candied peel, apricots, pineapple, and orange rind to the nuts and mix well.

5. Sift the flour, cocoa, cinnamon, coriander, nutmeg, and cloves into the bowl and mix well.

6. Put the sugar and honey into a saucepan and set over low heat, stirring, until the sugar has dissolved. Bring to a boil and cook for 5 minutes, until thickened and beginning to darken.

7. Stir the nut mixture into the saucepan and remove from the heat.

8. Spoon the batter into the prepared cake pan and smooth the surface. Bake in the oven for 1 hour, then transfer to a wire rack to cool. When cold, carefully remove from the pan and peel off the parchment paper.

# 12 DECEMBER

# GOLDEN CHRISTMAS CAKE

**SERVES: 16–18     PREP TIME: 50 MIN.     COOK TIME: 2 HR.**

### INGREDIENTS

1⅓ cups chopped dried apricots

⅔ cup chopped dried mango

½ cup chopped dried pineapple

1¼ cups golden raisins

4 pieces preserved ginger, chopped

⅓ cup chopped candied peel

finely grated rind and juice of 1 orange

¼ cup brandy

1½ sticks unsalted butter

½ cup firmly packed light brown sugar

4 eggs, beaten

2 tablespoons honey

1⅓ cups all-purpose flour

2 teaspoons baking powder

2 teaspoons ground allspice

1 cup pecans

1. Place the chopped apricots, mango, and pineapple in a bowl with the golden raisins, preserved ginger, and candied peel. Stir in the orange rind, orange juice, and brandy. Cover the bowl and let soak overnight.

2. Preheat the oven to 325°F. Grease a 9-inch round springform cake pan and line with parchment paper.

3. Cream together the butter and sugar until the mixture is pale and fluffy. Add the eggs to the mixture, one at a time, beating well between each addition. Stir in the honey.

4. Sift the flour and baking powder with the allspice and fold into the mixture, using a metal spoon. Add the soaked fruit and pecans and mix well. Spoon the batter into the prepared pan, spreading evenly, then make a slight dip in the center.

5. Place the pan in the center of the preheated oven and bake for 1½–2 hours, or until golden brown and firm to the touch and a toothpick inserted into the center comes out clean. Let cool in the pan.

6. Invert the cake, remove the parchment paper, and rewrap in clean parchment paper and aluminum foil. Store in a cool place for at least 1 month before serving.

TUSCAN
CHRISTMAS CAKE

# POTATO PANCAKES

**SERVES: 8**   **PREP TIME: 10 MIN.**   **COOK TIME: 10–15 MIN.**

## INGREDIENTS

8 Yukon gold potatoes (about 2¼ pounds)

1 onion

¼ cup all-purpose flour

1 egg, beaten

sunflower oil, for pan-frying

salt and pepper

sour cream, to serve

**1.** Finely grate the potatoes and onion. Put them into a strainer and press out as much liquid as possible, then spread out on a clean dish towel. Roll and twist to remove any remaining moisture.

**2.** Place the grated vegetables in a bowl and stir in the flour. Stir in the egg and season well with salt and pepper.

**3.** Heat a shallow depth of oil in a skillet until medium–hot. Drop heaping tablespoonfuls of the mixture into the pan, pressing with a spatula to flatten, and cook in batches, turning once, for 8–10 minutes, until golden brown and cooked through.

**4.** Drain the pancakes on paper towels and keep warm while you cook the remaining mixture. Serve hot with sour cream.

# COMPOTE OF DRIED FRUITS

SERVES: 4–6     PREP TIME: 5 MIN.     COOK TIME: 20 MIN.

### INGREDIENTS

1 cup dried apricots

1 cup pitted prunes

2 cups halved dried apple slices

⅓ cup dried cranberries

2 cups orange juice

2 pieces preserved ginger in syrup, drained and chopped, 2 tablespoons syrup reserved

whipped cream or yogurt, to serve

**1.** Put the dried apricots, prunes, apple, and cranberries into a saucepan and pour the orange juice over them.

**2.** Bring to a boil over medium heat, then stir in the ginger and reserved syrup. Reduce the heat to low, cover, and simmer gently for about 15 minutes, until the fruit is soft.

**3.** Lift out the fruit with a slotted spoon and place in a serving dish. Simmer the juice, uncovered, for 3–4 minutes, until reduced and slightly thickened.

**4.** Pour the syrup over the fruit and serve warm or cold with whipped cream.

# CRANBERRY APPLE MERINGUES

SERVES: 4 · PREP TIME: **10 MIN.** · COOK TIME: **20 MIN.**

### INGREDIENTS

3 Granny Smith or Pippin apples

1 tablespoon apple juice

1 cup superfine sugar
or granulated sugar

⅔ cup dried cranberries

2 egg whites

**1.** Preheat the oven to 400°F. Peel, core, and chop the apples, place in a saucepan, and sprinkle with the apple juice.

**2.** Add ⅓ cup of the sugar and the cranberries, stir, and heat gently until boiling. Cover the pan, reduce the heat, and simmer gently, stirring occasionally, for 8–10 minutes, until the fruit is just tender.

**3.** Divide the fruit among four 1½-cup ovenproof dishes and place on a baking sheet.

**4.** Put the egg whites into a grease-free bowl and beat until they hold soft peaks. Gradually beat in the remaining sugar until the mixture holds stiff peaks.

**5.** Spoon the meringue on top of the fruit, swirling with a knife. Bake in the preheated oven for 10–12 minutes, until the meringue is lightly browned. Serve warm.

# 16 DECEMBER

# MIXED NUT ROAST

SERVES: 4     PREP TIME: 35 MIN.     COOK TIME: 35 MIN.

## INGREDIENTS

2 tablespoons butter, plus extra for greasing

2 garlic cloves, chopped

1 large onion, chopped

⅓ cup pine nuts, toasted

¾ cup hazelnuts, toasted

¾ cup ground walnuts

½ cup ground cashew nuts

2 cups fresh whole wheat bread crumbs

1 egg, lightly beaten

2 tablespoons chopped fresh thyme

1 cup vegetable stock

salt and pepper

fresh thyme sprigs, to garnish

cranberry sauce, to serve

1. Preheat the oven to 350°F. Grease an 8-inch loaf pan with butter and line it with parchment paper. Melt the butter in a saucepan over medium heat. Add the garlic and onion and cook, stirring, for 5 minutes, until softened. Remove from the heat. Grind the pine nuts and hazelnuts. Stir all the nuts into the saucepan, add the bread crumbs, egg, thyme, and stock, and season with salt and pepper.

2. Spoon the mixture into the loaf pan and level the surface. Cook in the preheated oven for 30 minutes, or until cooked through and golden. The loaf is cooked when the tines of a fork inserted into the center come out clean.

3. Remove the nut roast from the oven and invert onto a serving dish. Garnish with thyme sprigs and serve with cranberry sauce.

# 17 DECEMBER

# POACHED SALMON

SERVES: 8–12     PREP TIME: 15 MIN.     COOK TIME: 25 MIN.

## INGREDIENTS

16 cups water

⅓ cup white wine vinegar

1 large onion, sliced

2 carrots, sliced

1½ tablespoons salt

1 teaspoon black peppercorns

6-pound salmon, cleaned, with gills and eyes removed

## TO SERVE

salad greens

1 cucumber, thinly sliced

lemon wedges

1. To make a stock in which to poach the fish, put the water, vinegar, onion, carrots, salt, and peppercorns in a large fish poacher or covered roasting pan and bring to a boil. Reduce the heat and simmer for 20 minutes. Remove the trivet (if using a fish poacher) and lay the salmon on it. Lower it into the stock, cover, return to simmering point, and cook for 5 minutes. Turn off the heat and let the fish rest in it, covered, to cool in the liquid.

2. When the fish is cold, lift it out of the poacher on the trivet and drain well. Using two spatulas, carefully transfer to a board. Using a sharp knife, remove the head, then slit the skin along the backbone and peel off. Carefully turn the fish over and peel off the skin on the other side.

3. To serve, line a serving platter with salad greens and cucumber and carefully transfer the salmon to the platter. Serve with lemon wedges.

**MIXED NUT
ROAST**

# CHOCOLATE BRANDY TRUFFLES

**MAKES: ABOUT 26**     **PREP TIME: 20 MIN. PLUS COOLING TIME**     **COOK TIME: 5 MIN.**

### INGREDIENTS

8 ounces semisweet dark chocolate

¾ cup heavy cream

3 tablespoons brandy

2 tablespoons confectioners' sugar

unsweetened cocoa powder, for dusting

**1.** Break the chocolate into small pieces and place in a bowl.

**2.** Pour the cream into a small saucepan and heat over low heat until almost boiling. Remove from the heat and add the chocolate, stirring until melted and smooth.

**3.** Stir in the brandy and sugar and beat well with a wooden spoon. Let cool until the mixture is firm enough to hold its shape.

**4.** Put the cocoa powder into a shallow bowl and use some to lightly dust your hands. Use a teaspoon to scoop small pieces of mixture and roll into balls with your hands.

**5.** Roll the balls in the cocoa powder until lightly coated, then chill until firm.

**6.** Serve the truffles piled on a dish, or in small paper liners.

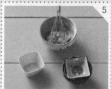

# CHRISTMAS MACARONS

MAKES: 16    PREP TIME: 40 MIN. PLUS 30 MIN. STANDING TIME    COOK TIME: 15 MIN.

## INGREDIENTS

¾ cup almond meal (ground almonds)

1 cup confectioners' sugar

1 teaspoon ground allspice

2 extra-large egg whites

¼ cup superfine sugar
or granulated sugar

½ teaspoon freshly grated nutmeg

1 teaspoon golden balls

## FILLING

4 tablespoons unsalted butter,
softened

juice and finely grated
rind of ½ orange

1 teaspoon ground allspice

1 cup confectioners' sugar, sifted

2 tablespoons finely chopped
candied cherries

**1.** Place the almond meal, confectioners' sugar, and allspice in a food processor and process for 15 seconds. Sift the mixture into a bowl. Line two baking sheets with parchment paper.

**2.** Place the egg whites in a large bowl and beat until they hold soft peaks. Gradually beat in the superfine sugar to make a firm, glossy meringue. Using a spatula, fold the almond mixture into the meringue one-third at a time. When all the dry ingredients are thoroughly incorporated, continue to cut and fold the mixture until it forms a shiny batter with a thick, ribbonlike consistency.

**3.** Pour the mixture into a pastry bag fitted with a ½-inch plain tip. Pipe 32 small mounds onto the prepared baking sheets. Tap the baking sheets firmly onto a work surface to remove air bubbles. Sprinkle half the macarons with the grated nutmeg and golden balls. Let stand at room temperature for 30 minutes. Meanwhile, preheat the oven to 325°F.

**4.** Bake in the preheated oven for 10–15 minutes. Cool for 10 minutes, then carefully peel the macarons off the paper. Let cool completely.

**5.** To make the filling, beat the butter, orange juice, and orange rind in a bowl until fluffy. Gradually beat in the allspice and confectioners' sugar until smooth and creamy. Fold in the candied cherries. Use to sandwich together pairs of macarons.

# BRUSSELS SPROUTS WITH CHESTNUTS

SERVES: 4    PREP TIME: 10 MIN.    COOK TIME: 10 MIN.

## INGREDIENTS

4 cups Brussels sprouts (about 12 ounces), trimmed

3 tablespoons butter

1 cup canned whole chestnuts

pinch of grated nutmeg

salt and pepper

slivered almonds, to garnish

1. Bring a large saucepan of lightly salted water to a boil. Add the Brussels sprouts and cook for 5 minutes. Drain thoroughly.

2. Melt the butter in a large saucepan over medium heat. Add the Brussels sprouts and cook, stirring, for 3 minutes, then add the chestnuts and nutmeg. Season with salt and pepper and stir well. Cook for an additional 2 minutes, stirring, then remove from the heat. Transfer to a serving dish, sprinkle the almonds over them and serve.

# PORK, CRANBERRY & HERB STUFFING

SERVES: 6    PREP TIME: 20 MIN.    COOK TIME: 35 MIN.

## INGREDIENTS

1 tablespoon vegetable oil, plus extra for oiling

1 onion, finely chopped

2 celery stalks, chopped

1 pound bulk sausage or sausage meat with the casings removed

1 cup fresh white or whole-wheat bread crumbs

⅓ cup dried cranberries

¾ cup fresh cranberries

1 tablespoon chopped fresh parsley

1 tablespoon chopped fresh sage

1 tablespoon chopped fresh thyme

1 extra-large egg, beaten

salt and pepper

1. Heat the oil in a heavy skillet over medium heat, add the onion and celery, and cook, stirring frequently, for 10 minutes, until the onion is transparent and soft.

2. Meanwhile, preheat the oven to 375°F and oil a baking sheet. Break up the sausage meat in a large bowl. Add the bread crumbs, dried and fresh cranberries, and the herbs and mix together well. Add the cooked onion and celery, then the egg. Season well with salt and pepper and mix together thoroughly.

3. Form the stuffing into balls, place on the prepared baking sheet, and bake in the preheated oven for 25 minutes. Alternatively, spoon into two disposable foil pans, level the surface, and bake for 45 minutes.

# MANGO & MACADAMIA STUFFING

SERVES: 4–6    PREP TIME: 10 MIN.    COOK TIME: 30 MIN.

### INGREDIENTS

2 tablespoons butter,
plus extra for greasing

1 small onion, finely chopped

1 celery stalk, diced

4 cups fresh white bread crumbs

1 egg, beaten

1 tablespoon Dijon mustard

1 small mango,
peeled, pitted, and diced

½ cup chopped macadamia nuts

salt and pepper

**1.** Preheat the oven to 400°F. Grease a 1-quart ovenproof dish.

**2.** Melt the butter in a saucepan, add the onion, and sauté, stirring, for 3–4 minutes, until soft. Add the celery and cook for an additional 2 minutes.

**3.** Remove from the heat and stir in the bread crumbs, egg, and mustard. Add the mango and nuts, then season with salt and pepper.

**4.** Spread the mixture into the prepared dish and bake in the preheated oven for 20–25 minutes, until golden and bubbling.

# CRANBERRY SAUCE

SERVES: 8　　PREP TIME: 20 MIN.　　COOK TIME: 5 MIN.

### INGREDIENTS

thinly pared rind and juice
of 1 lemon

thinly pared rind and juice
of 1 orange

3½ cups cranberries,
thawed if frozen

¾ cup granulated sugar

2 tablespoons arrowroot, mixed with
3 tablespoons cold water

1. Place the lemon and orange rind in a heavy saucepan. If using fresh cranberries, rinse well and remove any stems. Add the cranberries, lemon juice, orange juice, and sugar to the saucepan and cook over medium heat, stirring occasionally, for 5 minutes, or until the cranberries begin to burst.

2. Strain the juice into a clean saucepan and reserve the cranberries. Stir the arrowroot mixture into the juice, then bring to a boil, stirring continuously, until the sauce is smooth and thickened. Remove from the heat and stir in the reserved cranberries.

3. Transfer the cranberry sauce to a bowl and let cool, then cover with plastic wrap and chill in the refrigerator until ready to use.

# BAKED GLAZED HAM

SERVES: 8　　PREP TIME: 20 MIN.　　COOK TIME: 4 HR. 20 MIN.

### INGREDIENTS

8¾-pound uncooked ham

1 apple, cored and chopped

1 onion, chopped

1¼ cups beer

6 black peppercorns

1 bouquet garni of sprigs of parsley
and thyme tied together

1 bay leaf

about 50 cloves

¼ cup raw brown sugar

1. Put the ham in a large saucepan and add enough cold water to cover. Bring to a boil and skim off the scum that rises to the surface. Reduce the heat and simmer for 30 minutes. Drain the ham and return to the saucepan. Add the apple, onion, beer, peppercorns, bouquet garni, bay leaf, and a few of the cloves. Pour in enough fresh water to cover and return to a boil. Reduce the heat, cover, and simmer for 3 hours 20 minutes.

2. Preheat the oven to 400°F. Take the saucepan off the heat and set aside to cool slightly. Remove the ham from the cooking liquid and, while it is still warm, loosen the rind with a sharp knife, then peel it off and discard. Score the fat into diamond shapes and stud with the remaining cloves. Place the ham on a rack in a roasting pan and sprinkle with the sugar. Roast in the oven, basting occasionally with the cooking liquid, for 20 minutes. Serve hot, or cold later.

CRANBERRY
SAUCE

# TRADITIONAL ROASTED TURKEY

SERVES: 4    PREP TIME: 25 MIN. PLUS 25 MIN. STANDING TIME    COOK TIME: 3 HR. 15 MIN.

## INGREDIENTS

10–12-pound oven-ready turkey

1 garlic clove, finely chopped

½ cup red wine

6 tablespoons butter

seasonal vegetables, to serve

## STUFFING

1½ cups white button mushrooms

1 onion, chopped

1 garlic clove, chopped

6 tablespoons butter

2 cups fresh bread crumbs

2 tablespoons finely chopped fresh sage

1 tablespoon lemon juice

salt and pepper

## PORT & CRANBERRY SAUCE

½ cup granulated sugar

1 cup port

2 cups fresh cranberries

1. Preheat the oven to 400°F.

2. To make the stuffing, clean and chop the mushrooms, put them in a saucepan with the onion, garlic, and butter, and cook for 3 minutes. Remove from the heat and stir in the remaining stuffing ingredients, including salt and pepper to taste. Rinse the turkey and pat dry with paper towels. Fill the neck end with stuffing and truss with string.

3. Put the turkey in a roasting pan. Rub the garlic over the bird and pour the wine over it. Add the butter and roast in the oven for 30 minutes. Baste, then reduce the temperature to 350°F and roast for an additional 40 minutes. Baste again and cover with aluminum foil. Roast for an additional 2 hours, basting regularly, or until a meat thermometer inserted into the thickest part of the meat—in the inner thigh area near the breast—without touching the bone, has a reading of 180°F. The stuffing is ready when a meat thermometer inserted into the stuffing in the cavity reads 165°F. If you don't have a meat thermometer, cook until the turkey is tender and the juices run clear when the tip of a sharp knife is inserted into the thickest part of the meat. Gently pull the leg away from the body; the leg should give and no traces of pink or blood should remain. Remove from the oven, cover with foil, and let stand for 25 minutes.

4. Meanwhile, put the sugar, port, and cranberries in a saucepan. Heat over medium heat until almost boiling. Serve the turkey with seasonal vegetables and the port-and-cranberry sauce.

TRADITIONAL
ROASTED TURKEY

# TURKEY CLUB SANDWICHES

MAKES: 6   PREP TIME: 30 MIN.   COOK TIME: 10 MIN.

### INGREDIENTS

12 bacon strips

18 slices white bread

12 slices cooked turkey breast

3 plum tomatoes, sliced

6 Boston lettuce leaves

6 stuffed olives

salt and pepper

### MAYONNAISE

2 extra-large egg yolks

1 teaspoon dried mustard

1 teaspoon salt

1¼ cups olive oil

1 teaspoon white wine vinegar

1. First make the mayonnaise. Put the egg yolks in a bowl, add the mustard and salt, season with pepper, and beat together well. Pour the oil into a bowl. Using an electric mixer, begin to beat the egg yolks, adding just one drop of the oil. Make sure that this has been thoroughly absorbed before adding another drop and beating well.

2. Continue adding the oil, a drop at a time, until the mixture thickens and stiffens—at this point, beat in the vinegar and then continue to dribble in the remaining oil slowly in a thin stream, beating continuously, until you have used all the oil and you have a thick mayonnaise. Cover and refrigerate while you prepare the other sandwich components.

3. Broil or fry the bacon until crisp, drain on paper towels, and keep warm. Toast the bread until golden, then cut off the crusts. You will need three slices of toast for each sandwich. For each sandwich, spread the first piece of toast with a generous amount of mayonnaise, top with two slices of turkey, keeping the edges neat, and then top with a couple of slices of tomato. Season with salt and pepper. Add another slice of toast and top with two bacon strips and one lettuce leaf. Season again, add a little more mayonnaise, then top with the final piece of toast. Push a decorative toothpick through a stuffed olive, and then push this through the sandwich to hold it together.

# CRANBERRY & ORANGE PIES

MAKES: 12   PREP TIME: 25 MIN.   COOK TIME: 30 MIN.

### INGREDIENTS

butter, for greasing

1¾ cups frozen cranberries

1 tablespoon cornstarch

3 tablespoons freshly squeezed orange juice

2 star anise

¼ cup granulated sugar, plus extra for sprinkling

1 sheet rolled dough pie crust, chilled

flour, for dusting

milk, for glazing

1. Preheat the oven to 350°F. Lightly grease a 12-cup mini muffin pan.

2. Put the still-frozen cranberries in a medium saucepan with the cornstarch and orange juice. Add the star anise and cook uncovered, over low heat, stirring from time to time, for 5 minutes, or until the cranberries have softened. Add the sugar and cook for an additional 5 minutes, then let cool.

3. Roll out the dough thinly on a lightly floured surface. Using a fluted pastry cutter, stamp out 12 circles, each 2½ inches in diameter. Press these gently into the prepared pan, rerolling the trimmings as needed. Squeeze together any remaining trimmings and reserve. Brush the top edges of the pie shells with a little milk. Discard the star anise, then spoon in the filling.

4. Roll out the remaining dough thinly on a lightly floured surface. Using a fluted pastry wheel, cut thin strips of pastry. Arrange these over each pie and brush with a little milk. Sprinkle with a little sugar. Bake in the preheated oven for 20 minutes, covering with aluminum foil after 10 minutes if the tops brown too quickly. Let cool in the pan for 10 minutes, then loosen with a blunt knife and transfer to a wire rack to cool.

**TURKEY CLUB
SANDWICHES**

# MULLED WINE

MAKES: 14 cups (3½ quarts)    PREP TIME: 20 MIN.    COOK TIME: 15 MIN.

### INGREDIENTS

5 oranges

50 cloves

thinly pared rind and juice of 4 lemons

3½ cups water

½ cup granulated sugar

2 cinnamon sticks

2 standard-size bottles red wine

⅔ cup brandy

**1.** Prick the skins of three of the oranges all over with a fork and stud with the cloves, then set aside. Thinly pare the rind and squeeze the juice from the remaining oranges.

**2.** Put the orange rind, orange juice, lemon rind, lemon juice, water, sugar, and cinnamon in a heavy saucepan and bring to a boil over medium heat, stirring occasionally, until the sugar has dissolved. Boil for 2 minutes without stirring, then remove from the heat, stir once, and let stand for 10 minutes. Strain the liquid into a heatproof bowl, pushing down on the contents of the strainer to extract all the juice.

**3.** Pour the wine into a separate saucepan and add the strained spiced juices, the brandy, and the clove-studded oranges. Simmer gently without boiling, then remove the saucepan from the heat. Strain into heatproof glasses and serve.

# EGGNOG

SERVES: 4–6    PREP TIME: 5 MIN.    COOK TIME: NO COOKING

### INGREDIENTS

1 egg

1 tablespoon confectioners' sugar

⅓ cup brandy

warm milk

freshly grated nutmeg, to decorate

**1.** Beat together the first three ingredients, strain into tall glasses, and fill with milk. Sprinkle with the nutmeg and serve.

# RICH CHICKEN CASSEROLE

SERVES: 4          PREP TIME: 15 MIN.          COOK TIME: ABOUT 1 HR. 10 MIN.

## INGREDIENTS

2 tablespoons olive oil

8 chicken thighs

1 medium red onion, sliced

2 garlic cloves, crushed

1 large red bell pepper, seeded and thickly sliced

thinly pared rind and juice of 1 small orange

½ cup chicken stock

1 (14½-ounce) can diced tomatoes

½ cup thinly sliced sun-dried tomatoes

1 tablespoon chopped fresh thyme

½ cup pitted ripe black olives

salt and pepper

thyme sprigs and orange rind, to garnish

1. In a heavy or nonstick large skillet, heat the oil and cook the chicken over high heat, turning occasionally until golden brown. Using a slotted spoon, drain off any excess fat from the chicken and transfer to a flameproof casserole dish.

2. Sauté the onion, garlic, and red bell pepper in the skillet over moderate heat for 3–4 minutes. Transfer the vegetables to the casserole dish.

3. Add the orange rind, orange juice, chicken stock, canned tomatoes, and sun-dried tomatoes and stir to combine.

4. Bring to a boil on the stove, then cover the casserole dish with a lid and simmer gently over low heat for about 1 hour, stirring occasionally. Add the thyme and olives, then season with salt and pepper.

5. The chicken is done when a fork can be easily inserted into the thickest part of the meat with ease and the juices run clear. A meat thermometer inserted into the thickest part of the meat, without touching the bone, should read 170°F. Sprinkle with the thyme sprigs and orange rind to garnish and serve.

# TROPICAL FRUIT DESSERT

**SERVES: 6**     **PREP TIME: 20 MIN.**     **COOK TIME: NO COOKING**

## INGREDIENTS

14 amaretti cookies

3 tablespoons white rum

½ cup orange juice

1 papaya, halved, seeded, peeled, and chopped

½ small pineapple, cored and chopped

2 kiwis, peeled and chopped

1¼ cups heavy whipping cream

1 teaspoon vanilla extract

toasted flaked dried coconut, to decorate

**1.** Coarsely crumble the amaretti into a glass serving bowl and sprinkle with the rum and orange juice.

**2.** Mix together the papaya, pineapple, and kiwis and spread over the amaretti.

**3.** Beat the cream with the vanilla extract until it just holds its shape, then spoon over the fruit.

**4.** Sprinkle the toasted coconut over the cream and serve chilled.

# Quick Reference Index

Turbot Steaks with Parsley, Lemon & Garlic 114
Wine-Steamed Mussels 194

## Ham

Bacon & Chicken Burgers 238
Bacon-Wrapped Italian-Style sausages 351
Baked Glazed Ham 370
Baked Ham with Hoisin & Honey Glaze 8
Bacon Cheeseburgers 194
Chorizo & Cheese Quesadillas 294
Farfalle with Blue Cheese & Ham 334
Ham & Mushroom Quiche 324
Meatloaf 300
Paprika Pork 304
Pork Chops Braised with Shallots 64
Pork Chops with Applesauce 286
Pork, Cranberry & Herb Stuffing 368
Quick Ham & Pineapple Stir-Fry 110
Romaine, Bacon & Blue Cheese Salad 210
Sausage & beer casserole 270
Slow-Cooked Potato Stew 28
Toasted Muffins with Blueberries
   & Bacon 152

## Lamb

Irish Stew 82
Lamb Casserole with Dates 112
Lamb Chops in Tomato Sauce 290
Lamb Koftas with Thyme & Lemon Dip 207
Lamb Stew 47
Meatloaf 300
Peppered Lamb 107

## Pasta

Chicken & Wild Mushroom Cannelloni 279
Farfalle with Blue Cheese & Ham 334
Fresh Tomato Soup with Pasta 299
Fusilli with Zucchini & Lemon 132
Ham & Spinach Pasta 44
Honey & Mustard Chicken Pasta Salad 149
Lasagna 276
Macaroni & Seafood Casserole 92
Pasta with Pesto 74
Pasta with Arugula & Mozzarella 170
Penne in Tomato sauce with
   Two Cheeses 15
Penne with Turkey Meatballs 84
Pepperoni Pasta 110
Salami Pasta Salad 269
Spaghetti Carbonara 14
Spaghetti with Meat Sauce 58
Spaghetti with Fresh Pea Pesto 146
Spaghetti with Meatballs 122
Spaghetti with Tomatoes &
   Black Olives 214

## Potatoes

Bean Casserole with Potatoes, Corn &
   Squash 309
Chunky Potato & Spinach Curry 326
Fish & Potato Stew 302
Fresh Potato Salad 139
Italian-Style Sausages & Mashed Potatoes 261
Mashed Potatoes 294
Mashed Potatoes with Scallions 82
New Potatoes with Garlic & Chile Butter 88
Potato & Bacon Casserole 92
Potato Gnocchi 262
Potato Kabobs with Feta 211
Potato Pancakes 360
Potato Stew, Slow-Cooked 28
Pot Roast with Potatoes & Dill 300
Roasted Potatoes 48
Scalloped Potatoes 254
Soufflé Baked Potatoes 284

## Soups

Barley, Lentil & Onion Soup 12
Broccoli & Blue Cheese Soup 53
Carrot & Cilantro Soup 74
Chicken & Corn Soup 320
Chicken Soup with Rice 18
Chilled Beet Soup 254
Chilled Pea Soup 217
French Onion Soup 308
Fresh Tomato Soup with Pasta 299
Gazpacho 205
Shrimp Noodle Soup 178
Squash, Sweet Potato & Garlic Soup 322
Turkey & Lentil Soup 10
Turkey Soup with Rice, Mushrooms
   & Sage 350

## Turkey

Chili-Spiced Maple-Glazed Turkey Cutlets 319
Creamy Turkey & Broccoli Gnocchi 34
Lemon Turkey with Spinach 111
Mexican Turkey Burgers 182
Mexican Turkey Cutlets 208
Paprika Turkey Strips 61
Penne with Turkey Meatballs 84
Spicy Turkey & Sausage Kabobs 208
Tarragon Turkey 238
Thanksgiving Roasted Turkey 338
Traditional Roasted Turkey 372
Turkey & Lentil Soup 10
Turkey Casserole with Cabbage & Dill 76
Turkey Club Sandwiches 374
Turkey Cutlets with Lima Beans 118
Turkey Cutlets with Tarragon Sauce 76
Turkey Salad Pita 184

Turkey Scallops with Prosciutto & Sage 34
Turkey Soup with Rice, Mushrooms
   & Sage 350
Turkey Teriyaki 168
Turkey with Mole Sauce 250

## Vegetarian Dishes (* see also Pasta, Potatoes, Soups)

Asparagus & Tomato Tart 134
Asparagus with Lemon Butter Sauce 106
Avocado, Feta & Arugula Salad 204
Baked Beans with Corn 276
Baked Pumpkin with Gruyère Cheese 311
Baked Sweet Potato with Garlic Salsa 334
Bean Casserole with Potatoes, Corn &
   Squash 309
Brussels Sprouts with Chestnuts 368
Caesar Salad 193
Caramelized Onion Tart 52
Chunky Potato & Spinach Curry 326
Coleslaw 224
Corn & Chive Fritters 112
Corn on the Cob with Blue Cheese
   Dressing 240
Creamed Spinach with Nutmeg 338
Green Bean Casserole 336
Garlic & Herb Bread Spiral 152
Hush Puppies 260
Layered Casserole 352
Leek & Goat Cheese Tarts 68
Mâche & Cucumber Salad with Figs 160
Mashed Potatoes with Scallions 82
Mashed Yams with Parsley Butter 337
Mixed Nut Roast 364
Mixed Vegetable Bruschetta 210
Mushroom & Walnut Open Tart 292
Nachos 138
Potato Gnocchi 262
Ratatouille 330
Red Salad with Beets & Radish 148
Roasted Butternut Squash 278
Roasted Bell Pepper & Garlic Focaccia 143
Roasted Summer Vegetables 196
Roasted Vegetables 290
Roasted Vegetable & Feta Cheese Wraps 245
Scallion & Ricotta Tarts 119
Summer Couscous Salad 237
Tofu Pockets 185
Vegetable & Black Bean Egg Rolls 335
Vegetable Couscous 118
Vegetable Kabobs with Blue Cheese 246
Vegetarian Chile Burgers 180
Vegetarian Hot Dogs 181
Warm Bulgur Wheat Salad 62
Winter Salad Slaw 16
Zucchini with Butter & Lemon 236